Advanced Studies in E-Commerce

Advanced Studies in E-Commerce takes a fresh and global viewpoint to E-Commerce development. It encompasses such issues as the basic concepts and principles of E-Commerce, the industry chain of E-Commerce, the security management of E-Commerce; the architecture of E-Commerce; the analytics of E-Commerce; and some cutting-edge topics of E-Commerce.

Li Xiong · Houcai Wang

User-Driven Cross-Border E-Commerce Platform Competition and Policy Analysis

西安交通大学出版社
XI'AN JIAOTONG UNIVERSITY PRESS

Springer

Li Xiong
School of Management
Shanghai University
Shanghai, China

Houcai Wang
School of Management
Shanghai University
Shanghai, China

Advanced Studies in E-Commerce
ISBN 978-981-97-3834-2 ISBN 978-981-97-3835-9 (eBook)
https://doi.org/10.1007/978-981-97-3835-9

Jointly published with Xi'an Jiaotong University Press
The print edition is not for sale in China Mainland. Customers from China Mainland please order the print book from: Xi'an Jiaotong University Press.

This Springer imprint is published by the registered company Springer Nature Singapore Pte Ltd.
The registered company address is: 152 Beach Road, #21-01/04 Gateway East, Singapore 189721, Singapore

Preface

With the rapid development of new generation information technologies such as big data, cloud computing, and artificial intelligence, global business management models have also undergone profound changes, especially in the digital economy era, cross-border e-commerce has gradually become one of the important trends in the development of global business activities. Cross-border e-commerce refers to an international commercial activity in which transaction subjects belonging to different customs territories reach transactions through e-commerce platforms, carry out electronic payment settlement, and deliver goods through cross-border e-commerce logistics and off-site warehousing. China has launched a series of supportive measures in taxation, customs clearance, and settlement. From 2015 to 2022, 165 cross-border e-commerce comprehensive experimental zones have been approved, covering all 31 provinces (regions, cities) in the country. Through innovative supervision methods and support policies, it helps with the rapid development of new forms of business such as cross-border e-commerce, and cross-border e-commerce has become a new highlight of China's foreign economic and trade cooperation.

This book takes cross-border e-commerce enabling international business as the situational basis, studies consumers' purchase decision-making and preferences for cross-border products from the perspective of customer perceived value, and compares the value drivers of consumers under non-cross-border e-commerce platforms. This helps cross-border e-commerce companies to choose more effective business models, achieve fine-grained and personalized marketing for cross-border users, meet the diversified consumption needs of domestic users for quality, and achieve commercial intelligence. By analyzing the online comments of cross-border purchase users on different imported cross-border e-commerce platforms, we can explore consumers' emotional tendencies toward different feature attributes of the platform, and then analyze the competitive advantages of the platform; sentiment analysis of online comments on imported cross-border e-commerce platforms helps platform operators discover the shortcomings of the platform, help them improve their own functions, increase user satisfaction, thereby enhancing their competitive advantage, and promoting the rapid and healthy development of the cross-border e-commerce industry. Discuss the structure and evolution rules of cross-border e-commerce policies, analyze the cooperation of policy subjects in cross-border e-commerce, the application of policy tools, and explore the characteristics of each stage of policy evolution. At the same time, analyze the implementation effect of cross-border e-commerce policies in the comprehensive experimental zone, study the influence mechanism of environmental factors in cross-border e-commerce on the implementation of policies in the comprehensive experimental zone, and the factors affecting the development differences of cross-border e-commerce in different comprehensive experimental zones, to provide reference for the formulation and implementation of policies in subsequent comprehensive experimental zones. The book is divided into four parts: introduction, cross-border e-commerce retail import user chapter, imported cross-border e-commerce platform chapter, and cross-border e-commerce policy chapter.

Introduction: Overview of the book. This includes the research background of the book, the current state of cross-border e-commerce research, the main research content, etc.

Cross-border E-commerce Retail Import User Chapter: Through Python language, data is scraped from relevant cross-border retail import platforms. Natural language processing is used to extract key information from unstructured comment information, construct customer perceived value models and indicators, and quantify scores for consumer focus on main attributes and sentiment analysis. Using existing user behavior to explore consumer preferences when shopping cross-border. The Bayesian network is continuously trained and learned to construct a Bayesian network model of cross-border user consumption preferences, thereby deriving the correlation between various driving factors, and quantifying the importance of each indicator, which serves as a portrait of cross-border user behavior.

Import Cross-border E-commerce Platform Chapter: Construct a research model from the perspective of platform companies and propose related hypotheses. Collect and organize qualitative data from import cross-border e-commerce platforms and convert it into quantitative analyzable data. Use contingency table analysis to analyze the impact of different factors and the matching between factors on platform competitive advantage, and test research hypotheses. The online comments on Jingdong Fresh platform were taken as the research object and preprocessed with normalization, word segmentation, and part-of-speech tagging. The emotion dictionary was constructed based on HowNet dictionary and ECSD e-commerce sentiment dictionary of Soochow University. The time window was divided based on the number of positive tests on imported fresh packaging, official conference notices, and news. Normal control period S1, epidemic outbreak period S2, imported fresh incident outbreak peak S3, imported fresh incident spread control period S4; finally, the emotional diffusion value and emotional energy value of consumers under different time Windows are analyzed, and the influence of events on different types of imported fresh products is excavated and compared.

Cross-border E-commerce Policy Chapter: Based on the current situation of cross-border e-commerce development and policy evaluation theory, policy analysis is conducted, and a cross-border e-commerce policy evaluation model is constructed. This chapter introduces the cross-border e-commerce policy evaluation methods used, including policy literature metrology analysis, metrology visualization methods, and econometric methods. It mainly elaborates on how to encode policy units, and visualizes cross-border e-commerce policies from the perspectives of policy subject visualization, policy action field visualization, and policy tool visualization, and explains the evolution process and rules of cross-border e-commerce policies. The multi-period difference-in-differences method is used to evaluate the policy effects of the pilot zone, and the parallel trend test and placebo test are used to demonstrate the validity of the experiment. The mediating effect analysis of cross-border e-commerce environmental factors is carried out, and the heterogeneity test of the policy effect of the pilot zone is conducted.

Conclusion section. The four-dimensional customer perceived value driving model is composed of value-driven, technology-driven, brand-driven, and service-driven components. From the consumer's perspective, it is found that the importance of customer perceived value driving factors is inconsistent. Through the data modeling comparison between cross-border and non-cross-border platforms, it is found that the customer perceived value of non-cross-border platforms tends to be value-driven, far greater than technology-driven and brand-driven factors. The estimated technology-driven factor is related to the relatively complete domestic logistics system, while the customer perceived value of cross-border platforms can be classified from large to small as: value-driven factors, brand-driven factors, and technology-driven factors, but the importance of the three the numerical deviation is relatively small. Based on the perspective of platform companies, the product category and the degree of product popularity have a significant impact on the competitive advantage of the platform, and the website traffic of comprehensive e-commerce and long-tail e-commerce is larger and more competitive; in addition, the mixed import model and long-tail e-commerce. The matching can better meet consumer needs, promote consumer use of the platform, and help improve the competitive advantage of the platform. Based on the user's perspective, users' focus on imported cross-border e-commerce platforms mainly focuses on products, prices, channels, interactions, and services. Through the measurement and visualization analysis of cross-border e-commerce policies, it is concluded that each cross-border e-commerce comprehensive experimental area needs to pay attention to the implementation effect of policies and promote the high-quality development of the industry. Through the evaluation of the policy implementation effect of the cross-border e-commerce comprehensive experimental area, it is found that in the process of policy formulation and implementation, the comprehensive experimental area should fully combine the advantages and disadvantages of various aspects of the city and the impact of related strategies to maximize the implementation effect of the policy.

During the writing process of this book, many references and data resources were referred to. The author has listed them as detailed as possible in the references, and hereby expresses deep gratitude to these experts and research organizations. At the same time, the students who participated in the research and writing of this book also include graduate students Dan Wei, Meiqi Li, Wenjing Ma, etc., and hereby express sincere gratitude. This book has made beneficial explorations in the field of cross-border e-commerce enabling international business, but at the same time, some references may not point out the source of the materials due to negligence. If such a situation occurs, I hereby express my deepest apologies.

September 2024

Li Xiong
School of Management
Shanghai University
Shanghai, China

Introduction

With the international business transformation and cross-border trade development triggered by the new generation of information technology, cross-border e-commerce has become an important direction for global business activities. This book constructs a four-dimensional driving model of customer perception of cross-border e-commerce retail imports from the consumer's perspective, and builds a secondary index of the four-dimensional driving model of customer perception of cross-border e-commerce retail imports based on product and service theme attributes. It studies the competitive advantage of cross-border e-commerce from the perspectives of platform companies and users. At the same time, by constructing a cross-border e-commerce policy evaluation research model, it analyzes the inherent logic and evolution rules of China's cross-border e-commerce policy text, conducts an effect evaluation analysis of the implementation effect of the cross-border e-commerce comprehensive experimental zone policy, and studies the influence mechanism of environmental factors on policy implementation. This is of great theoretical significance and practical value for further understanding the execution of cross-border e-commerce policies, comparing the differences in policy implementation in different comprehensive experimental zones, improving the precision of policy formulation, optimizing, and improving the cross-border e-commerce policy system, and promoting foreign economic development.

Contents

1 The Current Status and Trends of Cross-Border E-commerce Development 1

2 Analysis of User-Driven Factors in Cross-Border E-commerce Retail Imports 69

3 Construction and Analysis of Cross-Border E-commerce Retail Import User Preference Model 95

4 Analysis of Competitive Advantage of Cross-Border E-commerce Platforms from the Perspective of Platform Enterprises 119

5 Analysis of Competitive Advantage of Cross-Border E-commerce Platforms from the User Perspective 131

6 Construction of Cross-Border E-commerce Policy Evaluation Model 147

7 Cross-Border E-commerce Policy Metrics and Visualization Research 159

8 Study on the Policy Effect Evaluation of Cross-Border E-commerce 185

Appendix 1: 2013–2022 Cross-Border E-commerce Core Policies 215

Appendix 2: Multi-agent Formulation of Cross-Border E-commerce Policies 223

Appendix 3: Classification of Cross-Border E-commerce Policy Tools 225

Appendix 4: Coding of Cross-Border E-commerce Policy Tools 227

Appendix 5: | Part of the Code 231

Chapter 1
The Current Status and Trends of Cross-Border E-commerce Development

Cross-border e-commerce refers to transaction entities belonging to different customs, realizing order placement and electronic payment settlement through e-commerce platforms, and completing transactions through cross-border logistics to circulate goods, a type of international commercial activity. With the rapid development of new generation information technologies such as big data, cloud computing, and artificial intelligence, the global business management model has also undergone profound changes. Especially in the digital economy era, cross-border e-commerce has gradually become one of the important trends in global business development [[1]].

1.1 Research Background and Significance

Consumers in the process of cross-border shopping will try to get relevant information about the product, the most direct and effective way is to choose to view the online reviews of users who have already purchased. The information source formed by online reviews affects consumer behavior motivation and consumption preferences, and contains consumers' emotional attitudes toward products and the environment. Based on the massive data of online reviews, it is a hot topic to conduct holistic, mixed, and related mining and analysis, and to predict user behavior by analyzing massive information.

1.1.1 Research Background

Cross-border e-commerce is a vital force empowering global business and is also an important trend in the development of international trade. In recent years, the

L. Xiong and H. Wang, *User Driven Cross-Border E-Commerce Platform Competition and Policy Analysis*, Advanced Studies in E-Commerce,
https://doi.org/10.1007/978-981-97-3835-9_1

development of the digital economy has driven the transformation of global business, cross-border e-commerce has shown a good development trend, and the mode of international business activities has also undergone profound changes. According to Dynata's survey of cross-border shoppers in 39 countries worldwide, China is the most popular online cross-border shopping market, with 30% of respondents saying they shop through Chinese e-commerce platforms. Germany ranks second with a vote rate of 14%, followed by the UK and the United States, both at 10%.

(1) Cross-Border E-commerce Imports Promote New Development of International Business

The empowerment of cross-border e-commerce in international business stems from the major achievements of China's opening up. China has become the world's second largest economy, the largest industrial country, the largest trading nation in goods, and the largest foreign exchange reserve country. Imported overseas goods have always attracted consumers' attention, with different forms such as personal shopping agents, overseas online shopping, and import cross-border e-commerce. Personal shopping agents refer to groups who often travel abroad to purchase overseas goods for others and sell them through online channels. "Overseas online shopping" refers to domestic consumers directly purchasing overseas goods on foreign websites and transporting them back to the country through international logistics. Both methods have an import "gray area". With the effectiveness of the General Administration of Customs Announcement No. 56 of 2014 (Announcement on the Supervision of Cross-border Trade E-commerce Import and Export Goods and Articles) and No. 57 (Announcement on Adding Customs Supervision Mode Codes), the cross-border e-commerce model has become an important channel for consumers to purchase imported products and a new mode and new form of international business.

From the perspective of the government and enterprises, cross-border e-commerce is a more transparent retail import method, which is more conducive to government supervision of cross-border import behavior, product traceability, and consumer rights protection. However, for consumers, is there a fundamental difference between purchasing overseas goods on cross-border e-commerce platforms and other platforms for purchasing imported goods? And this difference on how cross-border e-commerce companies adopt more focused business models to gain competitive advantages, therefore, exploring the driving factors of consumers buying overseas products from the consumer's perspective, and analyzing their behavior preferences most directly affect the intrinsic mechanism of cross-border consumption behavior, which is of great significance for empowering national business development.

The global retail e-commerce market size nearly tripled from 2014 to 2022. In 2014, the General Administration of Customs issued Announcement No. 12 (Announcement on Adding Customs Supervision Mode Codes), which clearly stated that the added customs supervision mode code "9610", fully named "Cross-border Trade E-commerce", abbreviated as "E-commerce", applies to domestic individuals or e-commerce companies that carry out transactions through e-commerce trading platforms and adopt the "list clearance, summary declaration" mode to handle customs clearance procedures for e-commerce retail import and export goods (excluding e-commerce retail import and export goods through customs special supervision areas or bonded supervision places); e-commerce companies, operating companies, payment companies, and logistics companies that carry out e-commerce retail import and export business with the "9610" customs supervision mode should register with the customs as required, and transmit transaction, payment, warehousing, and logistics data to the e-commerce customs clearance management platform in real time through the e-commerce customs clearance service platform. In 2020, the General Administration of Customs issued Announcement No. 75, namely "Announcement on Carrying out the Pilot Program of Cross-border E-commerce Companies for Enterprise Export Supervision", adding the customs supervision mode code "9710", fully named "Cross-border E-commerce Enterprise Direct Export", abbreviated as "Cross-border E-commerce B2B Direct Export", applicable to goods of cross-border e-commerce B2B direct export. The customs supervision mode code "9810" was added, fully named "Cross-border E-commerce Export Overseas Warehouse", abbreviated as "Cross-border E-commerce Export Overseas Warehouse", applicable to goods of cross-border e-commerce overseas warehouses.

Consumers will try their best to get information about the value attributes and brand value of recommended products during the cross-border shopping process, among which the most direct and effective way is to choose to view the online reviews of users who have already purchased. Online reviews form an information source that influences consumer behavior motives and consumption preferences. Based on the massive data of online reviews, comprehensive, mixed, and relevant mining and analysis are carried out, and at the same time, predicting user behavior through the analysis of massive information has become a hot spot of current research, which has profound research value in the fields of economic management science and international business.

The popularity of cross-border e-commerce shows the strong consumption potential of the domestic market, and the online reviews of cross-border e-commerce products are an important source of information for exploring the direction of international business development. What are the influencing factors that consumers consider when purchasing overseas products? Among these influencing factors, which factor preference is more important? There are various channels for purchasing overseas products, and they can also be purchased on non-cross-border platforms (such as purchasing agents, overseas shopping). So where is the importance and necessity of cross-border e-commerce platforms reflected? In the twenty-first century, the network economy is socialized and content-oriented. Consumers, as the main body of cross-border consumption behavior, play more roles in content production and dissemination in the entire product purchase and consumption experience, and the production content of online reviews fundamentally comes from what consumers perceive in the entire process of purchasing products and using experiences. Therefore, this book's research is based on the perspective of customer perceived value, and this method is also more conducive to discovering the real driving factors of consumer purchase preferences. This book takes cross-border e-commerce as the situational basis, from the perspective of customer perceived value, studies consumer purchase behavior decisions and preferences for cross-border products, compares consumer value drivers under different overseas international business platforms, helps cross-border e-commerce companies choose more effective business models, realizes refined and personalized marketing for cross-border users, meets the diversified consumption needs of domestic users for quality, and realizes international business intelligence manufacturing.

(2) Cross-Border E-commerce Has Become a New Driving Force for the Development of International Business

The reduction in cross-border e-commerce transaction costs and the improvement in trade facilitation have led to its unprecedentedly rapid development, gradually penetrating production, circulation, and people's livelihoods. It meets the growing consumer demand for high-quality, cost-effective, and diverse overseas goods, becoming a new driving force for international business growth. The China International Import Expo, which has been successfully held in Shanghai for four consecutive years from 2018 to 2021, has turned exhibits into commodities and exhibitors into investors, exchanged ideas and concepts, connected China and the world, and become an international business platform for international procurement, investment promotion, cultural exchange, and open cooperation. It fully embodies the important value of the China International Import Expo, which is "not only to be held annually, but also to improve the level, achieve results, and get better and better". It has become a globally shared international business public product and is a concrete practice of fully building a trade liberalization, economic globalization industry chain, and new international business pattern. New formats and models such as cross-border e-commerce and overseas warehouses are booming, providing new growth points for our country's foreign trade development. By the end of the third quarter of 2021, cross-border e-commerce imports and exports and market procurement exports achieved growth of 20.1% and 37.7%, respectively, and the number of overseas warehouses exceeded 2,000, covering an area of more than 16 million square meters [[2]].

In recent years, with the successive introduction and continuous improvement of cross-border e-commerce policies, the rapid development, and continuous expansion of the cross-border e-commerce market, more and more enterprises have joined the import cross-border e-commerce industry, making the competition between platforms increasingly fierce. Each platform follows market and policy changes, trying to occupy a place in cross-border e-commerce imports, and platforms with a larger market share continue to increase their competitive advantages. The competition pattern of China's import cross-border e-commerce retail market has initially formed, and small and medium-sized cross-border e-commerce platform enterprises are occupying a larger market share [[3]]. With the intensification of this effect, the market share of some platforms gradually declines, and even some small and medium-sized platforms are gradually eliminated from the market, showing the intensity of competition in the import cross-border e-commerce industry.

The core reliance of cross-border e-commerce companies to carry out related businesses is the trading platform. The number of cross-border platform companies in our country has already reached 5,000, and more and more companies are using cross-border platforms to engage in cross-border e-commerce [[4]]. In the face of increasingly fierce market competition, enhancing the competitive advantage of international business platforms has become the key to promoting their sustainable development. There are obvious differences between import cross-border e-commerce platforms and general e-commerce platforms. On the one hand, consumers expect to purchase goods from abroad with a wide variety; on the other hand, goods purchased by consumers on import cross-border e-commerce platforms must go through inspection and quarantine, customs clearance, and taxation before receiving. At the same time, different import cross-border e-commerce platforms have differences in goods, payment, logistics, and other competitive advantages, which make consumers' willingness to use different platforms vastly different [[5]]. From the perspective of platform companies, which type of platform model can increase the innovative ways of international business and thus enhance competitive advantage? From the user's perspective, what factors directly affect their use behavior and purchasing behavior on the import cross-border e-commerce platform? These factors are of great significance for import cross-border e-commerce platforms to choose a more focused business model to gain international business competitive advantage. Therefore, this monograph explores the influencing factors of the competitive advantage of import cross-border e-commerce platforms from the perspectives of platform companies and users.

Cross-border e-commerce in China not only empowers international business but also provides a stable driving force for the recovery of the world economy. With a population of over 1.4 billion and more than 400 million middle-income groups, China imports about 2.5 trillion US dollars of goods and services each year, making it a huge market. The process of consumers making cross-border purchases not only involves the selection of goods but also the choice of import cross-border e-commerce platforms. The platforms adopt different types of transaction entities and import modes, representing different self-positioning, operation modes, and regulatory modes of the platforms [[6]]. Therefore, this article first analyzes the relationship between different types of transaction entities, import modes, and their matching with website traffic, to identify key factors that can enhance the competitive advantage of the platform from the perspective of the platform company itself. On the other hand, with the rapid development of the Internet and the popularity of mobile terminals, more and more consumers are making online purchases through mobile phones, tablets, and other mobile terminals. When choosing an import cross-border e-commerce platform, consumers tend to choose cross-border e-commerce apps with good reputations (hereinafter referred to as "import cross-border e-commerce platforms"). The most direct and effective way to understand the reputation of import cross-border e-commerce platforms is to view the online reviews of the platform by users who have used it in the app store. Online reviews, as direct and easily obtainable raw information, directly affect consumer behavior motives and consumption preferences. Text mining and analysis based on online reviews have profound research significance and value. Therefore, this article again analyzes the online reviews of cross-border purchase users on different import cross-border e-commerce platforms, explores the emotional tendencies of consumers toward different feature attributes of the platform, and then analyzes the competitive advantages of the platform. Using text mining technology to conduct sentiment analysis on the online reviews of import cross-border e-commerce platforms can help platform operators discover the shortcomings of the platform, help them improve their own functions, increase user satisfaction, enhance their competitive advantages, and promote the rapid and healthy development of the cross-border e-commerce industry.

Cross-border e-commerce involves transaction parties from different borders, uses e-commerce platforms to complete transaction settlements, and delivers goods through overseas warehousing and cross-border logistics to complete a kind of international commercial activity. In the overseas warehouse model of cross-border e-commerce exports, the main participants include cross-border e-commerce export enterprises, logistics enterprises, foreign trade integrated service enterprises, public overseas warehouse operating enterprises, cross-border e-commerce platform enterprises (domestic or overseas B2C platforms), overseas logistics enterprises, overseas consumers, etc.

(3) Cross-Border E-commerce Policy Combination Escorts International Business

The development of cross-border e-commerce empowering international business cannot be separated from policy support and market environment. In recent years, China's foreign trade has developed rapidly, and the scale of the cross-border e-commerce industry has shown a trend of continuous expansion. The State Council has proposed to cultivate new forms of cross-border e-commerce through continuous deployment and improvement of cross-border e-commerce policies, to support the healthy and rapid development of the cross-border e-commerce industry, and thus promote the upgrade and transformation of foreign trade and open up a diversified international market. In terms of cultivating new forms and models of trade, the "Notice on Implementing Policies to Support Cross-border E-commerce Retail Exports" issued by the General Office of the State Council in 2013 indicates that the state officially supports cross-border e-commerce retail and pays close attention to cross-border e-commerce payment to ensure smooth and safe transactions [[7]]. In 2015, the State Council pointed out that it should gradually increase imports by expanding domestic consumption reasonably [[8]], and established Hangzhou, Tianjin, Shanghai, and other cross-border e-commerce comprehensive pilot zones in batches (hereinafter referred to as "cross-border e-commerce pilot zones" or "pilot zones"). In terms of the policy system for cross-border e-commerce, in 2019, Premier Li Keqiang proposed to deploy and improve the promotion policies for new forms of business such as cross-border e-commerce, to develop diversified markets, optimize international layout, and the Ministry of Commerce also proposed to continuously improve the policy system for new forms of business such as cross-border e-commerce, and strengthen policy support to adapt to the new trend of industrial revolution [[9]]. In the face of the impact of the global epidemic on the economy, the State Council executive meeting decided to establish 46 new cross-border e-commerce comprehensive pilot zones in 2020 [[10]], to enhance the role of online platform transactions and air logistics transportation to stabilize the international business supply chain.

In the process of the state supporting local development of cross-border e-commerce, the establishment of cross-border e-commerce comprehensive pilot zones is the most direct and effective promotion measure. The cross-border e-commerce comprehensive pilot zone is applied by the city, approved by the State Council, and is a pioneering experimental area with comprehensive nature of cross-border e-commerce [[11]]. It reflects our country's active promotion of the participation and activity of cross-border e-commerce, cultivation of new forms of cross-border e-commerce, promotion of cross-border e-commerce development in various places, and determination to effectively promote the deepening of reform in the field of foreign trade, optimize our country's industrial structure, and accelerate structural transformation.

The cross-border e-commerce comprehensive pilot zone in China is a city area with the pioneering and experimental nature of comprehensive cross-border e-commerce established by China, aiming at the technical standards, business processes, regulatory models and informatization construction in cross-border e-commerce transactions, payments, logistics, customs clearance, tax refunds, and foreign exchange settlement. Through system innovation, management innovation, service innovation, and coordinated development, it solves the deep-seated contradictions and systemic difficulties in the development of cross-border e-commerce, builds a complete industrial chain and ecological chain of cross-border e-commerce, gradually forms a set of management systems and rules that adapt to and lead the global development of cross-border e-commerce, and provides replicable and promotable experience for promoting the healthy development of cross-border e-commerce in China. From 2015 to 2022, a total of 165 cities in five batches have been included in the list of China's cross-border e-commerce comprehensive pilot zones, as shown in Table 1.1.

Data source: Official website of the Central People's Government of the People's Republic of China.

In addition to the continuous strengthening of support for cross-border e-commerce comprehensive pilot zones at the national level, local governments of each pilot zone have also issued relevant policy documents to promote the development of the cross-border e-commerce industry, gradually forming a new situation of promoting the facilitation of cross-border e-commerce and regulating the healthy development of the industry nationwide. In 2014, Hangzhou City, Zhejiang Province applied to the State Council to become the first cross-border e-commerce comprehensive pilot zone in our country to strive for more facilitation policies, and in 2015 formulated the "Implementation Plan for China (Hangzhou) Cross-Border E-Commerce Comprehensive Pilot Zone" [[12]] and "Development Plan for China (Hangzhou) Cross-Border E-Commerce Comprehensive Pilot Zone", actively exploring in the areas of cross-border e-commerce system innovation, management innovation, service innovation [[13]]. In 2019, Hangzhou City also passed the "Implementation Opinions on Accelerating the Development of Cross-Border E-Commerce", strengthening the cultivation of cross-border e-commerce from the aspects of subjects, brands, talents, industrial parks, and logistics [[14]]. In 2015, Shanghai issued the "Several Opinions on Promoting the Development of Cross-Border E-Commerce in the City" [[15]], by leveraging the innovative reform advantages of the free trade zone and the advantages of the Shanghai port, promoting the

Table 1.1 Distribution of comprehensive pilot zones for cross-border e-commerce in China

Batch	Time	City
First batch	2015	Hangzhou City (Zhejiang)
Second batch (12)	2016	Tianjin City, Shanghai City, Chongqing City, Hefei City, Zhengzhou City, Guangzhou City, Chengdu City, Dalian City, Ningbo City, Qingdao City, Shenzhen City, Suzhou City
The third batch (22)	2018	Beijing City, Hohhot City, Shenyang City, Changchun City, Harbin City, Nanjing City, Wuxi City, Nanchang City, Wuhan City, Changsha City, Nanning City, Haikou City, Guiyang City, Kunming City, Xi 'an City, Lanzhou City, Xiamen City, Tangshan City, Weihai City, Zhuhai City, Dongguan City, Yiwu City
The fourth batch (24)	2019	Shijiazhuang City, Taiyuan City, Chifeng City, Fushun City, Hunchun City, Suifenhe City, Xuzhou City, Nantong City, Wenzhou City, Shaoxing City, Wuhu City, Fuzhou City, Quanzhou City, Ganzhou City, Jinan City, Yantai City, Luoyang City, Huangshi City, Yueyang City, Shantou City, Foshan City, Luzhou City, Haidong City, Yinchuan City
The fifth batch (46)	2020	Xiong'an New Area, Datong City, Manzhouli City, Yingkou City, Panjin City, Jilin City, Heihe City, Changzhou City, Lianyungang City, Huai 'an City, Yancheng City, Suqian City, Huzhou City, Jiaxing City, Quzhou City, Taizhou City, Lishui City, Anqing City, Zhangzhou City, Putian City, Longyan City, Jiujiang City, Dongying City, Weifang City, Linyi City, Yichang City, Xiangtan City, Chenzhou City, Meizhou City, Huizhou City, Zhongshan, Jiangmen City, Zhanjiang City, Maoming City, Zhaoqing City, Chongzuo City, Sanya City, Deyang City, Mianyang City, Zunyi City, Dehong Dai and Jingpo Autonomous Prefecture, Yan 'an City, Tianshui City, Xining City, Urumqi City
The sixth batch (27)	January 2022	Ordos City, Yangzhou City, Zhenjiang City, Taizhou City, Jinhua City, Zhoushan City, Ma 'anshan City, Xuancheng City, Jingdezhen City, Shangrao City, Zibo City, Rizhao City, Xiangyang City, Shaoguan City, Shanwei City, Heyuan City, Yangjiang City, Qingyuan City, Chaozhou City, Jieyang City, Yunfu City, Nanchong City, Meishan City, Honghe Hani and Yi Autonomous Prefecture, Baoji City, Kashgar Prefecture, Alashankou City
The seventh batch (33)	November 2022	Langfang City, Cangzhou City, Yuncheng City, Baotou City, Anshan City, Yanji City, Tongjiang City, Bengbu City, Nanping City, Ningde City, Pingxiang City, Xinyu City, Yichun City, Ji 'an City, Zaozhuang City, Jining City, Tai 'an City, Dezhou City, Liaocheng City, Binzhou City, Heze City, Jiaozuo City, Xuchang City, Hengyang City, Zhuzhou City, Liuzhou City, Hezhou City, Yibin City, Dazhou City, Tongren City, Dali Bai Autonomous Prefecture, Lhasa City, Ili Kazak Autonomous Prefecture

innovative cross-border e-commerce policy system, optimizing customs supervision, innovative research and talent construction, creating a fair competition environment to form an ecological environment conducive to the development of cross-border e-commerce. In 2020, the Shanghai Municipal Commerce Commission organized the recognition of the Shanghai Cross-Border E-commerce Demonstration Park [[16]], aiming to guide the further development of cross-border e-commerce toward scale, standardization, clustering, and normalization. In July 2021, the China Cross-Border E-commerce Comprehensive Pilot Zone will establish a comprehensive pilot zone assessment and exit mechanism, organize the first assessment of the comprehensive pilot zone, and promote survival of the fittest.

The China Cross-Border E-commerce Comprehensive Pilot Zone is a city area set up by China for the pioneering and trial of cross-border e-commerce, aiming to pioneer and trial in technical standards, business processes, regulatory models, and informatization construction in cross-border e-commerce transactions, payments, logistics, customs clearance, tax refunds, and foreign exchange settlement. Through system innovation, management innovation, service innovation, and coordinated development, it solves deep-seated contradictions and systemic difficulties in the development of cross-border e-commerce, creates a complete industrial chain and ecological chain of cross-border e-commerce, gradually forms a set of management systems and rules that adapt to and lead the global development of cross-border e-commerce, and provides replicable and promotable experiences for promoting the healthy development of China's cross-border e-commerce.

1.1.2 Research Significance

(1) Theoretical Significance

First, it expands the research approach to the competitive advantage of import cross-border e-commerce platforms. This book provides two relatively unique analytical perspectives for studying the competitive advantage of import cross-border e-commerce platforms, and uses sentiment analysis methods in text mining to quantitatively analyze platform competitive advantages, expanding the existing academic achievements on the quantitative research of cross-border e-commerce platform competitive advantages, filling the gap in the literature on online reviews and competitive advantages under cross-border e-commerce platforms, expanding the boundary conditions of online evaluation and competitive advantage research, clarifying the features of cross-border e-commerce platforms that current users are concerned about, and leading future-related research.

Second, it expands the situational basis of online consumer behavior research. Domestic and foreign scholars have not conducted much research on the consumer needs of cross-border e-commerce retail import websites with online reviews as the medium, but it will receive more and more attention in the future. This article fills the gap in the literature on online reviews and user demand preferences under cross-border platform websites, expands the boundary conditions of online reviews and consumer behavior demand preference research, clarifies the demand features that current users are concerned about, and leads future-related research.

Third, it expands theoretical perspectives and behavior research models. It validates the user perceived value theory and TAN Bayesian network model in the field of cross-border e-commerce retail import economy, enriches the research perspective of customer perceived value, constructs a Bayesian network model for cross-border e-commerce retail import, provides empirical verification for these two theories in the business field, broadens the application field of the Bayesian model, further enriches and supplements these two theories, and is beneficial to further in-depth research in related fields.

Fourth, it is based on econometric analysis of cross-border e-commerce policy research. Under the support of relevant policies, cross-border e-commerce has become a new economic growth point and gradually become a hot spot for academic research in international business. At the same time, helping import cross-border e-commerce platforms to enhance their competitive advantages and discover the key factors affecting platform competitiveness has become a very worthwhile issue in academic research. However, this book not only visualizes the analysis of China's cross-border e-commerce policies from the perspective of bibliometrics, but also evaluates the policy implementation effects of the comprehensive test area from the perspective of policy effect evaluation, using econometric methods, forming a new paradigm for cross-border e-commerce policy evaluation, and providing ideas for subsequent research on cross-border e-commerce policies.

(2) Practical Significance

First, it consolidates the diversification and individualization of business decisions on cross-border e-commerce platforms. Cross-border e-commerce connects merchants of various brands around the world and is about to become the main method of global trade in the future. The competition between major cross-border platforms and merchant enterprises is very fierce. Through research, understanding consumer demand behavior characteristics and preferences, further expanding the depth and breadth of cross-border e-commerce development, and predicting the next stage of popular products based on the high probability of changes in cross-border import retail, optimizing website UI design, stimulating and guiding user consumption demand, predicting derivative products, enhancing related value-added services, understanding user psychological changes more accurately, providing side support for the business decisions of cross-border platforms and merchants, adopting more effective management methods, and helping to more rationally understand the development and expansion of cross-border online shopping market.

Second, it assists the government in making regulatory decisions on cross-border e-commerce retail import behavior. By studying user demand characteristics and comparing the preference changes of users on cross-border platforms and non-cross-border platforms, it helps to discover their competitive advantages and deficiencies in different aspects. Cross-border e-commerce connects merchants of various brands around the world and becomes an important method of global trade in the future. Exploring the importance and necessity of cross-border e-commerce import platforms provides a certain reference value for national policy decisions, and explores new economic characteristics based on prediction results, occupies a leading position in the international cross-border e-commerce field, and expands global trade influence and competitive position.

Third, it assists import cross-border e-commerce platforms in choosing a platform model that is more conducive to development. With the continuous increase of various types of import cross-border e-commerce platforms in China and the intensification of market competition, how to make major cross-border e-commerce platforms stand out and gain competitive advantages in such a fierce competition environment has become the focus of each platform. Therefore, this book uses the contingency table analysis method to find a platform model that is more conducive to the development of import cross-border e-commerce platforms, helps to improve business efficiency, uses sentiment analysis methods in text mining to explore users' emotional tendencies toward different feature attributes of import cross-border e-commerce platforms, helps platform operators understand consumer behavior motives and demand characteristics, discovers the deficiencies in various competitive advantages of the platform, further improves functions, improves service quality, and thus enhances competitive advantages.

Fourth, it provides an evaluation of the application effects of cross-border e-commerce policies. For policy makers, this book helps to clarify the structural features and evolutionary laws of cross-border e-commerce policies through visual analysis of cross-border e-commerce policy literature and development context, providing ideas for further improving the cross-border e-commerce policy system. In addition, this book analyzes the policy mechanism of the cross-border e-commerce comprehensive pilot zone, and the research results can provide reference for the formulation and implementation of policies for subsequent pilot zones.

1.2 Cross-Border E-commerce Industry Development and Research

With the rapid cross-development of the global economy and the popularization of big data application technology, cross-border e-commerce is promoting the vigorous development of international business worldwide. However, as a new research field, cross-border e-commerce involves complex situations such as the economic level of member countries involved in cross-border online shopping, religious and cultural habits, consumer behavior, and network technology level. The depth and breadth of research on cross-border e-commerce and international business are constantly strengthening. Foreign research mainly includes the following directions.

1.2.1 Research on Cross-Border E-commerce

Cross-border e-commerce research started late in China, but with the gradual introduction of national policies, it has developed rapidly. Current domestic research mainly includes the following directions.

(1) The role of cross-border e-commerce in international trade and suggested measures. For example, Wang Wailian, Wang Mingyu, and Liu Shuzhen (2013) focused on analyzing the development advantages of China's cross-border e-commerce and some accompanying problems, and proposed exploratory suggestions [[17]]; Chen Yunbo (2013) tried to sort out the current situation of China's cross-border e-commerce development from the perspective of international e-commerce development trends, and proposed relevant countermeasures for problems encountered in the development process [[18]]; Liu Jiaguo et al. (2015), based on grounded theory, analyzed the influencing factors of Sino-Russian cross-border e-commerce development and proposed feasible suggestions [[19]]; Wang et al. (2017) found that cross-border e-commerce has a positive effect on the growth of China's international trade [[20]].

(2) Relevant research on the adaptability of small and medium-sized enterprises to carry out cross-border e-commerce. As an important supplement to China's import and export trade system, the rise and development of small-scale cross-border e-commerce is very rapid and performs well. Wang Cong, Ma Qing, and Liu Yi (2012) analyzed and defined the concept, profit model, reasons for the rise, and factors restricting the development of small-scale cross-border e-commerce, and finally proposed corresponding development strategies and future prospects [[21]]; Liu Juan (2012) analyzed the reasons for the rise of small-scale cross-border foreign trade e-commerce and discussed the feasibility of its development. She believes that small-scale cross-border foreign trade e-commerce, as a new attempt channel in the field of import and export trade, currently has no technical obstacles and China has already taken the lead [[22]].

(3) Research on cross-border e-commerce in terms of payment, channels, government regulation, taxes, logistics, or other aspects. For example, Yang Jianzheng and Liu Han (2014) analyzed the level and existing problems of cross-border e-commerce applications in cross-border transactions of enterprises with different scale structures in China. A survey questionnaire on the four main links of cross-border e-commerce implementation revealed differences in the development of cross-border e-commerce among enterprises with different scale structures, and there are also significant differences in the ability of enterprises with the same scale structure to use e-commerce in different links of cross-border transactions [[23]]; Yang Jianzheng and Yu Lu (2014) also conducted a specific analysis of the application of cross-border e-commerce by Chinese foreign trade enterprises from the aspects of network marketing factors, international payment condition factors, electronic customs clearance factors, and logistics factors. The study shows that Chinese foreign trade enterprises are still in a conservative stage in the use of cross-border network marketing channels and there are many problems [[24]]; W Ai et al. (2016) found from the e-commerce logistics

performance evaluation model that cross-border payment and regulatory coordination are the bottlenecks in the development of cross-border e-commerce [[25]]; Wang Xuping et al. (2017) explored and studied the dual-channel pricing game model of cross-border e-commerce retail imports under the O2O model [[26]].

(4) The research on the influencing factors of cross-border e-commerce mainly focuses on innovation, model, organization, and performance. Luo Y (2001) showed through empirical research that there is a strong correlation between the entrepreneurial model and innovation performance of cross-border e-commerce; Wu Wei (2009), based on case analysis, constructed a model of the factors affecting the choice of cross-border e-commerce entrepreneurial model on the basis of past literature, and the research results summarized the external and internal influencing factors of the choice of cross-border e-commerce entrepreneurial model, which are the market, production, policy, etc. of the product sales country and institutional factors, products, corporate decision-makers, etc., the research found that the choice of model and development requires corporate decision-makers to consider both internal and external factors [[27]]; Wang Lin, Yang Lifan, Yang Jianzheng (2013), based on the structural equation model, conducted an empirical analysis of the enterprises participating in the Canton Fair in 2013, the factors affecting cross-border e-commerce transactions, and rule requirements are subject to multiple aspects of synergistic effects. Empirical evidence shows that cross-border marketing capability is the key to conducting international trade, and cross-border logistics is its capability bottleneck, which does not include cross-border payment capability; in addition, the demand for cross-border transaction activity rules is strong and urgent, and the development and growth of China's cross-border e-commerce requires the joint action of the government and platforms/companies; Yang Jianzheng, Li Zi (2014) based on the mean method and gray correlation degree analysis method, conducted a questionnaire survey of the enterprises participating in the Canton Fair in 2013, the research results show that the most significant factors affecting cross-border e-commerce include: legal system and international trade economic environment; the least influential factors are: consumers, customs clearance, taxation and other factors [[29]]; Wang et al. (2016) based on the theory of two-sided markets and geographical location research, constructed two competition theory models using the Dalian and Tianjin Cross-border E-commerce Comprehensive Pilot Zones as examples [[30]], and further through equilibrium analysis in-depth research found that the endogenous value of the cross-border e-commerce comprehensive pilot zone is affected by the agglomeration effect, competition effect, and spatial structure effect [[31]]; Chen N et al. (2107) studied the mediating role of innovation support policies and corporate performance in the innovation of cross-border e-commerce business models [[32]].

1.2.2 Cross-Border E-commerce Industry Development Status

In recent years, the global cross-border e-commerce industry has been continuously developing, and scholars at home and abroad have increasingly focused on cross-border e-commerce. There are many research results on cross-border e-commerce, and the research field covers a wide range, mainly including studies on the cross-border e-commerce ecosystem, development level, and influencing factors. In the process of cross-border e-commerce enabling the evolution of international business ecology, not only are there more and more participating entities, but it is also affected by a more complex environment. Firstly, in the exploration and development stage, our country began to integrate into the international market, and suppliers, consumers, and cross-border purchasing agents and cross-border e-commerce platforms that facilitate transactions have developed new business forms; secondly, in the standard expansion stage, relevant departments of our government began to intervene in cross-border e-commerce supervision, and our cross-border e-commerce import and export platforms also gradually grew, with more suppliers and consumers entering the system; thirdly, in the coordination and promotion stage, the government led the establishment of public service platforms, and the foreign exchange bureau issued cross-border foreign exchange payment licenses to payment companies, etc., and the positioning of each entity in the cross-border e-commerce ecosystem gradually became clear; fourthly, in the update and evolution stage, customs declaration companies, marketing companies, logistics companies and other service providers for cross-border e-commerce gradually gathered, and the species in the cross-border e-commerce ecosystem became more abundant.

Gao Lan and others have conducted quantitative analysis on the e-commerce ecosystem based on information ecology theory [[33]]; Wang Huimin believes that cross-border e-commerce can promote the transformation and upgrading of our country's foreign trade [[34]]; Xiong Li and others proposed a four-stage model of cross-border e-commerce ecosystem evolution [[35]]: exploration and development, standard expansion, coordination and promotion, update and evolution (as shown in Fig. 1.1).

(1) Cross-Border E-commerce Industry Research

In terms of merchants and consumers, Ding Feng and others, based on the perspective of cross-border supply chain with dual channels, used game models to analyze the impact of consumer preferences on the differentiated competition strategies of cross-border e-commerce merchants [[36]]; Han JeongHugh and others theoretically analyzed the connection between different types of cross-border e-commerce behavior motives, information technology usage patterns, consumer informativeness, and purchase intentions [[37]]. In terms of logistics, Wang Ying and others established a hierarchical evaluation system for city logistics competitiveness and evaluated the performance of alternative cities under quantitative evaluation indicators [[38]]; Chen Xuhua established a complete transportation efficiency evaluation system based on the Analytic Hierarchy Process to evaluate cross-border e-commerce logistics, and

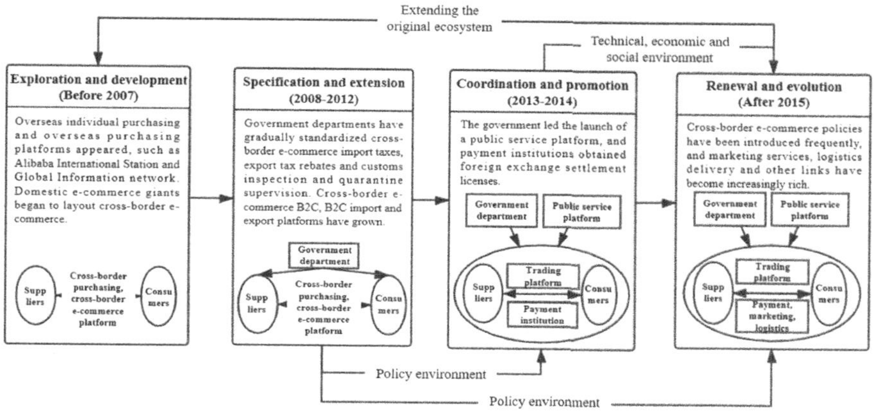

Fig. 1.1 Evolutionary model of cross-border e-commerce ecosystem

applied it to the port of Qingdao, China, to analyze the efficiency of port loading and unloading, and sea vessels [[39]]. In terms of input factors, Zhang Xiaoheng and others empirically analyzed the efficiency of input factors in the development of cross-border e-commerce by constructing an evaluation index system and a multiple linear regression model [[40]].

(2) Cross-Border E-commerce Influencing Factors Research

In terms of technological development, Gomez-Herrera E and others pointed out that the popularization of the Internet and computer skills, and the use of efficient and flexible cross-border payment systems are positive factors for the development of cross-border e-commerce [[41]]; Strzelecki and others pointed out that not all key features of online electronic retail stores have been developed, and the different characteristics of online stores have different utilities for customers to purchase goods [[42]]; Zhang Xibao pointed out that the improvement of informatization level is conducive to the further development of cross-border e-commerce comprehensive experimental zone [[43]]. In social aspects, Cardona M and others found that the increase in transaction costs related to overcoming language barriers, the regional integration of digital markets being constrained by the lack of integration of traditional physical markets will inhibit the development of cross-border e-commerce [[44]]; Thanh-Tuyen Tran found through statistical tests that trust and loyalty contribute to the development of cross-border e-commerce [[45]]. Economically, He Yugang and others took ASEAN countries as an example, discussed the determining factors of cross-border e-commerce trade from both export and import aspects, and found that GDP and real exchange rate have been affecting the development of cross-border e-commerce trade [[46]]. In terms of government regulation, Sun Lei and others believe that China's cross-border e-commerce needs to be regulated, including how to solve tax evasion, inspection and quarantine, market order, and other issues [[47]].

Research on the development level of cross-border e-commerce. In terms of development evaluation indicators, there are few studies on the evaluation indicators for the development of cross-border e-commerce, mainly evaluating from the indicators of cross-border e-commerce process, enterprises, and environment. Foreign scholars Lutz and Su combined the frequency of use of the Internet and e-commerce, etc., to conduct exploratory spatial data analysis on EU cross-border e-commerce [[48]]; Fan Jin and others examined the main factors affecting the development performance of manufacturing enterprises in Henan Province from five aspects: enterprise transaction scale, industry penetration, supporting environment, etc. [[49]]. Domestic scholar Wu Fen studied the development level of China's cross-border e-commerce imports and exports from the perspective of trade facilitation [[50]]; such as Ma Shuzhong and others evaluated the comprehensive performance of Chinese cross-border e-commerce enterprises by analyzing the financial data of Chinese cross-border e-commerce enterprises [[51]]; Yang Jianzheng and others constructed a cross-border e-commerce evaluation indicator system based on the cross-border e-commerce transaction process [[52]]; Zhao Zhitian and others conducted an empirical analysis on the development level of cross-border e-commerce of related enterprises in Zhejiang and Guangdong through the construction of a comprehensive evaluation model of the capability level of cross-border e-commerce [[53]]; Xiong Li and others constructed a comprehensive development level evaluation indicator system covering infrastructure, logistics development, customs clearance speed, payment environment, and transaction environment [[54]].

Since cross-border e-commerce entered the research field, a large number of scholars have explored the development status of cross-border e-commerce in our country. Sun Lei and others (2015), Tian Aiguo (2016) and Pan Yong (2017), and other scholars have analyzed the development status of cross-border e-commerce in our country in different periods, pointing out that cross-border e-commerce has the advantages of disintermediation, not being restricted by geographical space, reducing transaction costs [[55]], found that cross-border e-commerce has restrictive factors in logistics, customs efficiency, payment and settlement, credit and dispute handling, informatization construction, legal regulation, industry norms, etc. [[56]], and gave a series of solutions and suggestions [[57]]. Wang Fei (2019) addressed the issues in cross-border e-commerce in terms of logistics transportation, payment, product quality control, etc., and proposed the use of blockchain technology with features such as point-to-point networking, trustlessness, consensus algorithms, public and private key encryption algorithms, and smart contracts to solve these problems [[58]]. Zhang Weinian et al. (2019) used multiple regression method to study the influencing factors of the development of cross-border e-commerce in China, and concluded that the most important factors affecting the development of cross-border e-commerce are national policies, internet penetration rate, and logistics development level. Based on this, they proposed corresponding suggestions from legal, safety, talent, policy, and regulatory aspects [[59]].

1.2.3 Cross-Border E-commerce Platform Research

With the increasing number of cross-border e-commerce platforms and the increasingly fierce market competition, how the platform, as one of the main bodies of e-commerce market transactions, can highlight its own characteristics and gain competitive advantages that can compete with other platforms has become one of the problems that must be solved in the development of the platform. However, there is relatively little research on the competitive advantages of cross-border e-commerce platforms by scholars. Customer experience is one of the important factors measuring the competitive advantage of cross-border e-commerce companies. Zhang Lijuan (2015) found that consumer characteristic analysis through traditional questionnaire surveys and market research data can effectively explore its influencing factors [[60]]. From the perspective of market operation, Sun Shaoye (2016) found that users' attention to the platform and consumption tendency directly affect the competitive advantage of cross-border e-commerce companies. With the improvement of transaction processes and the increase of information transparency, consumers' perception of cross-border e-commerce services extends not only to marketing and after-sales, but also to the entire supply chain. Therefore, accurately identifying and exploring consumer characteristics, improving the overall customer experience level, has become the key to cross-border e-commerce companies gaining market competitive advantages [[61]]. From the perspective of cross-border e-commerce in the manufacturing industry, Liu Jinfei (2018) found that companies of different industry types have their own focuses when improving their competitiveness, but all companies must strengthen their cross-border marketing capabilities and technology adoption capabilities [[62]]. From the perspective of cross-border e-commerce logistics companies, Wen Liqin et al. (2019) constructed an evaluation index system for the international competitiveness of cross-border e-commerce logistics companies based on the network hierarchy method, and proposed a path for such companies to enhance their international competitiveness [[63]].

1.2.4 Cross-Border E-commerce Logistics Research

Cross-border e-commerce logistics is an important link to ensure the smooth completion of cross-border purchases. At present, scholars' research on cross-border e-commerce logistics mainly focuses on development status, logistics information matching, logistics network characteristics, logistics mode selection, etc. Zhang Bin et al. (2015) and Zhang Xia Heng et al. (2015) mainly discussed the logistics operation mode and development status [[64]], and found that there are urgent problems to be solved in terms of policy support, infrastructure construction, professional services, logistics costs, distribution cycle, returns and exchanges, etc. [[65]]. To optimize cross-border logistics distribution schemes and improve user experience, Guo Ren et al. (2018) used dynamic clustering method to establish a framework for cross-border e-commerce logistics information matching, and conducted empirical analysis [[66]]. Lu Yuduo et al. (2018) established a logistics network model based on the characteristics of cross-border logistics networks, and used simulation technology to analyze the resilience of the network [[67]]. To more accurately find the fault source of the cross-border e-commerce logistics system, Guo Ren et al. (2018) established a fault tree model for the system and conducted a detection of the fault system [[68]]. Wei Jie et al. (2017) and Xiao Jianhui (2018), respectively, sorted out the characteristics and pros and cons of different cross-border e-commerce logistics modes [[69]], and compared various logistics modes through multiple indicators, finally deriving the selection criteria for various logistics channels [[70]]; Zhang Duo et al. (2019) based on the fuzzy comprehensive evaluation method, analyzed the impact of different risks on the cross-border e-commerce logistics mode [[71]]. Hsiao et al. (2016) used text mining technology to analyze the online content of cross-border e-commerce logistics services, identifying the relationship between cross-border logistics service elements and customer feelings [[72]].

1.2.5 Research on Cross-Border E-commerce Payment and Pricing Strategy

The payment link is the last step for consumers to purchase on the cross-border e-commerce platform. The diversity, security, and convenience of payment methods directly affect the final completion of cross-border e-commerce transactions. In terms of research on cross-border e-commerce payment, Zhang Xiaoheng (2017) discussed the influencing factors of cross-border e-commerce payment after analyzing the development characteristics and business models of cross-border e-commerce payment, and found that factors such as usage preferences and costs affect the choice of cross-border payment methods [[73]]; Weng Dongling (2018) conducted research on third-party cross-border payment institutions, found problems in authenticity verification, reserve funds, network connection mode, anti-money laundering, regulatory regulations, information and data security, etc., and proposed a series of countermeasures and suggestions [[74]]; Wang Juanjuan et al. (2018) proposed that blockchain technology can solve the problems existing in the "Belt and Road" regional cross-border payment, and simulated the index system constructed based on the characteristics of the blockchain [[75]].

Compared with buying domestic goods, consumers need to pay a certain amount of taxes when buying overseas goods from cross-border e-commerce platforms, and the cost of cross-border logistics is relatively high. How to price the goods sold on the cross-border e-commerce platform is one of the key issues for platform operators and platform merchants. In terms of research on cross-border e-commerce pricing strategies, Wang Xuping et al. (2017) studied the dual-channel pricing game model of cross-border e-commerce retail import under the O2O model, and explored the impact of different power structures on the pricing and income of supply chain members [[76]]; Zhang Xuanxuan et al. (2015) first analyzed the evolutionary game equilibrium of cross-border e-commerce companies and regulatory departments, and then used the Bertrand model to analyze the sales pricing strategy of cross-border e-commerce stock channels and traditional trade stock channels [[77]].

1.2.6 Research on Cross-Border E-Commerce Tax and Supervision Policy

Taxation is an indispensable part of cross-border e-commerce purchases and is one of the very important features that distinguish cross-border e-commerce from domestic e-commerce. Changes in tax policy will directly affect the development of the cross-border e-commerce industry. Many scholars have conducted related research on cross-border e-commerce taxation. Among them, Hou Huan (2017) proposed that there are difficulties in the standardization, definition of tax elements, and implementation of the process in the tax collection and management of cross-border B2C e-commerce. He thought about tax fairness from micro, meso, and macro perspectives, and proposed corresponding solutions from the aspects of equalization, standardization, and cooperation [[78]]; Wang Lei (2017) proposed that the new customs tax policy will affect the price and category of goods of imported cross-border e-commerce [[79]]; Zhang Li (2018) mainly sorted out the cross-border e-commerce export, import and other related tax policies in various periods of our country, and proposed suggestions from multiple aspects such as improving laws and regulations and tax policies, classified supervision, and improving the level of informatization construction of customs supervision [[80]]; Sun Ruihua et al. (2018) focused on the analysis of the new customs tax policy, and studied the impact of changes in tax policy on cross-border import retail e-commerce platforms [[81]]; Kreos et al. (2019) targeted the problems existing in VAT declaration among enterprises, tax bureaus, customers and other related stakeholders in cross-border e-commerce, and proposed to establish a VAT automatic declaration system for non-EU small and medium-sized enterprises through cooperation with various e-commerce platforms to solve the above problems [[82]].

As a new field of economic development, cross-border e-commerce is bound to develop a trend of formulating perfect regulatory policies. At the same time, the improvement of regulatory policies will help the cross-border e-commerce industry to develop in a more scaled, standardized, and compliant direction. For the research on cross-border e-commerce regulatory policies, the research team of the Shanghai Academy of Social Sciences Economic Research Institute (2014) focused on the issues of tax evasion, inspection and quarantine, market order, etc. in the current regulatory system, and proposed to build a multi-level regulatory system, formulate special management measures, build a public information platform and other government regulatory suggestions [[83]]; Xu Lei (2018) mainly analyzed the impact of the policy dividend era, customs regulatory system on the cost of imported cross-border e-commerce, customs clearance efficiency, product access, development of small and medium-sized platforms, market polarization, industrial upgrading, etc. [[84]]; Hu Rong et al. (2017) analyzed the customs risks of cross-border e-commerce, and based on the Bayesian network, analyzed the regulatory risks of cross-border e-commerce customs [[85]].

1.2.7 Research on the Purchasing Intention of Consumers on Cross-Border E-commerce Platforms

Cross-border e-commerce platforms are one of the main ways for consumers to purchase overseas goods, and consumers' purchasing intentions on the platform directly affect the platform's competitive advantage and its economic benefits. Therefore, more and more scholars are studying the purchasing intentions of consumers on cross-border e-commerce platforms. Saprikis V (2015) took consumers as the guide, studied the views of Greek Internet users on e-commerce platforms, aiming to reveal the purchasing behavior of users on Greek and international e-commerce platforms [[86]]. Han et al. (2018) based their research on the theory of planned behavior, studying the relationship between beliefs in electronic service quality, consumer uniqueness needs, perceived behavioral control, significant others' expectations, and the intention to engage in cross-border e-commerce [[87]]. Huang et al. (2019) integrated signal transmission theory, attachment theory, and the consumer perceived value model to establish a research model for the influencing factors of consumers' shopping intentions on foreign websites. They concluded that trust and perceived value are the key factors driving consumers to shop on foreign websites, and that price competitiveness, product uniqueness, communication costs, and waiting costs determine the perceived value of consumers shopping on foreign websites [[88]]. Han et al. (2019) established a specific research model for cross-border e-commerce, theoretically analyzing the connections between different types of cross-border e-commerce motivations, information technology usage patterns, consumer informativeness, and purchase intentions [[89]]. Xiao et al. (2019) innovatively identified four cues that promote cross-border e-commerce consumer behavior, including online promotion cues, content marketing cues, personalized recommendation cues, and social comment cues. They proposed a theoretical model based on cue utilization theory and the stimulus-organism-response model, introducing these four cues and brand familiarity into the analysis of the impact of cross-border online shopping on consumer purchase intentions [[90]].

1.3 Cross-Border E-commerce Online Shopping Behavior Research

1.3.1 Cross-Border E-commerce Shopping Influencing Factors Research

Internationally, Jarvenpaa et al. (1996) conducted an open-ended survey of 220 online shopping consumers to analyze the impact of various factors such as their shopping experiences, product and e-commerce website service experiences on their online shopping behavior [[91]]; Schaupp et al. (2005) conducted a study of 188 young consumers and found that the three important factors influencing consumer online shopping satisfaction were: technical factors, product factors, and shopping factors [[92]]; similarly, Ha et al. (2009), based on the TAM model, conducted an online survey of 298 college students and found that technology, product, and shopping environment have a significant effect on consumer shopping intentions and behavior expression [[93]]. Domestically, Cheng Hua (2003), based on the TAM model, found through empirical analysis that the main influencing factors of online shopping behavior intention are the perceived usefulness and safety value during the consumer's online shopping process [[94]]; Xu Ruqing et al. (2009) found through empirical research that technical factors (website security and reliability) are the most important influencing factors on consumer purchase intentions and behavior expression, and that online shopping convenience and webpage design aesthetics have different effects on different products [[95]]; Chen Jie (2012) based on the Eroglu background framework, constructed the SOR model, specifically analyzing the role of the consumer's perceived experience during the online shopping process on their perceived risk and behavior expression [[96]]; Zhang Lingying (2014) divided the consumer purchase process in B2C online shopping into different behavioral stages, and independently explored the influencing factors of different behavioral stages [[97]].

1.3.2 Cross-Border E-commerce Shopping Behavior Mechanism Research

Based on the factors influencing online shopping behavior, many scholars have further explored the characteristics related to online shopping behavior, focusing on feasibility studies based on models and moderating variables (such as perceived risk, perceived value, and trust). In 2000, Geoffrey and others summarized four key features of early user behavior modeling and predicting future user behavior directions, namely the need for large data sets, labeled feature data, the existence of concept drift, and computational complexity [[98]]; Pavlou et al. (2003) integrated TRA and TAM theory variables to establish a related model and found that perceived usefulness, perceived ease of use, and perceived risk are important factors driving consumers' online shopping [[99]]; Baecke et al. (2010) found through research that the addition of situational variable data for purchasing occasions can significantly improve the accuracy of consumer purchase behavior prediction [[100]]; Kim et al. (2012) found that the online shopping behavior intentions of consumers (new customers and repeat customers) are influenced by perceived price and perceived trust, and the influence of perceived trust is greater than that of perceived price [[101]]; Zhang Yue (2012) found that the mediating role of perceived benefits affects consumers' willingness to shop again, while perceived risk has a negative correlation with the behavior intention of first-time buyers [[102]]; Chen Si (2013) analyzed the principles, methods, and models of past consumer behavior research through literature reading and summarizing comparisons, focusing on the methods of data standardization, and summarized how to explore consumer behavior research in the era of big data based on the above background and further refined this research theoretical framework [[103]]; Chen Chuanhong (2013) found through questionnaire survey and model empirical testing that consumer perceived risk is affected by website risk control, and there is a negative correlation between the two [[104]]; Feng Zhiyan et al. (2013) analyzed the opportunities and difficulties faced by e-commerce in the era of big data, explored the behavioral characteristics in the social network environment, the mechanism of the enterprise network ecosystem, the channel selection in the era of big data and consumer insights, and summarized and refined the feasible mode innovation methods based on the big data industry [[105]].

Currently, there is very few literature on consumer behavior research in the field of cross-border e-commerce retail imports, and a few scholars have conducted related exploratory research, such as Yang Chaojun et al. (2015) found through questionnaire cross-analysis that satisfaction is the mediating variable of Amazon website quality and has an indirect impact on consumer shopping behavior [[106]]; Lv Xueqing (2015) studied the pricing issue of cross-border e-commerce import retail based on grounded theory, and proposed suggestions such as brand differentiation and reasonable pricing on this basis [[107]].

1.4 Current Status of Cross-Border E-commerce Policy Research

In recent years, scholars have analyzed and discussed current policies from the two perspectives of existing cross-border e-commerce policies and industry development status, providing policy suggestions for further standardizing, and optimizing the cross-border e-commerce industry.

(1) Cross-border e-commerce policy. To study the policy of cross-border e-commerce, we must first clarify the meaning of the policy. A policy is the guiding ideology and action measures adopted by the state government organs to achieve certain goals or to handle certain affairs. The cross-border e-commerce policy is the state's guidance in the cross-border e-commerce industry, and it is the guidelines

formulated by the government to promote the healthy development of cross-border e-commerce. It determines the overall direction and goals of regulating and guiding cross-border e-commerce activities. The cross-border e-commerce policies studied in this article include the norms and policy documents for promoting the development of cross-border e-commerce formulated by the State Council and its subordinate departments, and the government departments of various comprehensive test zones.

(2) Policy evaluation. Policy evaluation includes the evaluation of policy proposals, the evaluation of the entire process of the policy, and the evaluation of policy effects. The narrow sense of policy evaluation is based on certain standards and procedures to analyze the effects of policy implementation, while the broad sense of policy evaluation includes judgments on the amount of work input, policy effects, sufficiency, and overall social development goals. The amount of work input represents the distribution of the quality and quantity of resources invested in the policy implementation process; the policy effect is the impact of the policy on objective things and the policy environment; the policy efficiency reflects the ratio of policy input to policy effect within a unit time. This study uses the broad definition of policy evaluation, and the content of the evaluation includes policy subjects, policy action fields, policy proposals, and policy implementation effects.

(3) Policy effect. The policy effect studied in this article is the change in economic effects before and after the implementation of the policy in the cross-border e-commerce comprehensive experimental zone. Researchers are often interested in the effects produced after the implementation of a policy, plan, or project, which is usually referred to as the policy effect in the field of econometrics. The policy effect refers to the impact of the implementation of the policy on the object of action. The evaluation of the policy effect includes two aspects: one is the speed of the effect, also known as the time effect of the policy, which measures the effect of the policy from time; the other is the size of the effect, also known as the quantity effect of the policy. Since the quantity effect of the policy can reflect the time effect, this article focuses on the evaluation of the quantity effect of the policy.

(4) Discuss and analyze existing policies. Wei Shuang and others proposed suggestions for improving the legislation of cross-border e-commerce in China in terms of transaction subject supervision and information privacy protection by comparing and analyzing domestic and foreign measures and explorations in cross-border e-commerce legislation [[108]]; Zhang Mingfei and Yang Jianzheng and others used the policy evaluation standards proposed by William to analyze and evaluate the supervision policy of cross-border e-commerce, and proposed suggestions for the supervision policy of cross-border e-commerce [[109]]; Su Weihua and others used social network analysis methods to study and found that the policy of cross-border e-commerce involving service content lacks long-term strategic planning, especially policies related to taxation and warehousing [[110]].

(5) Based on the current situation of China's cross-border e-commerce development, policy suggestions are proposed. Lai Youwei proposed policy suggestions such as optimizing the service support and supervision system of cross-border e-commerce, the development environment of cross-border e-commerce, promoting the development of new formats such as direct import of cross-border

e-commerce, bonded stockpiling, strengthening international cooperation in cross-border e-commerce, and improving the development level and international competitiveness of China's cross-border e-commerce service industry by analyzing the current situation and trend of China's cross-border e-commerce development [[111]]. Xu Yingnan and others, through their research on China's cross-border e-commerce pilot cities, evaluated the innovativeness of policies in areas such as cross-border e-commerce business process optimization, platform construction, and government regulation, and discussed policy gaps in areas such as talent training and standard management of foreign trade enterprises [[112]].

In summary, domestic and foreign research on cross-border e-commerce mainly focuses on four aspects: first, research on the cross-border e-commerce industry, such as consumers, suppliers, platforms, and logistics; second, research on the ecological environment of cross-border e-commerce, including technology, economy, society, and political environment; third, research on the development level of cross-border e-commerce, mainly based on the construction and evaluation of the indicator system; fourth, research on cross-border e-commerce policies and suggestions, proposing policy suggestions from the perspective of regulations and industry development status. However, research on the evaluation of cross-border e-commerce policies is relatively rare, so it is of practical and theoretical significance to study the development of cross-border e-commerce from the perspective of policy evaluation.

1.4.1 Research Status of Policy Implementation Process

To evaluate policies, it is necessary to understand the policy operation process, factors affecting the policy execution effect, commonly adopted evaluation standards, and research ideas. The policy operation process includes three stages: policy formulation, policy decision, and policy implementation [[113]], as shown in Fig. 1.2.

The policy formulation stage revolves around specific economic and social issues, proposes corresponding goals and plans, and conducts detailed evaluations. The policy plans that pass the evaluation will be decided to be implemented. The policy implementation stage begins with policy announcement and publicity. Government departments will decompose the policy and implement it specifically, and evaluate the effect of policy implementation, feedback, and analysis to further optimize and improve related policies.

Smith refined the specific process of policy implementation into a classic model of policy analysis (see Fig. 1.3). Smith's policy execution model points out that the main factors affecting policy execution are four aspects: ideal policy plan, executing agency, target group, and environmental factors [[114]], these four parts interact and feedback on the policy. The ideal policy plan is reasonable, legal, and feasible, including the goals, types, forms, and scope of the policy. The executing agency is the institution responsible for the policy goals, including organizational structure, cooperation division, organizational leadership mode, etc. The target group is the object of the policy, usually the group that needs to adjust its behavior due to a

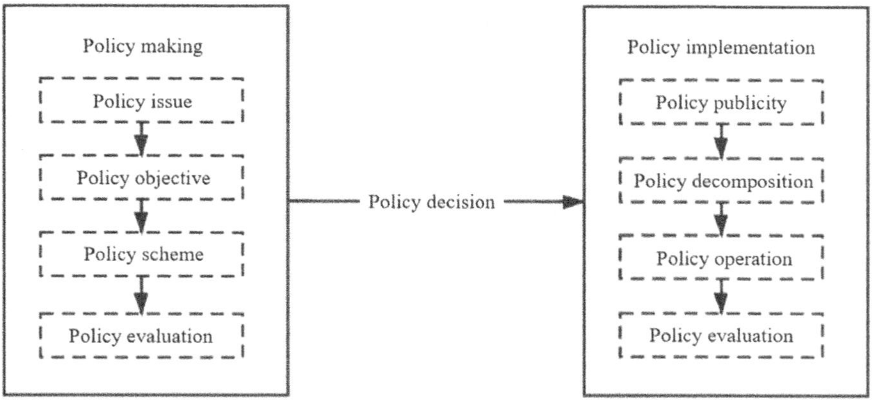

Fig. 1.2 Policy operation process

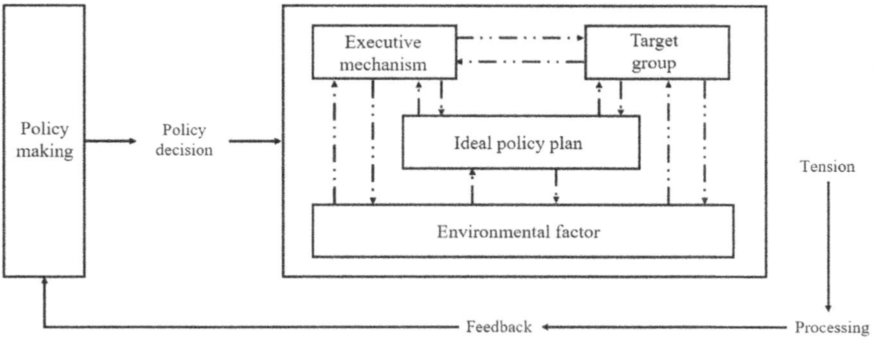

Fig. 1.3 Smith's policy implementation process

certain policy. Environmental factors are a series of factors related to policy execution, including political, economic, cultural, and social environments.

1.4.2 Research Status of Policy Effect Evaluation

The effect is the expected and unexpected results caused by specific behavior interventions such as policies, plans, projects, and effect evaluation is the process of analyzing and monitoring the changes caused by this behavior [[115]]. Effect evaluation attempts to find changes in results directly attributable to specific behavior interventions, which helps to analyze the key issues of policy, planning, and other interventions: that is, whether the intervention works? Where does it work? Why can it work?

The core idea of effect evaluation is to consider what the outcome would be if no intervention had taken place, i.e., assuming a specific intervention does not exist, what changes would occur to the original subjects of the intervention. This unobservable hypothetical fact is called the counterfactual outcome. Although the counterfactual outcome cannot be directly measured normally, at the same point in time, an individual can only exist in one of two states: either subjected to intervention or not subjected to intervention. However, a reasonable control group can be used to simulate the situation of individuals under the other state, which is also the method commonly widely adopted by researchers.

Therefore, the evaluation of policy effects can draw on the idea of effect evaluation, that is, to analyze the effects on individuals who have not been subjected to a certain policy as a hypothetical fact. In this way, the measurable effect of a policy can be the difference between the actual policy outcome and the hypothetical fact [[116]]. The idea is that individuals who are affected by the policy and those who are not affected by the policy may be affected by the same factors and produce similar structural changes. Therefore, using individuals who have not been affected by the policy as a control group to obtain counterfactual results and then estimate the policy effect of the experimental group.

The difference-in-differences model and the multi-period difference-in-differences model have been used by scholars at home and abroad in recent years for research in economics, finance, urban planning, and other fields. Foreign scholars Cole and Megan used the difference-in-differences method and the treatment weight inverse probability method to compare the results of children who received primary health care policies with children who received primary health care at the control point [[117]]; Grafova used the difference method to explore the impact of community economic environment on the self-assessment of health in the elderly [[118]]; Pippel identified the relationship between research and development cooperation in research institutions and the performance of corporate product and process innovation through the difference-in-differences method [[119]]; Thorsten B and others evaluated the impact of bank supervision on income distribution from the perspective of the multi-period difference-in-differences method [[120]]; Cerulli G researched and developed a new Stata command representing the difference-in-differences method of fixed-time multiple treatments to implement the application of the multi-period difference-in-differences model [[121]].

Domestic scholar Zhang Yingying used the difference-in-differences method to test the impact of smart city construction on the upgrading of the manufacturing industry and its mechanisms and effects [[122]]; Chen Haiqiang used the difference-in-differences method to analyze the policy disposal effect of the introduction of margin trading system [[123]]; Wu Jianzu used the difference-in-differences method to test the relationship between the environmental talk system and the efficiency of local government environmental governance [[124]]; Ye Jingjing used the difference-in-differences method and the fixed effects model to study the relationship between income tax reform and individual labor participation rate and working hours [[125]]. Chen Renjun and others used the multi-period difference-in-differences method to find that overall, the central environmental protection supervision can improve the performance of listed industrial companies through innovation drive, and it still maintains a significant positive effect after the inspection [[126]]; Yang Yong and others established a multi-period difference-in-differences model to analyze the impact of free trade agreements on the quality of China's export products [[127]]; Lv Hongyan and others used the multi-period difference-in-differences model to examine the impact of institutional innovation in free trade pilot zones on the total factor productivity of regional enterprises [[128]].

Zhao Caijing and others used the multi-period double difference method to verify the impact of smart city construction on the quality of urban development [[129]]; An Hui and others constructed a multi-period double difference model to empirically analyze the effect of sales restriction policies on housing prices and their heterogeneity from both the national and city levels [[130]].

In summary of the above studies, the multi-period double difference method is widely used in the field of social economy, and the use of the multi-period double difference model to estimate the effects of pilot policies is effective. However, research on the implementation effect of cross-border e-commerce policy is still in its infancy, and the above research provides research ideas and methods for the evaluation of cross-border e-commerce policy effects. In the process of implementing cross-border e-commerce policies, the main method adopted from the national to the local level is to promote the establishment of cross-border e-commerce comprehensive pilot zones. Considering the characteristic of multiple batches of comprehensive pilot zones, this article uses the multi-period double difference method to evaluate policy effects.

1.5 Theoretical Basis of Cross-Border E-commerce

The research on cross-border e-commerce mainly relies on the theoretical basis of network word-of-mouth information dissemination, customer perceived value theory, Bayesian network in graph model, sentiment analysis in text mining, competitive advantage theory, double difference model, intermediary effect model, policy literature measurement, data visualization analysis, etc.

1.5.1 Network Word-Of-Mouth Dissemination

Word-of-mouth is a way of information dissemination. In the era when the degree of information sharing was low, word-of-mouth was the main way for people to obtain information. The earliest scholar to conduct academic research on word-of-mouth was Armdt (1967), who defined word-of-mouth as non-commercial communication between word-of-mouth disseminators and receivers about factory brands, products, and services [[131]]. With the deepening of word-of-mouth research, its definition has been continuously expanded, such as Westbrook (1987) believes that word-of-mouth refers to the way people discuss their feelings about products or services in informal occasions [[132]]; Prince (1992) believes that word-of-mouth refers to people's exchange of information about their purchase of products or services [[133]]. After the theory of word-of-mouth was proposed, it was widely used in the field of marketing and became one of the very important research issues in this field. Bristor (1990) found that compared with formal information, people are more willing to choose informal word-of-mouth dissemination, and found that word-of-mouth dissemination is more persuasive and credible [[134]]. Brown et al. (2005) used retailers as research objects and empirically analyzed that the intention and behavior of positive word-of-mouth dissemination will be affected by customer commitment factors [[135]]. The research of Yang Xiaodong et al. (2006) and Qu Lezhang (2008) shows that word-of-mouth marketing can enhance the competitiveness of enterprises in a low-cost and efficient way [[136]].

(1) The Impact of Network Word-of-Mouth on Consumer Buying Behavior.

With the advancement of communication technology and the rapid development of network informatization, user network social platforms such as WeChat, Tieba, and forums are increasingly emerging, and more and more consumers express their opinions and views through the Internet. Word-of-mouth has gradually developed from the initial offline word-of-mouth to network word-of-mouth, breaking the limitations of traditional word-of-mouth and expanding the influence of word-of-mouth [[137]]. Stauss (1997) defined network word-of-mouth as non-commercial communication realized by consumers based on the Internet [[138]]. Compared to traditional word-of-mouth, the characteristics of online word-of-mouth are as follows (Hennig-Thurau et al., 2004): (1) Fast dissemination: online word-of-mouth is easy to replicate, and the participants in the dissemination are both receivers and disseminators of information; (2) Wide range of information: the spread of online word-of-mouth is not limited by time and space, making it easier to expand its influence; (3) Tangibility: online word-of-mouth is recorded in tangible forms such as text, pictures, videos, etc.; (4) Anonymity: the virtuality and anonymity of the internet result in the generation and dissemination of online word-of-mouth being anonymous [[139]]. With the continuous development of online word-of-mouth, its quantity has increased dramatically, greatly affecting the operation of the consumer market, and attracting a large number of scholars to use online word-of-mouth to study consumer purchasing behavior. Lazarus et al. (1991) found that different types of online word-of-mouth have different degrees of impact on user purchasing behavior [[140]]. Godes et al. (2004) found that the degree of difference in online word-of-mouth has an impact on user purchasing decisions and behavior [[141]]. Song Yafei et al. (2011), Huang Wenyuan et al. (2013), and Xie Guangming et al. (2018), respectively, explored the impact of online word-of-mouth on consumer purchase intention from three different perspectives: negative online word-of-mouth [[142]], the quality of online word-of-mouth [[143]], and the dispersion of online word-of-mouth [[144]]. Wang Jianjun et al. (2019), based on the S–O-R model, mainly studied online word-of-mouth from different sources, aiming to discover its impact on consumer purchase intention from different perspectives [[145]].

Online word-of-mouth has evolved from traditional word-of-mouth. Arndt (1967) defined word-of-mouth as non-commercial or informal information dissemination about manufacturers' brands, products, and services between individuals [[146]]. Past word-of-mouth often occurred in familiar interpersonal interactions, with obvious geographical limitations and temporal decay characteristics [[147]]. With the development of network information and social platforms, online word-of-mouth has emerged and broken the limitations of interpersonal communication. Hanson (2000) believes that the biggest difference between online word-of-mouth and traditional word-of-mouth is that most online word-of-mouth is disseminated through chat messaging software, forum posts, microblogs, and other internet platforms as media [[148]]. Similarly, Chatteijee (2001) believes that online word-of-mouth is consumers or technology users communicating effective information with each other through the internet as a medium [[149]]. Stephen (2007) believes that online word-of-mouth includes consumers' expectations and comments on product characteristics and prices, and potential consumers can understand relatively real product suggestions through online comment systems, and interact and communicate with consumer comments [[150]]. This definition highlights the interactivity of online word-of-mouth. Chen Yubo and Xie Jinhong (2008) also emphasized that consumers' online comments have behavioral orientation toward other potential consumers, which strengthens the connection between online comments and consumer behavioral intention [[151]]. Chen believes that reviewers comment on product features based on their own product usage, disseminate word-of-mouth from the consumer's perspective, highlight the role of zero-cost "marketing channels", and can assist potential consumers (especially new online shoppers) to quickly find and determine products that match their preference needs [[152]]. Walsh et al. (2004) and Bi Jidong (2010) define it as: existing customers, current users, and future potential users exchange text, pictures, emojis, videos, etc. through synchronous or asynchronous internet platforms to record, publish, and share information about the price, cost-effectiveness, and other attributes of products or services [[153]].

Combining the explanations of online word-of-mouth from past literature, this book defines online word-of-mouth as follows: in a narrow sense, online word-of-mouth is also known as online reviews or ratings [[154]], referring to consumers or users informally and non-economically disseminating multimedia information about products or services through online reviews, forwarding, sharing, or other behaviors, providing decision support to other potential users [[155]]. The research direction and content of online word-of-mouth are classified, and current research mainly reflects the relationship between the quantity, benefits, and consistency of word-of-mouth and sales. The more online word-of-mouth, the higher the possibility for consumers to understand effective information about products or services. For example, Chen et al. (2004) proved that the number of online reviews has a positive effect on the relative sales ranking of books [[157]], Liu (2006) found that the number of word-of-mouth has a large explanatory power for box office when studying the relationship between online word-of-mouth and box office [[156]], Duan et al. (2008) found that movie ratings do not have a significant impact on the box office, while the number of online reviews affects box office sales [[158]], which is similar to the results of Wang

H et al. (2017) [[159]], Qin (2011) proved that the number of blogs is both a predictor and a consequence of the box office [[160]]; Singh V Kd et al. (2016) found that the number of friends and fans has a positive effect on the number of user online reviews based on Yelp website data [[161]]; Huang N et al. (2017) found that the integration of social networks in online reviews increases the number of user-generated online reviews, but the quality of reviews decreases [[162]].

(2) The Effect and Consistency of Online Word-of-Mouth.

The benefit of online word-of-mouth is more about how it influences consumers' attitudes, intentions, and behaviors toward products or services. Zhang et al. (2006) found that the benefit of online word-of-mouth, not the quantity, has a significant effect on the box office [[163]], Chintagunta (2010) believes that using national unified box office data for serial-themed movies will cause a series of endogenous problems, so local box office data was used to obtain similar research results to Zhang et al. (2006) [[164]]; Chevalier and Mayzlin (2006) proved that the impact of negative word-of-mouth is greater than that of positive word-of-mouth [[165]]; Luca (2011) used the Yelp platform as the research object, and the breakpoint regression estimation method better explained the causal effect of ratings. The results show that improving the rating by one step can increase performance by 5%–9%, and the benefit of ratings will be strengthened with the increase of online reviews [[166]]; Baek H et al. (2012) collected 75,226 online reviews from Amazon using a page scraping tool, and conducted sentiment analysis on the text information. The results show that the user's website level, acceptance, and online review text content have an impact on the usefulness of online review value [[167]]; Jeong Deng et al. (2015) used model detection to show that there is a positive regulatory effect on consumer behavior and platform impact by online reviews' valence and objectivity/subjectivity [[168]]; Zhang et al. (2016) identified non-linguistic features of online reviews through research, and compared to linguistic features, these improve the performance of online fake review detection models, thereby affecting the value and utility of online reviews [[169]]; Li X (2107) found that there are average value differences between different products, and when consumers have relative heterogeneity in product valuation and companies have the ability to coordinate product prices, platforms or companies that display online review scores generate higher profits than those that do not take this measure [[170]].

Regarding word-of-mouth consistency, some literature focuses on direct impacts, while others explore the moderating role of online word-of-mouth consistency. The role of online word-of-mouth consistency presents a diversified situation, such as inconsistent online word-of-mouth predictions can stimulate the curiosity of recipients, highlight the target group of products or services, and affect the trust of purchased consumers or potential users in word-of-mouth, [[171]] etc. If the overall online reviews are positive, it may cause consumers to doubt the authenticity of the reviews. At this time, the appearance of irrelevant or impurity information or negative word-of-mouth may reduce this doubt. Lee (2015) found that when the information entropy of online reviews is less than or equal to a certain threshold, the increase in online review information entropy will strengthen the impact on the box office. When the online review information entropy exceeds a certain threshold, the impact may weaken or even become insignificant as the value increases [[172]]; Sun (2012) explored the role of online word-of-mouth consistency under different rated products, and found that for higher-rated products, there are already many consumers interested in them, and the inconsistency of word-of-mouth will offset some consumers, while for lower-rated products, it may attract certain specific consumer groups whose preferences match exactly; Zhao X et al. (2015) used factor analysis from online review content to derive five secondary driving indicators and one secondary driving indicator from online review sources (a total of six predictive variables), and the research results found that negative information in online reviews has a negative correlation with online booking behavior, while positive information has a statistically insignificant relationship with online booking behavior [[173]]; Pang J et al. (2016) studied the impact of the "price" factor in online reviews on consumer attitudes and behaviors toward purchasing products, and found that there is inconsistency in the effect of different thinking motives on consumers [[174]]; Zhou W et al. (2016) found through a mediation model that online professional reviews have a positive effect on user online word-of-mouth, enhancing user online review activity and indirectly affecting the download volume of related apps [[175]]. Some literature has also conducted extended research, such as comparing the effects of word-of-mouth on the market based on different cultural backgrounds (domestic and foreign) [[176]]; comparing and interacting the effects of online word-of-mouth with other marketing channels [[177]]; comparing the effects of word-of-mouth on different online platforms, [[178]] etc.

1.5.2 Customer Perceived Value Theoretical Model

Regarding the definition of customer perceived value, there are two views in academia. The first view believes that customer perceived value is a sub-concept of customer value, that is, customer value includes but is not limited to customer perceived value; the second view believes that customer value is equivalent to the concept of customer perceived value, and the two are equivalent.

(1) Customer Perceived Value.

Anderson et al. (1992) defined value based on the market: value is the economic, technical, service, and social benefits expressed in monetary form that customers obtain by purchasing a certain market offering with a certain amount of money [[179]]. This value refers to the benefits obtained after weighing against the costs paid, but the costs here do not include the price of the product or service; Gale (1994) understands customer value as a function of the perceived quality and price of the product or service [[180]]; Gronroos (1996), starting from relationship marketing, supplemented the explanation that in long-term buying and selling relationships, attention needs to be paid to the overall relationship between each other, including the energy expended to maintain the relationship, which is defined as "total situational value" [[181]]; Kotler [[182]] and Kotler [[183]] explain and analyze customer value from the perspective of customer value transfer.

"Perceived value" was proposed in the 1990s based on psychological and sociological research and the characteristics of industrial service marketing research, among which the definition proposed by American scholar Zeithaml is widely accepted and used. Zeithaml and Monroe define it from the consumer's perspective. Zeithaml (1988) believes that customer value is equivalent to customer perceived value, referring to the overall value evaluation after the customer balances the perceived utility benefits of the product and the various costs incurred in obtaining the product or service [[184]], which laid the foundation for later research on the two; Monroe (1990) formulated the customer perceived value: customer perceived value = benefits/sacrifice, which is a kind of exchange relationship between the two [[185]]; Woodruff (1997) emphasized the experiential and empirical nature of customer perceived value [[186]], similarly, Holbrook (1999) explained from the experience perspective that customer perceived value is the behavioral result of the interaction between the customer and the merchant's product or service [[187]]; Wu Yonghong et al. (2004) believe that customer value is the overall value evaluation formed after individuals or groups with specific needs and behavioral intentions perceive the various benefits and costs of a specific market offering provided by a specific company in a specific situation [[188]].

From the above analysis, it is found that there are differences in the specific measurement dimensions or theories of customer value and customer perceived value, but the core ideas of the two are consistent, that is, both are a balance comparison between perceived gains and perceived losses. The focus of this study is the evaluation after the customer balances gains and losses, rather than measuring the specific situation of customer gains and losses.

Therefore, based on the definition by Zeithaml and Woodruff, and considering the specific context of cross-border e-commerce retail imports, customer perceived value is defined as: the overall evaluation or rating by customers after weighing the benefits and costs incurred when obtaining product information, seller communication services, and platform technical services on a cross-border platform. This refers to the customer's perception of certain characteristics conveyed by the product or service, preference for these characteristics, and evaluation of features that promote or hinder the achievement of individual customer goals and behavioral intentions in specific actual cases. This is consistent with the initial intention of cross-border users' online comments. It is the overall evaluation of gains and losses perceived during the entire product "purchase process" and "after using the product", representing the difference between total customer value and total customer cost. The total customer value refers to the specific benefits that customers expect to obtain from a specific product or service, and the total customer cost refers to the total expected cost incurred by customers in investigating, evaluating, testing, obtaining, and using the product or service.

(2) Theoretical Research on Customer Perceived Value.

There are many drivers of customer perceived value, mainly including price value, competitive value, emotional value, functional value, and social value. Current literature on customer perceived value mainly divides into the emotional perspective and the rational perspective [[189]]. The emotional perspective of perceived value emphasizes the experiential value that consumers obtain throughout the process of purchasing a product, emphasizing the realization of individual emotions and the satisfaction of individual needs, which is always accompanied by the experience process of orientation, interaction, and preference [[190]]. The rational perspective assumes that consumers are rational and emphasizes that consumer behavior is goal-oriented. The typical models of customer perceived value mainly include the following.

Zeithaml's theory of customer perceived value. Zeithaml believes that when a company designs, creates, and provides value for customers, it should stand from the consumer's perspective, emphasizing the perception of value by customers as a determinant. This is done by integrating psychology and economics to enrich and change the perspective of the concept of value, with the core being the balance between perceived benefits and perceived losses. This theory expresses two meanings: first, it acknowledges that value is experiential in nature, and different customers perceive different values or sacrifices for the same product or service, indicating individual differences; second, value represents the balance of gains and losses, and customers decide their behavior expression based on various perceived driving factors, not just a single factor. The theoretical model is shown in Fig. 1.4.

Woodruff's theory of customer value cognition. Woodruff integrates the "channel-goal" method into the basic theory of customer value, and based on data processing cognition logic and cross-feedback system, proposes a hierarchical model of customer perceived value, as shown in Fig. 1.5. This model believes that customers can form expected value through the "channel-goal", dividing customer perceived value into three levels: at the lowest level, customers will consider the specific characteristics and performance of the product; at the second level, the usage result level, customers form expectations based on product characteristics and performance for the expected realization of product effects; the third level, the goal level (top level),

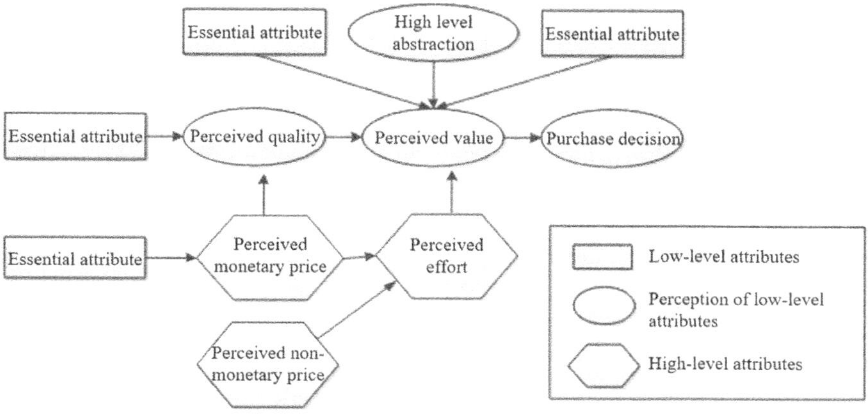

Fig. 1.4 Zeithaml's theoretical model of customer perceived value

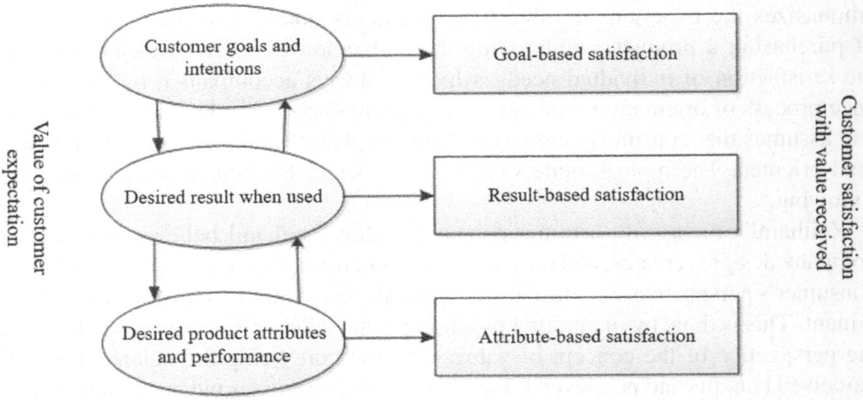

Fig. 1.5 Woodruff's customer value hierarchy model

includes the core values of consumers, which are the final results of customers using products and services.

The most valuable contribution of this model is that: the product is merely a means for customers to achieve their goals, the value of the product lies in its satisfaction of the expected goal value that customers want to achieve, indicating that customer satisfaction with product characteristics, performance, usage results, and goals will positively or negatively affect perceived value.

Gronroos's theory of customer value process. Gronroos innovatively supplemented the theory of customer perceived value from the perspective of relationship marketing. The process of relationship maintenance is the starting point and result of customer perceived value. Customer value not only comes from the core functions of the product and additional services, but also includes the maintenance of the overall relationship, that is, relationship value. It is necessary to pay attention to its full situational value, thus forming a customer value model, as shown in formula (1.1)–(1.3):

$$FullSituationalValue = \frac{SituationalGains + RelationalGains}{SituationalLosses + RelationalLosses} \tag{1.1}$$

$$CustomerPerceivedValue(CPV) = \frac{CoreSolution + AdditionalService}{Price + RelationshipCost} \tag{1.2}$$

$$CustomerPerceivedValue(CPV) = CoreValue + / - AddedValue \tag{1.3}$$

The model explains that all gains and losses related to the relationship itself are determinants of customer perceived value, and the value of core products and specific services is also presented in the process of relationship maintenance.

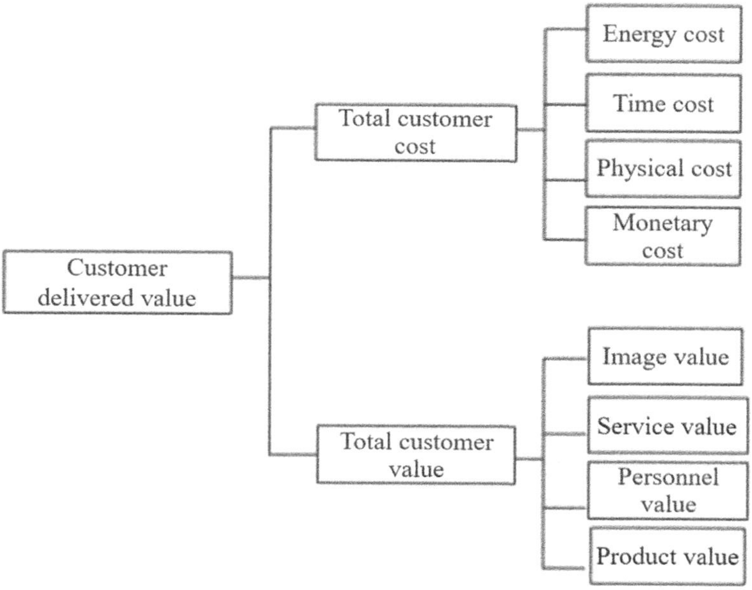

Fig. 1.6 Kotler's customer delivered value model

Kotler's theory of customer surrender value. Kotler explains customer value from the two dimensions of customer surrender value and satisfaction. He believes that when customers face different products and corporate brands under the goal of purchase, they always hope to pay the lowest cost and get the maximum utility, to achieve the greatest satisfaction. That is, under the constraints of limited knowledge framework and certain search costs, customers are individuals or groups oriented by value maximization. He proposed the customer surrender value model, as shown in Fig. 1.6:

Research on domestic customer perceived value theory. Domestic research started late. With the further development and deepening of foreign research on customer perceived value theory, more and more domestic scholars are conducting research and exploration. For example, Yang Long (2002), based on the theory of customer value, analyzed the secondary driving factors under its key driving factors and established a value-driven model from the perspectives of suppliers and customers [[191]]; Dong Dahai et al. (2004) through market survey data empirical research found that customer value is the cause of customer loyalty, which in turn affects the supplier's advantage [[192]], and further research (2008) constructed a three-part model of customer perceived value in the network environment, namely emotional value, procedural value, and result value [[192]]; Wang Yonggui (2005) based on customer rights and interests to build a value-oriented CRM model, empirical findings of the mediating effect of relationship quality on customer value [[193]]; Wang Chong (2011) found that product quality is an important influencing factor of online shopping consumers' perceived utility [[194]]; Lei Ting et al. (2012) through questionnaire survey, using factor analysis and other methods to establish a model suitable for the characteristics of B2C e-commerce transaction platform customer perceived value, customer satisfaction and customer loyalty interrelationship [[195]]; Zhang Ruijin et al. (2014) through empirical construction of the structural model of customer perceived value, to study the proposal of mobile data business platform upstream and downstream acquisition of customers, maintain customers and competitive strategy [[196]]; Ma Baolong (2015) took the car as the research object, the results show that the brand competitive advantage based on customer perceived value has no significant impact in practice [[197]]; Ding Yong et al. (2017) reconstructed the driving factors of customer perceived value and explored the positive proactive role of social value in customer perception on brand preference [[198]].

Customer perceived value is an important predictive variable of consumer willingness and behavior, and its impact on behavior-oriented changes has been supported by a large number of theoretical studies and empirical tests. Customer perceived value has a direct impact on consumer behavioral intention, and indirectly affects current and future behavioral intentions through user satisfaction [[199]]. Pan Yu and others (2009) found that lifestyle affects consumer purchasing behavior decisions by acting on customer perceived value factors [[200]]. The consumer's perception of customer value before purchasing a product will directly affect changes in their purchasing intention [[201]], and directly lead to changes in user loyalty [[202]]; Wei Wei and others (2011) defined a new customer value concept based on the theory of customer perceived value, and tried to analyze consumer purchasing and evaluation behavior patterns with customer value [[203]]; Zhang Hongmei and others (2016) explored the indirect effect of perceived quality and perceived value on tourist behavior intention through the variable of satisfaction in the context of tourism [[204]]; Zhang Xin (2017) found that user trust has a partial mediating effect between perceived value and browsing intention based on the study of WeChat users' perceived value [[205]].

(3) Four-Dimensional Driving Model of Customer Perception.

The theory of customer perceived value occurs before the customer purchases a product, or ends after the use of the product, increasing or decreasing with time, which may involve product value, relationship value, etc. Based on past literature research, this article can conclude that the perceived value in the process of product purchase mainly includes "service", "price", and "brand" value driving elements. Customers first choose shopping targets through brand trust or word of mouth. After determining the purchase product, because cross-border online shopping is different from offline physical purchases, customers cannot obtain the target object in time, they will highly depend on the network system to pay attention to product logistics delivery and feedback system, and produce network evaluation feedback in the whole shopping process. Therefore, the past literature theory is sorted out and summarized, and classified according to dimensions, as shown in Table 1.2.

From Table 1.2 and this research, it is found that for the new environment of cross-border e-commerce retail imports, past theories and models have not been able to cover all dimensions or factors of customer perception in the entire shopping process. Therefore, this article draws on classic theories and combines cross-border

Table 1.2 Classic customer perceived value theory

Scholar	Customer perceived value dimension	The number of dimensions
Zeithaml (1988)[184]	Perceived gains, perceived losses	Two dimensions
Kotler (1991)[182]	Total customer cost, total customer value	
Yang Long (2002)[191]	Perceived utility, perceived cost	
Rust (2000)[206]	General value, brand value and relationship value	Three dimensions
Dong Dahai et al. (2008)[189]	Emotional value, procedural value, and consequential value	
Kotler (1998)[207]	Product value, personnel value, service value, and image value	Four dimensions
Sweeney (1999)[208]	Quality value, emotional value, price value, and social value	
Heinonen (2004)[209]	Time, space, function, and technology	
Wang Yonggui (2005)[193]	Functional value, social value, emotional value, and perceived losses	
Sheth (1991)[210]	Functional value, cognitive value, emotional value, social value, and conditional value	Multiple dimensions
Meng Qingliang (2005)[211]	Functional value, social value, knowledge value, emotional value, and perceived sacrifice	
Zhang Ruijin et al. (2014)[196]	Quality value, service value, emotional value, self-actualization value, security value, monetary cost, and non-monetary cost	

e-commerce application scenarios to improve the above theoretical models. The driving factors of customer perceived value consist of brand driving elements, service driving elements, value driving elements, and technology driving elements, forming a four-dimensional driving model, as shown in Fig. 1.7.

This model is based on the consumer's perspective, with online reviews as the object, to achieve a comprehensive measurement of consumer behavior needs and preferences under cross-border e-commerce retail imports. The driving factors include the following: service driving factors include merchant services, product packaging, etc.; value driving factors include product quality, price, etc.; brand driving factors include brand recognition and reputation; technology driving factors include platform convenience and logistics feedback services, etc. The specific secondary driving indicators are verified in the practice of this book and the model is improved, see Chapter 2 for details.

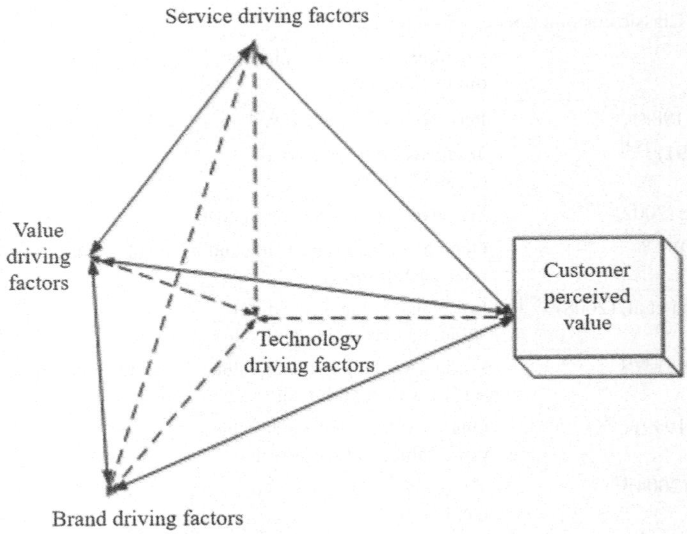

Fig. 1.7 Four-dimensional driving model of customer perceived value

1.5.3 Bayesian Network Model

The category of graph models is wide, and it visualizes the probability relationship between various predictive variables in a graphical way. It can be divided into directed graphs and undirected graphs based on edges, and models that combine directed edges and undirected edges are called chain graphs. The position of the Bayesian network in the graph model is shown in Fig. 1.8. Pearl (1986) proposed that the Bayesian network is the result of the fusion of probability theory and graph theory [[212]], modular representation can simplify complex systems. Bayesian networks are an important branch of business intelligence used to predict uncertainty, and due to their model flexibility, they are widely used in various fields such as economics, industry, and medicine.

(1) Basic Concepts of Bayesian Theory.

The Bayesian theory can be simplified through classical probability relationships. That is, Bayesian probability refers to the speculative probability of an event object for a specific event occurrence. First, the event object estimates the possibility of unknown events based on existing specific knowledge (prior information) and current statistical data, rather than the probability of event occurrence obtained by conducting repeated experiments (objective probability). Bayesian probability is a prediction of unknown events based on existing objective factual data.

Consider events A and B, and assume $A = A_1 \cup A_2 \cup \cdots \cup A_n$, and when $i \neq j$ exists $A_i \cap A_j = \varphi$, then the probability of A_i occurring under condition B is as shown in formula 1.4:

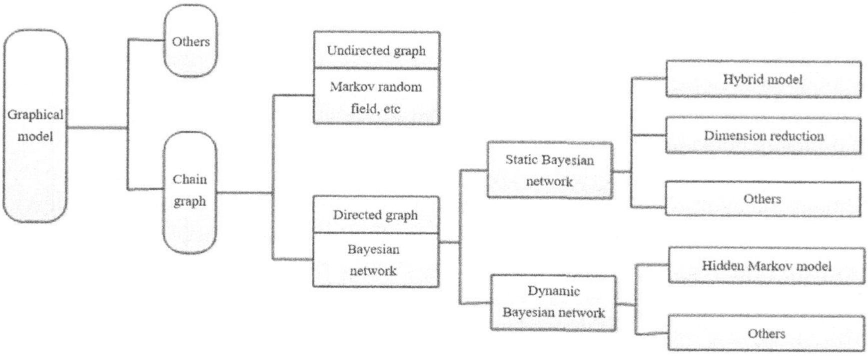

Fig. 1.8 Hierarchy diagram of the graphical model

$$P(A_i|B) = \frac{P(B|A_i)P(A_i)}{P(B)} = \frac{P(B|A_i)P(A_i)}{\sum_{i=1}^{n} P(B|A_i)P(A_i)} \tag{1.4}$$

Considering events A and B as arbitrary events, it can be expressed in a general form as shown in formula 1.5:

$$P(A|B) = \frac{P(B|A)P(A)}{P(B)} \propto P(B|A)P(A) \tag{1.5}$$

where: $P(A_i)$ is the prior probability, which is obtained from historical data statistics or expert knowledge statistics, and needs to meet two conditions: one is that all possible outcomes of the event must be finite; the second is that the possibility of each outcome occurring is independent and equal;

$P(A_i|B)$ is the posterior probability, which can be obtained by correcting and adjusting the prior probability $P(A_i)$ and observed data.

Based on the above, it can be found that the posterior probability, as the prior probability of the next time, is corrected as the data continues to increase. At the same time, the probability of the event result occurring under specific conditions can be inferred as the possibility of the event result occurring under specific conditions.

(2) Bayesian Network Learning.

Bayesian Network (BN) is a non-cyclic directed graph, composed of nodes and related parameters. The nodes are connected by directed edges, with the parent node pointing to the child node with a single arrow. Each node is a predictive variable, and the directed edge represents the conditional occurrence probability between predictive variables. Therefore, the overall structure of the Bayesian network can be divided into model structure and parameter attributes.

The Bayesian model structure is composed of several network nodes and single arrows. The nodes represent predictive variables, and the single arrows represent conditional dependencies. For example, suppose there are three nodes L, X, and Y, and there is a single arrow between L and X from L to X, then L is called the parent node of X. If L also points to Y, L is also called the parent node of Y, and X and Y are both child nodes of L. There are two possibilities for X and Y. One is that there is a separate directed arrow between the two, indicating that there is a dependency relationship between the two; the second is that there is no directed edge, then X and Y have a conditional independent relationship. This shows that the Bayesian network includes the conditional independence relationship between predictive variables.

The parameters of a Bayesian network are the probability distribution tables for each node (predictive variable). In the Bayesian network diagram, each predictive variable has its own probability distribution table, which lists in detail the causal relationships between variables. The probability distribution table of the root node explains the marginal distribution of the connected predictive variables, while the probability distribution table of the non-root nodes explains the conditional probability of the occurrence of the node result when the parent node is known, i.e., the likelihood of one variable affecting another. Therefore, the probability of other nodes can be derived from the known probabilities of some nodes, which is known as probability propagation. For specific examples of Bayesian networks, see Fig. 1.9.

In Fig. 1.9, the five variables L, X, Y, Z, and A are represented by nodes, and the relationships between the five variables are shown in the figure, with the conditional probability distribution of each node listed on the side. Variable L is the parent node of variable X, X and A are the parent nodes of Y, X is the parent node of Z, that is, Z depends on X, Y depends on both X and A, and X depends on L. Given L, X and A are conditionally independent; given X and A, Y is conditionally independent of L, and Z and Y are conditionally independent. The probability distribution table of L explains the marginal probability distribution of L, and the probability distribution table of X

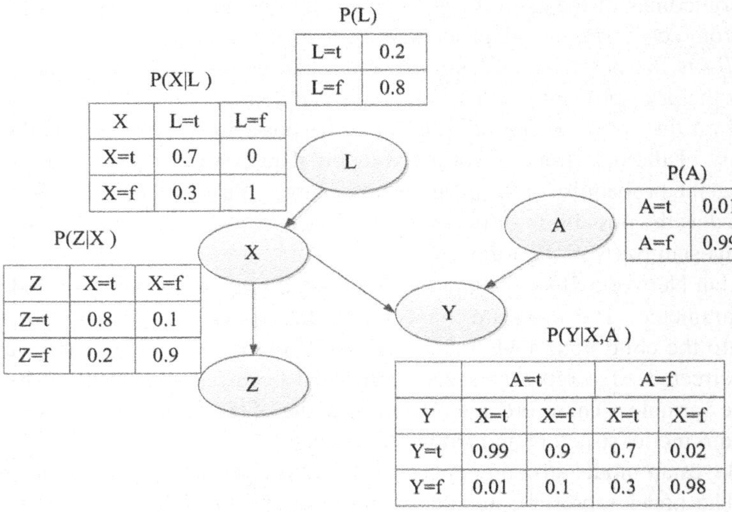

Fig. 1.9 Bayesian network example result

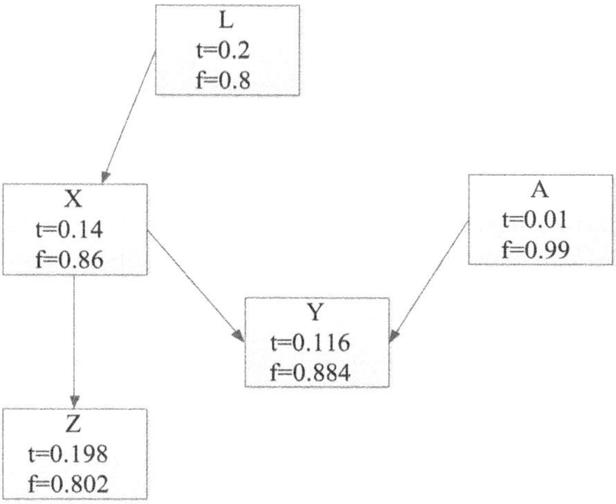

Fig. 1.10 Joint probabilistic propagation network of nodes

is the conditional probability distribution when L is known, i.e., $P(X|L)$, , and so on. Finally, the probabilities of each node (predictive variable) can be calculated, and the joint probability propagation of each node can be obtained, as shown in Fig. 1.10.

Bayesian networks are suitable for uncertainty and probabilistic events, and can learn causal or other relationships to predict future events [[213]]. Bayesian learning is the process of constructing a Bayesian network structure suitable for data input and output and calculating the parameter tables of each predictive variable in this structure through data cleaning, desensitization, and analysis training. In other words, the learning process includes network structure learning and conditional parameter learning. Through continuous network structure reconstruction and continuous data input learning training, new conditional parameters are obtained until the best results are achieved [[214]].

The most used Bayesian classifier is the Naive Bayesian classifier, which assumes that each node (predictive variable) is conditionally independent of each other. Although this greatly simplifies the calculation process, it is difficult for different attributes in daily life to meet this condition. The TAN (Tree Augmented Naive Bayesian) network is an improved model proposed by Fridmanl (1997). The essence of the TAN algorithm is to retain the structural characteristics of the Naive Bayesian algorithm while extending the model tree dependency, further relaxing the independence assumption of the Naive Bayesian network, and fully considering the dependency information between predictive variables when modeling [[215]]. From a practical life case point of view, the assumption of the TAN Bayesian network model is closer to life, its performance should be better than the Naive Bayesian network model, and it has the following notable features: (1) there is a dependency relationship between attribute nodes (predictive variables); (2) the class variable (root node) is the parent node of each predictive variable; (3) all attributes must be considered when modeling, even if some input variables do not significantly affect the output variables; (4) the class variable is the root node and has no parent nodes; (5)

attribute nodes (predictive variables) are allowed to have at most one other attribute as a parent node besides the class node; at the same time, common methods for parameter learning in Bayesian network models include maximum likelihood estimation, Bayesian parameter estimation, EM algorithm, and other classic algorithms. In Clementine, the main methods for parameter learning in Bayesian network models are maximum likelihood estimation (with consistency, efficiency, and invariance) and Bayesian parameter estimation (training and learning results).

This article selects the TAN Bayesian network model as a consumer behavior prediction tool for the following advantages: (1) it can simulate the complex relationships between important demand factors in online reviews, that is, the dimensions of the reviewer's comments; (2) it does not require prior assumption of data distribution, but obtains the matching model through autonomous learning and training of data; (3) this model can adapt to uncertainty, presenting results in the form of probability theory (data form), rather than a simple cause-and-effect relationship.

(3) Bayesian Network Research.

The Bayesian network model, as a combination of mathematical statistics and graphical reasoning, became popular in the late 1990s and has been widely used in behavioral learning and prediction in various disciplines since 2000. Bayesian networks are applicable to traffic safety, such as using dynamic Bayesian networks to predict changes in driver behavior [[216]], building behavior models in the field of autonomous driving, analyzing parking decision-making behavior, and studying behavior choices and characteristics of urban travel [[217]]; in the field of artificial intelligence, the focus is on using Bayesian networks to learn to manage robot behavior indicators [[218]], further exploring how Bayesian networks learn robot behavior and make predictions when sensors fail, and adaptive behavior learning under non-stationary conditions [[219]]; in the online education environment, the focus is on how to use Bayesian networks to learn to infer student behavior and predict learning styles [[220]]; in social networks, studying the influence of habits and patterns [[221]], analyzing the influencing factors of consumer behavior [[222]], and thus personalizing intelligent prediction of mobile phone user behavior [[223]]; in addition, it also includes supply chain risk propagation prediction [[224]] etc.

In the field of e-commerce online shopping research, the application of Bayesian networks for online review research has developed in recent years, but it focuses more on the impact or role of the product or online reviews themselves, such as Reshma's fully trained naive Bayesian classifier can accurately and truthfully refine effective reviews [[225]]; Khopkar discusses the predictability of early reviews on future product ratings in different models, finding that the Bayesian network model predicts well and the results of learning from less data have high credibility [[226]]; Chen found through Bayesian network analysis that free samples have a positive effect on online word-of-mouth [[227]]; Zhang Guangqian (2105) predicts consumer behavior and recommends new products based on the Bayesian network model established according to consumers' past shopping behavior [[228]].

1.5.4 Competitive Advantage Theory

The concept of competitive advantage was first proposed in the book "Theory of Monopolistic Competition" published by British economist Chamberlin in 1939 [[229]], but it did not attract the attention of the academic community at that time. It was not until the 1980s that Porter [[230]] Research on competitive advantage has been published, bringing competitive advantage back into the research field and becoming a hot topic in corporate strategic management. As research on competitive advantage deepens, Teece et al. (1997) believe that how to enable enterprises to obtain and maintain competitive advantage has become the core issue of strategic management [[231]]. The theory of corporate competitive advantage mainly answers the question of "why some companies can achieve better performance than other companies", that is, it explains the reasons for the performance differences between companies [[232]]. With the continuous deepening of research on competitive advantage, existing research explains the theory of competitive advantage from multiple perspectives, which can be mainly divided into three categories: the first is the theory of competitive advantage based on industry structure, the second is the theory of competitive advantage based on resources, and the third is the theory of competitive advantage based on capabilities.

(1) The theory of competitive advantage based on industry structure. The initial theory of competitive advantage research is the industry structure theory, its strategic thought originates from the industrial organization paradigm S-C-P (Structure-Conduct-Performance), this paradigm indicates that the market structure and behavior in the enterprise's industrial environment affect the performance of the enterprise [[233]]. Porter is one of the representative figures of this research. Porter's five forces model believes that the five forces of suppliers, customers, substitutes, complementors, and peers in the industry determine the scale and intensity of competition in the industry, and these five forces together affect the attractiveness of the industry and the competitive strategy decisions of enterprises.

(2) The theory of competitive advantage based on resources. In 1984, Wernerfelt's "Resource-Based View of the Firm" provided a theoretical basis for the research of competitive advantage theory, its goal is to find the competitive advantage of the enterprise from within the enterprise. The core of the resource-based view is that the enterprise is composed of a combination of various resources, and the competitive advantage of the enterprise comes from the resources it owns, especially heterogeneous resources. The external market structure and market opportunities can have a certain impact on the competitive advantage of the enterprise, but these two factors are not decisive [[234]]. The resource-based view focuses on the resources owned by the enterprise and explains the differences in competitive advantage.

(3) The theory of competitive advantage based on capabilities. Scholars have formed the theory of corporate capabilities based on the resource-based view. Prahalad and Hamel's 1990 article "Core Competence of the Corporation" indicates that the enterprise is composed of various capabilities, and these capabilities affect the competitive advantage and operating performance of the enterprise, and the core

competence of the enterprise refers to the integration of resources, technology, and knowledge [[235]].

1.5.5 *Sentiment Analysis in Text Mining*

Text sentiment analysis refers to the process of analyzing, processing, summarizing, and reasoning about texts with subjective emotional color about products, events, characters, etc. [[238]], its purpose is to discover the attitudes or opinions expressed by the texts generated by people, thereby judging the emotional tendency of the text, calculating and analyzing the emotional intensity of the text. This paper mainly analyzes the emotional polarity and intensity of different feature attributes of the import cross-border e-commerce platform, thereby discovering the competitive advantages of different platforms under different feature attributes.

When conducting sentiment analysis on text, it often requires the integration of technologies such as natural language processing, machine learning, and data mining. At the same time, with the rapid development of internet communication technology, more and more people express their views and attitudes toward characters, events, products, etc., through channels such as microblogs, forums, and e-commerce websites. This has led to many scholars obtaining online comment corpora that can be used for analysis from these channels and analyzing the key information hidden in them. The text corpus studied in this article is the online comments of related application software obtained from Apple's APP Store, and sentiment analysis is conducted on it. The process of sentiment analysis is based on the polarity of sentiment words, extracting feature opinion pairs from subjective sentences containing sentiment words, and then conducting sentiment analysis on the extracted feature opinion pairs.

(1) Feature Selection in Sentiment Analysis.

Different from feature extraction in text, feature selection in sentiment analysis includes two aspects. First, it is necessary to identify sentiment words and subjective sentences in the text with reasonable and effective methods. Secondly, it is necessary to identify the feature attributes related to sentiment words and judge the sentiment polarity of the feature attributes. When analyzing online comments, the focus is usually on the sentiment polarity of a certain feature attribute mentioned in the online comments. Therefore, it is necessary to extract feature opinion word pairs from online comments. At present, the commonly used methods for feature extraction in text sentiment analysis are: selection methods based on part-of-speech templates, and selection methods based on syntactic relationships.

(a) Selection method based on part-of-speech templates. In the online comments of cross-border e-commerce platforms, users usually use sentiment words to express their evaluations and views on different feature attributes of the platform, and feature words and sentiment words usually appear in pairs in comments. Therefore, when analyzing the sentiment tendency of the text, the collocation structure of feature words and sentiment words that often appear can be obtained based on statistical methods, and text sentiment analysis can be conducted by extracting the fixed collocation of feature sentiment words. In Chinese, the collocation of text part-of-speech is more complex, and it is not easy to obtain the collocation pattern between feature words and sentiment words using this method, and the calculation amount is large.

(b) Selection method based on syntactic relationships. In Chinese grammar, there are grammatical relationships between words. By using dependency syntax to analyze the grammatical relationships between words in a sentence, and locating the positions of various grammatical components in the sentence, a new research method is provided for accurately obtaining feature words and their corresponding sentiment words. Nie Hui et al. (2018) used dependency syntax analysis to build a feature dictionary for online comments in the catering industry, extracted user opinion pairs, calculated the sentiment extremes of different user opinions, and mined competitive intelligence in user opinions [[239]]. In dependency syntax relationships, subject-predicate relationships, verb-object relationships, prepositional phrase structures, and attributive relationships often exist between feature words and sentiment words.

Sentiment classification, also known as sentiment orientation classification, aims to identify users' opinions and views on events, products, etc., in the text, and judge the sentiment orientation of the text. It is the core of sentiment analysis technology. At present, there are mainly three types of sentiment classification methods, namely, dictionary-based methods, machine learning-based methods, and deep learning-based methods.

The first is the dictionary-based method. This method needs to build a sentiment dictionary of the text in advance, perform syntactic analysis on the preprocessed text, and identify sentiment words in the text according to certain matching rules. The polarity represented by different words is used to calculate the sentiment extreme value, and then the sentiment orientation of the text is determined based on the size of this value. This sentiment classification method is easy to implement, but its adaptability is relatively poor. A comprehensive sentiment dictionary must be built to ensure the accuracy of text sentiment analysis.

The second is a method based on machine learning. This method generally treats sentiment classification as a common classification problem, using machine learning algorithms to classify text sentiment. According to the labeling situation of the training samples used in machine learning, sentiment classification methods are mainly divided into three categories, including supervised learning methods, semi-supervised learning methods, and unsupervised learning methods. Supervised learning methods require training on many labeled samples, and finally obtain a sentiment classification model. This method requires manual labeling of many samples, which is time-consuming and laborious. Semi-supervised learning methods train on a small number of labeled samples and learn on many unlabeled samples to obtain a sentiment classification model. This method reduces the number of texts that need to be labeled to build a model, improving the performance of machine learning methods. Unsupervised learning methods refer to using unlabeled samples for sentiment classification modeling. In sentiment classification based on machine learning, the quality of labeled text affects the performance of the classification model, and the classification models used by this method mainly include support vector machines, naive Bayes, maximum entropy models, etc.

The third is a method based on deep learning. With the deepening of neural network research, more and more scholars apply deep learning technology to sentiment classification problems. The sentiment classification method based on deep learning includes two steps: first, the text to be classified is converted into semantic word vectors, then, using semantic synthesis rules to obtain the feature expression of the text corresponding to the word vector, and finally, the feature expression is classified for sentiment. This method avoids a lot of manual labeling work and has a great advantage in sentiment classification.

1.5.6 Double Difference Model Metric Analysis

The essence of the double difference model is the econometric analysis of panel data. Panel data is all sample data of the research object under multiple periods, forming a data matrix of time dimension and space dimension. The double difference model is an effective method to evaluate policy effects. The steps to evaluate policy effects with the double difference model are as follows:

First, select the experimental group and the control group. If the individual is affected by the policy, the value of its group dummy variable is 1, representing the experimental group; otherwise, the value is 0, representing the control group. The purpose of adding a control group is to avoid selection bias, that is, when the policy is not implemented, the experimental group may also be affected by other potential factors, resulting in the difference before and after the policy implementation not necessarily coming from the policy effect.

The analysis process is divided into the following two steps: The first step is to calculate the difference estimator of the experimental group, compare the difference before and after the policy implementation of the experimental group, as shown in formula (1.6). The second step is to calculate the difference estimator of the control group, as shown in formula (1.7).

$$\overline{y}_{treated,after} - \overline{y}_{treated,before} \tag{1.6}$$

$$\overline{y}_{control,after} - \overline{y}_{control,before} \tag{1.7}$$

By combining the two difference estimators and calculating the difference between the mean values of the experimental group and the control group, we can obtain the policy effect estimate *DID*, as shown in formula (1.8):

$$DID = \left(\overline{y}_{treated,after} - \overline{y}_{treated,before}\right) - \left(\overline{y}_{control,after} - \overline{y}_{control,before}\right) \tag{1.8}$$

If the experimental group, when not affected by the policy, has a similar change pattern over time as the control group, it indicates that the potential factors have the same impact on the individuals in both groups, that is, the parallel trend condition is satisfied [[240]], (as shown in Fig. 1.11), this is the premise for evaluating policy effects using the double difference model.

If the individuals in the experimental group are affected by the policy, they are marked as 1, and all other situations are marked as 0, as shown in Table 1.3.

In practical analysis, the policy effect *DID* in formula (1.9) cannot be directly observed, and is usually estimated using the method in formula (1.10). In the formula, y_{it} is the dependent variable of the policy effect, β is the coefficient of the explanatory variable, *Time* is the time variable, $Treated_i$ is the grouping variable, ε_{it} is the random error term, and the corresponding variables are controlled as needed.

$$y_{it} = \beta_0 + \beta_1 * Time + \beta_2 * Treated_i + \beta_3 * (Treated_i * Time) + \varepsilon_i \quad (1.9)$$

Time-differentiating formula (1.9) gives formula (1.10).

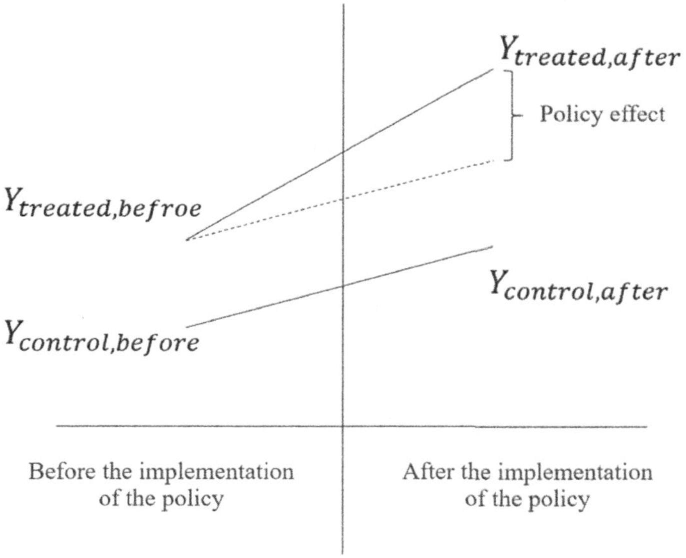

Fig. 1.11 Parallel trend conditions

Table 1.3 Policy intervention and non-policy intervention

Treated/Control	Control	Treated
Before	0	0
After	0	1

$$\Delta y_i = \beta_1 + \beta_3 * Treated_i + \Delta\varepsilon_i \tag{1.10}$$

Differentiating formula (1.11) again and taking the expectation, we know that β_3 is the policy effect *DID* we need to obtain.

$$E(\Delta y_{treated} - \Delta y_{control}) = \beta_3 \tag{1.11}$$

It is crucial to examine whether the evaluation results of the difference-in-differences model will change with the change of parameter settings. The robustness of the model is usually tested by changing a specific parameter and repeating the experiment to observe whether the sign and significance of the estimated coefficient will change. If changes occur, it indicates that the original experiment lacks robustness, and the model needs to be adjusted. Parallel trend tests and placebo tests are two commonly used methods for testing the robustness of the difference-in-differences model. The parallel trend test requires that if not affected by policy, the changes of individuals in the experimental group are consistent with the changes of individuals in the control group. If inconsistencies occur, it indicates that the results estimated by the difference-in-differences model are biased [[241]]. The essence of the placebo test is to change the data, re-estimate the experiment, and exclude the interference of other unobservable variables on the estimated results by constructing virtual time or virtual individuals. If the baseline model results are random, or there are potential factors affecting the reliability of the experimental results, the estimated coefficient of the re-experiment will be significant. If the estimated results of the virtual policy time point or virtual sample individuals are consistent with expectations, that is, the estimated coefficient is not significant, it means that the baseline results are robust [[242]].

The multi-period difference-in-differences model evolved from the difference-in-differences model. Unlike the difference-in-differences model, which is mainly suitable for consistent policy action times, the multi-period difference-in-differences model is suitable for multiple policy action times and is often used in policy effect evaluation studies where policy times are randomly distributed. Since the cross-border e-commerce policy has different action times in various pilot zones, this paper uses the multi-period difference-in-differences model to evaluate the policy effect. The specific method will be detailed in Chapter 3.

1.5.7 Mediation Effect Model

Unlike only analyzing the relationship between the explanatory variable and the dependent variable, the mediation effect model can introduce intermediate variables to analyze the process and mechanism of the influence of the explanatory variable on the dependent variable.

The principle of the mediation effect model is shown in formulas (1.12)–(1.14). In order to analyze the relationship between the dependent variable Y and the explanatory variable X, the variable M is introduced as an intermediary variable. First, with Y as the dependent variable, regress Y and X, test whether the explanatory variable significantly affects the dependent variable, the significance of the regression coefficient c indicates the significance of Y and X; then with M as the dependent variable, regress M and X, the significance of the coefficient a indicates the significance of M and X; finally, with Y as the dependent variable, X and M *To perform regression on the explanatory variables, observe the coefficients* c' *and b for significance. The significance of the coefficient b will indicate the significance of Y with respect to M; after the coefficients a and b are significant, test the significance of* c' *If significant, it indicates that the variable M plays a mediating role for Y.*

$$Y = cX + e_1 \tag{1.12}$$

$$M = aX + e_2 \tag{1.13}$$

$$Y = c'X + bM + e_3 \tag{1.14}$$

In the mediation effect model, the coefficient c is the total effect of the explanatory variable X on the dependent variable Y, as shown in Fig. 1.12. The coefficient c' represents the direct effect of X on Y after controlling for the mediating variable. The coefficient a is the effect of the explanatory variable on the mediating variable, and the coefficient b represents the effect of the mediating variable on the dependent variable. Therefore, the relationship between the total effect and the mediating effect is: $= c' + a * b$, $a * b$ is the mediating effect that needs to be analyzed, and the value of this mediating effect can also be represented by $c - c'$.

The stepwise regression test method is a commonly used mediating effect model by scholars

at home and abroad. This method was first proposed by Baron and Kenny, and it tests the role of mediating variables through three-step regression analysis [[243]]. The method of mediating effect analysis is widely used in the study of policy measures. This paper uses the stepwise regression test method to analyze the mediating effect model of environmental factors on cross-border e-commerce policy effects.

1.5.8 Policy Literature Metrology Analysis

Policy literature metrology is a discipline that uses mathematical statistics to quantitatively describe, evaluate the academic status quo, and predict development trends. The term "literature metrology" was first proposed by British scholar Pritchard, which is the science of applying mathematics and statistics to books and other text communication carriers [[244]]. In the process of development, it gradually developed

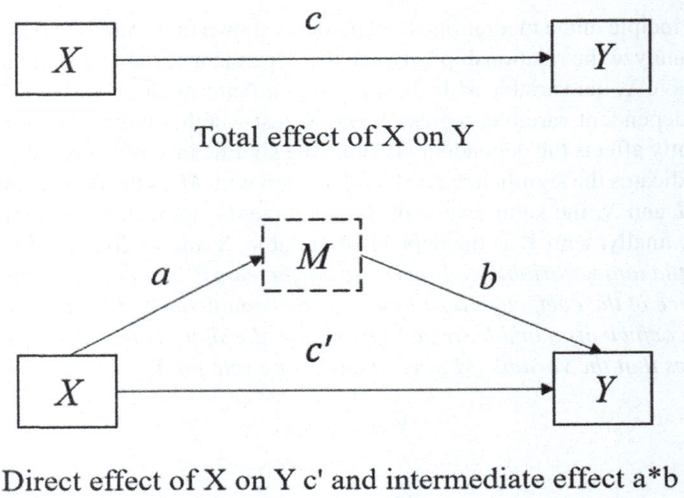

Fig. 1.12 Schematic diagram of mediation effect analysis

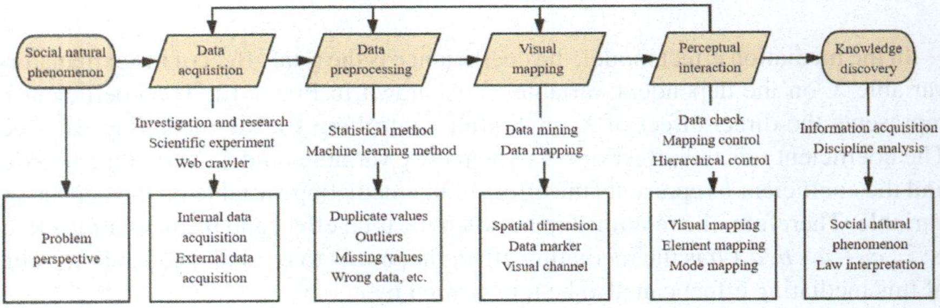

Fig. 1.13 Data visualization analysis process

from elementary statistical measurement to the science of quantitative research on literature with mathematical statistics and other mathematical tools, used to reveal the quantitative change rules and system structure of literature.

Policy literature metrology analysis refers to the research object based on literature information, using different methods to decompose and represent literature, and obtaining data units of different levels and types. Common methods of literature metrology analysis include feature analysis, content analysis, citation analysis, and relationship analysis [[245]].

(1) Feature Analysis of Policy Literature.

The n feature attributes of policy literature W are $a_1, a_2, \ldots, a_n$. $(a_1, a_2, \ldots, a_n)$ an be used to represent it. This ordered sequence is referred to as the metadata representation of the document W, and can be represented by the row matrix A (as shown in formula 1.15).

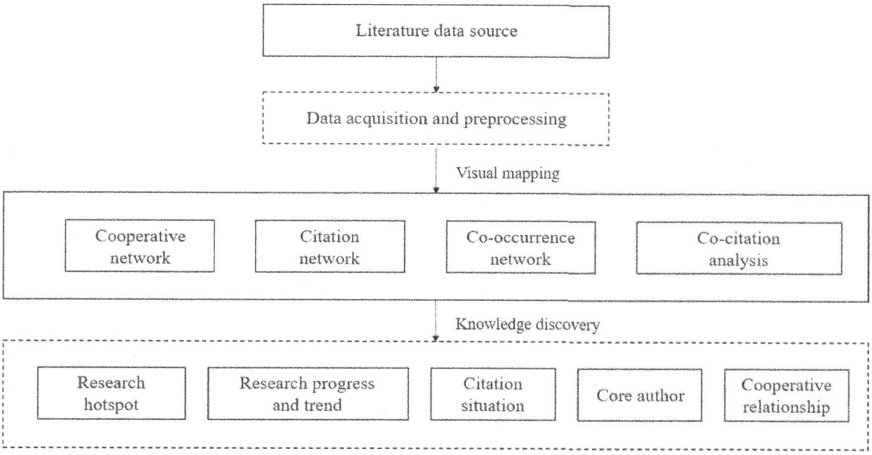

Fig. 1.14 Main contents of literature visualization methods

$$A = (a_1, a_2, \ldots, a_n) \tag{1.15}$$

Therefore, in a collection of m policy documents, a $m * n$ matrix can be used to represent the feature data of the document collection (as shown in formula 1.16).

$$A = \begin{bmatrix} a_{11} & \ldots & a_{1n} \\ \ldots & \ldots & \ldots \\ a_{m1} & \ldots & a_{mn} \end{bmatrix} \tag{1.16}$$

The feature measurement analysis of policy documents includes the analysis of author nationality, number of documents, quality of documents, field of documents, etc. Through these feature analyses, the research focus of this discipline can be grasped at a macro level.

(2) Policy Document Content Analysis.

Policy document content analysis is a method of systematically quantifying the content of policy documents, aiming to measure the essential facts or trends in policy documents. Content analysis can be divided into word frequency analysis and length analysis according to different analysis units. Word frequency analysis is the word frequency analysis of document theme words, keywords, and indicator words. Length analysis is the measurement of content units with independent meanings. After processing and tagging, policy document W forms x keywords or independent content units $c_1, c_2, \ldots, c_x$, with their frequencies of occurrence being $f_1, f_2, \ldots, f_x$, then we can conduct content analysis on the document W from the continuous set $\{(c_1, f_1), (c_2, f_2), \ldots, (c_x, f_x)\}$. Content analysis of the document can quantify the high-frequency words and emerging words to reflect the research hotspots and future trends in the discipline.

(3) Citation Analysis of Policy Documents.

Citation analysis studies the citation and cited relationships between documents, revealing quantitative characteristics and citation relationships. For journals, commonly used metrics in citation analysis include: citation rate, cited rate, impact factor, citation coupling strength, and co-citation strength, as shown in Table 1.4.

(4) Policy Document Relationship Analysis.

Relationship analysis refers to the cooperation relationship among authors in a set of documents. It can be measured by indicators of social network analysis methods, as shown in Table 1.5. Treating *N* documents as *N* nodes, the analysis is conducted from the indicators such as degree, network density, clustering coefficient, degree centrality, and betweenness centrality, achieving citation analysis, cooperation analysis, and other document relationships and research hotspots.

Connectivity indicators can explain the universality of cooperation phenomena in this document network. Network density and clustering coefficient can indicate the density and degree of cooperation in the document network. Average degree and centrality indicators can show the distribution of document cooperation in the document network. Through the analysis of document cooperation relationships, it can summarize the development trajectory and research focus of the research field, and judge the authoritative figures and authoritative views in this field.

From a research perspective, methods of document feature data analysis, content analysis, relationship analysis, and citation analysis are widely used in fields such as technological innovation, business management, and finance. This provides ideas for the application of bibliometric methods in cross-border e-commerce policy research.

(5) Policy Document Bibliometric Analysis Method.

Policy documents are the material carriers of policy thoughts. Policy documents have roughly the same basic elements as other documents, so policy documents can be considered a type of document, and can also be expanded from policy document features, content analysis, relationship analysis, and citation analysis. However,

Table 1.4 Common indexes of citation analysis in policy literature

Index	Definition
Citation rate	The number of references in the journal/total number of published articles refers to the average number of references per article, which measures the ability of the research object to absorb knowledge
Cited rate	The number of cited articles published in the journal in the statistical year/the number of articles published in the journal in the current year
Impact factor	The total number of citations of the papers published in the journal in these 2 years in the statistical year/the total number of papers published in the journal in these 2 years. In journals, it refers to the average number of times an article is cited
Citation coupling	If two or more articles jointly cite one or more references, the two articles form a coupling relationship, and the coupling strength depends on the number of references jointly cited
Co-citation	If two articles are cited by other articles at the same time, the two articles form a co-citation relationship, and the co-citation intensity depends on the number of citations of these two articles

Table 1.5 Applications of social network analysis methods in literature relationship analysis

Index	Definition	Formula
Connectivity	It represents the degree of connectivity of the network and analyzes the minimum number of nodes between specified nodes	$L(n_i) = \min\langle n_i, n_j\rangle$
Average degree	The degree of a node n_i is equal to the number of lines associated with the node in the network, and the degree of a literature node determines the influence of the node in the network. The average node degree is the average of all degrees in the network	$\overline{d} = \frac{\sum_{i=1}^{N} d(n_i)}{N}$
Network density	It represents the degree of connection between nodes, the ratio of the actual number of connections between network nodes L to the theoretical maximum number of connections	$\Delta = \frac{2L}{N*(N-1)}$
Clustering coefficient	It represents the degree of clustering of nodes in the network, and refers to the probability that node k_i directly connected to the node is directly connected in theory	$C(n_i) = \frac{2N}{\lvert k_i\rvert*(\lvert k_i\rvert-1)}$

policy documents differ from journal documents. Policies are the guiding principles and guidelines adopted by government departments for specific goals during a certain period, characterized by timeliness, goal orientation, and authority. Scholars at home and abroad have transformed the unstructured and non-quantitative content of policy documents into quantitative information and data for further analysis and processing [[246]].

The content analysis of policy documents usually uses policy tool research methods. Policy tool analysis is a specific application of content analysis methods in the field of policy research. Through systematic analysis and quantitative research on policy content, the meaning of policy units can be inferred from words and sentences with representative significance. According to the different impact levels, Rothwell and Zegveld proposed the theories of supply-type, environment-type, and demand-type policy tools, each type of policy tools as shown in Table 1.6 [[247]].

The research questions applicable to policy document metrics not only cover the three major elements of policy objects, policy goals, and implementation means, but also include policy implementation time, effectiveness level, document distribution, policy themes, subject cooperation models, the structure and evolution of the policy system, and other policy features, to scientifically evaluate policy schemes [[248]]. The research methods of policy document metrics include policy feature analysis, policy subject relationship analysis, policy citation association analysis, policy content analysis, policy tool analysis, etc., as shown in Table 1.7.

Bibliometric analysis helps to understand and comprehend the hotspots and development trends of disciplines, and it has been widely used in multiple disciplines and fields. However, there is less bibliometric analysis in the field of cross-border e-commerce, so it is of certain value to analyze the characteristic rules and development trends of cross-border e-commerce policies from the perspective of bibliometrics.

Table 1.6 Theory of three environmental policy instruments

Types of policy instruments	Implication	Classified keywords
Supply type	It covers the government's direct investment and support in manpower, capital, technology, services, and other aspects	Manpower, capital, technology, services
Environmental type	It emphasizes that the government provides a favorable external macro environment through various measures such as fiscal, tax, financial and regulatory measures	Finance, taxation, regulations
Demand type	The government reduces market uncertainty or creates new markets by means of procurement, outsourcing, and regulation, thus creating market demand for emerging economic formats or new scientific and technological products	Procurement, outsourcing, regulation

Table 1.7 Bibliometric research methods of policy

Research method	Bibliometrics	Policy bibliometrics
Feature analysis	Taking the number of documents as the object to analyze the time trend of the number of documents; Taking the author as the object to analyze the author's academic growth track	Taking policy literature as the object to analyze the time trend of the number of policies; Taking the policy subject as the object to analyze the function change of the policy subject; Analyzing the change of policy implementation efficiency with the target group as the orientation
Relationship analysis	Taking the author cooperation as the object to analyze the correlation characteristics and relations of the literature cooperation in the literature system	Taking the policy subject cooperation network as the object to analyze the correlation features and relations of subject cooperation in the policy literature system
Citation analysis	Taking the number of citations as the object to analyze the fluctuation and persistence of academic influences	Taking the reference times of policy as the object to analyze the fluctuation and persistence of policy influence
Content analysis	Taking keywords as the object to mine research topics and analyze the evolution characteristics of research hotspots	Taking keywords as the object to mine the policy theme and analyze the change rule of policy theme
Policy instrument analysis		Taking the combination of policy instruments as the object to analyze the allocation of government resources

1.5.9 Data Visualization Theory

Data visualization is divided into scientific visualization, information visualization, and visualization analysis [[249]]. Scientific visualization is the graphic rendering of scientific data in different disciplinary fields. These data have fixed data structure attributes and can discover patterns from the data; information visualization can handle both numerical and non-numerical data, usually with abstract data structures; visualization analysis is the ultimate goal of data visualization, emphasizing the exploration of social and natural phenomena behind the data through perceptual interaction, combining interactive visual representation with quantitative statistics, data mining, and other basic analysis processes to effectively implement reasoning, decision-making, and other complex behavioral activities.

With the continuous enrichment of data types and the exponential growth of data volume, visualization methods are also constantly improving. They can not only effectively select and express abstract and complex data, help users better understand data, and discover potential rules, but also provide decision support for governments, enterprises, scholars, and other groups through interactive means and assist academic research.

The data for visualization includes multidimensional data, spatiotemporal data, text data, relationship data, and other data types. In terms of multidimensional data, it is usually necessary to map multidimensional data to two-dimensional or three-dimensional graphics for analysis, such as scatter plot matrices, three-dimensional coordinates, and radar charts, etc.; in terms of spatiotemporal data, geographic information data and time series change data are important contents for visualizing real things; in terms of text data, the visualization objects are texts, such as keywords, phrases, topics, and time-varying texts; in terms of relationship data, more complex relationships such as radiation relationships and social network relationships can be represented through visualization methods.

The basic process of data visualization includes the stages of problem proposal, data collection, data preprocessing, visualization mapping (drawing), perceptual interaction, and knowledge discovery, as shown in Fig. 1.13. Data visualization starts from the problem perspective of social phenomena, obtains internal and external original data through survey research, scientific experiments, web crawlers, etc., and after preprocessing the data through statistical methods, machine learning, etc., maps the data from the perspective of spatial dimensions, data marking methods, and visual channels to visualization charts, controls the mapping of data through perceptual interaction, and thus achieves knowledge discovery in the process of visualization analysis, aiming to explain social and natural phenomena and rules.

Visual mapping is the process of mapping analyzed data onto graphics with attributes such as color, brightness, size, shape, position, area, and slope. It can also present the temporal attributes of data through dynamic graphs to further analyze abstract and complex data. The spatial dimensions include two-dimensional, three-dimensional, maps, etc., representing the degrees of freedom in space; data marking is the mapping of data attributes to visual geometric graphic elements, common geometric graphics include points, lines, surfaces, bodies, etc.; visual channels are the values of data attributes mapped to visual presentation parameters, reflecting the quantitative information of data attributes, including position, hue, shape, pattern, length, area, and saturation, etc. Visualization chart drawing includes three methods: original data drawing, statistical value plotting, and multi-view associated drawing. Original data drawing can adopt line charts, bar charts, scatter plots, bubble charts, radar charts, heat maps, etc., statistical value plotting can use box plots, coordinate charts, curve.

charts, etc., multi-view associated drawing refers to the joint drawing of data with different types of attributes on one chart, achieving joint data analysis.

The key technology of data visualization can be represented as: data visualization mapping (drawing) is the key step of data visualization, the current main data visualization methods include using web-based interactive drawing libraries, JavaScript-based interactive chart libraries, Java-based graphic databases, and mature visualization software, as shown in Table 1.8.

The purpose of data visualization is to obtain abstract information and achieve knowledge discovery. To achieve this goal, visualization drawing can be carried out through comparison, distribution, composition, and relationship analysis. First, comparative visualization analyzes the differences of the research object by comparing the values between different elements or at different times. The values between different elements can be represented by bar charts, line charts, etc., and the values at different times can be represented by timeline charts, line charts, heat maps, etc. Second, distribution visualization is to visualize the characteristics of data distribution according to specific charts, commonly used for data anomaly discovery, numerical filtering, and basic statistical feature analysis of data, for example, the distribution of multiple dimensions can be represented by scatter plots, and location data can be represented by maps. Third, composition visualization is the analysis of data proportions or inclusion situations, for example, data that increases or decreases relative to the whole can be represented by waterfall charts, paired factors from multi-dimensional problems can be represented by matrix charts, and data with multi-layer

Table 1.8 Main technology or software of data visualization

Main technology or software	Introduction	Main application field
Plotly, Matplotlib	Web-based interactive drawing library	Data statistics
Echarts, Highcharts	Interactive chart library based on JavaScript	Personalized visual interaction
Citespace Gephi, Ucinet	Visualization software based on Java environment	Bibliometrics
Power BI	Desktop software composed of Power Pivot, Power View and Power Query	Business intelligence
Neo4J	NOSQL graphic database based on Java language	Relationship analysis

inclusion relationships can be represented by nested ring charts. Fourth, relationship visualization often combines statistical correlation analysis methods to judge the influence relationship between multiple factors through visual mapping and scene requirements, common charts include relationship charts, path charts, network charts.

Analyze the intrinsic connection and evolution rules of related knowledge and research topics in this research field, and realize the effective sorting and prediction of research hotspots and development trends in this field.

Collaborative network analysis is to analyze the authors and publishing institutions of literature in the research field, and to mine the cooperation relationship between authors and publishing institutions; citation network analysis identifies the core authors, important literature, and citation situations in the research field by analyzing the citation relationship of literature; co-occurrence network analysis can filter out the keywords of literature content, explaining the research hotspots and research trends in a certain field; co-citation network analysis can explore the research progress and evolution dynamics of the field.

In the research of bibliometric visualization at home and abroad, scholars usually use visualization software such as Citespace, Gephi, Ucinet, to analyze the literature in the research field. Guo Xiaochun and others used Gephi software to systematically review the literature on cryptocurrency [250]; Vahidzadeh R visualized the co-occurrence relationship of keywords, hot topics, etc. in the research literature of regional industrial symbiosis in the Gephi environment [251]. Liu Hang and others used the Citespace analysis tool to draw a visualized knowledge structure network map of domestic and foreign scholars' research on innovation diffusion at home and abroad and conducted comparative analysis [252]; Xie Xuemei and others used CiteSpace and Ucinet software to visualize the analysis of domestic and foreign literature in the field of innovation ecosystem, and drew a co-occurrence map of keywords and a time zone map of co-cited literature [253]; Zang Qichao and others applied CiteSpace to draw a scientific knowledge map of the literature on team social networks in the Web of Science database and conducted visual analysis [254]; Lu Yuzhong and others targeted the literature related to venture capital research in international top journals, and explored the hotspots, evolution process, and new trends of international venture capital research through visualized bibliometric analysis [255].

In addition, some scholars have realized the visualization of bibliometrics through self-development, which can further measure literature outside of academic literature. Zeng Li and others comprehensively used bibliometric tools and self-developed systems to display the current situation, hotspots, and frontier trends in the field of science and technology policy research through visual analysis methods [256]; Huang Xiaobin and others collected, extracted metadata, clustered and visualized bibliometric analysis of China's think tank policy literature by using bibliometrics, knowledge maps, cluster analysis, visual analysis, etc. [257]; Xie Xiufang and others used Timeflow and Gephi tools to visualize empirical research results, and analyzed the development trend of global renewable energy technology field and the strategic planning of various countries in chronological order [258]; Xiong Li and others analyzed the related theories of domestic and foreign think tanks and data visualization, and analyzed the hotspot methods, application technologies, and innovation trends of big data visualization methods in think tank research [259]; Yang Yanan and others used a multi-view collaborative visualization method to extract information and conduct interactive visual exploration analysis on the policy sequence text of multiple policy subjects within the Beijing Zhongguancun Science Park Commission [260].

Combining the above research findings, data visualization methods can be applied to the analysis of various data types and data structures, and modern data analysis tools can be used to analyze and evaluate policy literature, which is currently mainly concentrated in the field of science and technology policy. Therefore, the related methods and existing research provide ideas for the research of policy literature in the field of cross-border e-commerce by data visualization.

References

1. Li X, Zhaoran X, Yiqun L (2020) Cross-border e-commerce[M].Higher Education Press, Beijing
2. Yu Z (2021) New journey to the "fourteenth five-year plan": china's foreign trade stabilizes and improves quality to achieve high-level opening up. [EB/OL] (2021–11–28). Retrived from http://www.gov.cn/xinwen/2021-11/28/content_5653875.htm.
3. Li X, Qian D, Zhaoran X (2019) Research on the matching of cross-border e-commerce transaction subjects and import modes—based on the data of 50 small and micro cross-border e-commerce platforms[J]. Price Monthly 09:46–52
4. Xiaojun L, Bin Z The collaborative development of cross-border e-commerce logistics between china and the countries along the "belt and road"[J]
5. Youwei L, Kaiqian K (2014) Development form, obstacles and next steps of cross-border e-commerce in China[J]. Reform 05:68–74
6. China Customs. (1) total value of import and export goods (rmb value) a: annual table[EB/OL]. Retrived from http://www.customs.gov.cn/customs/302249/zfxxgk/2799825/302274/302277/302276/4005480/index.html
7. Ministry of Commerce of the People's Republic Of China (2013) Opinions on implementing policies to support cross-border e-commerce retail exports transmitted by the general office of the state council[Z], Beijing, 29 August 2013
8. General office of the state council (2015) Guiding opinions of the general office of the state council on promoting the healthy and rapid development of cross-border e-commerce[Z]. Beijing 16 June 2015
9. Ministry of commerce of the people's Republic of China (2019) National import and export work conference 2019 held in beijing[z]. In: national import and export work conference, Beijing,18 March 2019
10. The central people's government of the people's Republic of China (2020) State council: 46 new cross-border e-commerce pilot zones established[z]. In: state council executive meeting, Beijing, 08 April 2020
11. Hangzhou Municipal People's Government (2016) Hangzhou practice of cross-border e-commerce pilot zone taking the lead[z]. Hangzhou daily, 10 January 2016
12. Zhejiang Provincial People's Government Office (2015) Notice of the zhejiang provincial people's government on issuing the implementation plan for the china (hangzhou) cross-border e-commerce comprehensive pilot zone[z]. Hangzhou, 25 June 2015
13. Hangzhou Municipal People's Government Office (2016) Notice of the hangzhou municipal people's government office on issuing the development plan for the china (hangzhou) cross-border e-commerce comprehensive pilot zone[z]. Hangzhou, 25 January 2016

14. Hangzhou Municipal People's Government Office (2019) Implementation opinions of the hangzhou municipal people's government on accelerating the development of cross-border e-commerce[z]. Hangzhou, 02 December 2019
15. Shanghai Municipal People's Government Office (2015) Notice of the shanghai municipal people's government office on issuing several opinions on promoting the development of cross-border e-commerce in the city[z]. Shanghai, 25 September 2015
16. Shanghai Municipal Commerce Commission (2020) Notice of the shanghai municipal commerce commission on organizing the identification of shanghai cross-border e-commerce demonstration park[z]. Shanghai, 04 August 2020
17. Wailian W, Mingyu W, Shuzhen L (2013) Analysis and suggestions on the current situation of cross-border e-commerce in china[J]. E-commerce 9:23–24
18. Yunbo C (2013) Discussion on the development trend of cross-border e-commerce in china under the international e-commerce development trend[J]. Business 13:295–296
19. Jiaguo L, Wei L, Xiaoxi L, Jinlou Z (2015) Research on the development of sino-russian cross-border e-commerce based on grounded theory method[J]. China Soft Sci 09:27–40
20. Wang Y, Lee SH (2017) The effect of cross-border e-commerce on china's international trade: an empirical study based on transaction cost analysis[J]. Sustainability 9(11):2028
21. Cong W, Qing M, Yi L (2012) Analysis of small amount cross-border e-commerce[J]. Value Eng 32:180–181
22. Juan L (2012) Discussion on the rise and development issues of small amount cross-border e-commerce in foreign trade[J]. Foreign Trade Prac 2:89–92
23. Jianzheng Y, Han L (2014) Survey analysis of cross-border e-commerce application status in different scale enterprises in China[j]. Contemp Econ Manag 1:25–29
24. Jianzheng Y, Lu Y (2014) Analysis of cross-border e-commerce application in china's foreign trade enterprises[j]. Contemp Econ Manag 6:58–63
25. Ai W, Yang J, Wang L (2016) Revelation of cross-border logistics performance for the manufacturing industry development[J]. Int J Mobile Commun 14(6):593–609
26. Luo Y (2001) Determinants of entry in an emerging economy: a multilevel approach[j]. J Manag Stud 38(3):443–472
27. Wei W (2009) Research on the influencing factors of international entrepreneurship mode selection of multinational corporations[d]. Jilin University
28. Lin W, Lifan Y, Jianzheng Y (2013) China information economics society annual conference paper collection[C]. 25 November 2013
29. Jianzheng Y, Zi L (2014) Research on the influencing factors of cross-border e-commerce in the yangtze river delta region[J].Observation 08:7–8
30. Lu B, Wang H (2016) Research on the competitive strategy of cross-border e-commerce comprehensive pilot area based on the spatial competition[j]. Sci Program 2016:12
31. Wang H, Xiao M, Huo Y (2017) Research on the construction strategy of cross-border e-commerce comprehensive pilot area based on salop mode [J]. Int J Innov Comput Inform Control 13(5):1563–1577
32. Chen N, Yang J (2017) Mechanism of government policies in cross-border e-commerce on firm performance and implications on m-commerce[J]. Int J Mobile Commun 15(1):69–84
33. Lan G, Jungsoo H (2019) A review of the research on e-commerce ecosystem in china[j]. J Digit Converg 17(8):141–148
34. Huimin W (2014) Cross-border e-commerce and transformation and upgrading of international trade[J]. Int Econ Cooperation 10:60–62
35. Li X, Kaiwen Y (2020) Research on the correlation between the development of cross-border e-commerce ecology and policy combination dimensions[J]. Soft Sci 34(02):129–136
36. Feng D, Jun C, Chao C (2019) Research on cross-border e-commerce competitive strategy based on differentiation strategy[J].Oper Res Manag (6):33–40
37. JeongHugh H, Hag-Min K (2020) The role of information technology use for increasing consumer informedness in cross-border electronic commerce: an empirical study[J]. Electronic commerce research and zhang xiaheng. Evaluation of the efficiency of input of production factors in cross-border e-commerce[J]. J Beijing Univ Post Telecommun (social sciences edition) 22(01):30–35

38. Xibao Z, Yitao S, Baochang X (2020) Trade facilitation and the development of china's cross-border e-commerce – an empirical analysis based on the double difference method[j]. East China Econ Manag 34(02):94–103
39. Lei S, Fang W (2015) The current situation and countermeasures of China's cross-border e-commerce development[J]. China Circulation Econ 3:38–41
40. Fen W (2017) Research on trade facilitation and the development of china's cross-border e-commerce[D]. Zhejiang University
41. Shuzhong M, Li C, Hongsheng Z (2018) Research on the comprehensive performance of China's cross-border e-commerce listed companies[J]. Int Bus Res 2:48–66
42. Jianzheng Y, Lu Y (2014) Application analysis of cross-border e-commerce in China's foreign trade enterprises[J]. Contemp Econ Manag 6:58–63
43. Zhitian Z, Jianzheng Y (2014) Identification, verification and comprehensive evaluation of cross-border e-commerce capabilities of small and medium-sized manufacturing enterprises[J]. Syst Eng 10:53–62
44. Li X, Lu Y (2016) The driving mechanism and strategy of the development of Shanghai's cross-border e-commerce platform[J]. Sci Technol Manag Res 13:159–163
45. Aiguo T (2016) Problems and countermeasures of cross-border retail e-commerce under the background of "Internet+"[J]. China Circulation Econ 30(05):99–105
46. Yong P (2017) The current situation, problems and future development of cross-border e-commerce in china[J]. Theoretical Vision 12:36–39
47. Fei W (2019) Research on new ideas for promoting the development of cross-border e-commerce in china with blockchain technology[J]. Theoretical Monthly 03:117–122
48. Weinian Z, Xiaojing L, Menghua L (2019) Research on the influencing factors of China's cross-border e-commerce development[J]. J Hainan Univ (humanities and social sciences) 37(03):57–63
49. Lijuan Z (2015) Empirical analysis of the influencing factors of cross-border e-commerce customer experience – from the perspective of consumer characteristics[J]. Int Bus (J Univ Int Bus Econ) 03:94–101
50. Shaoye S (2016) Research on the competitive advantage of cross-border b2c platforms from the perspective of bilateral markets[J]. Bus Econ Res 19:82–84
51. Jinfei L (2018) Construction and evaluation of the indicator system for the competitiveness of manufacturing cross-border e-commerce enterprises[J]. Reform 05:97–106
52. Liqin W, Jinyong L, Minjiao Y (2019) The path to enhance the international competitiveness of China's cross-border e-commerce logistics enterprises – based on the anp-topsis model[J]. Econ Issue 09:45–52
53. Bin Z, Xiaojun L, Zhang T (2015) The current situation and operation mode of cross-border e-commerce logistics in China[J]. China Circulation Econ 29(01):51–56
54. Xiaheng Z, Tianshan M (2015) The dilemma and countermeasures of China's cross-border e-commerce logistics[J]. Contemp Econ Manag 37(05):51–54
55. Ren G, Shurong H, Xiaogang C (2018) Research on cross-border e-commerce logistics information matching based on dynamic clustering[J]. Lib Sci Res 01:89–94
56. Yuduo L, Xiuying S (2018) Research on the resilience of cross-border e-commerce logistics network based on complex network[J]. Sci Technol Manag Res 38(20):195–200
57. Ren G, Qing W (2018) Research on the vulnerability of cross-border e-commerce logistics system:from the perspective of fault tree analysis[J]. J Huaqiao Univ (Philos Social Sci) 05:73–80
58. Jie W, Hang W (2017) Research on the selection of cross-border e-commerce logistics mode[J]. Sci Technol Manag Res 37(21):175–179
59. Jianhui X (2018) Selection and development of cross-border e-commerce logistics channels[j]. China Circulation Econ 32(09):30–40
60. Duo Z, Wujun C (2019) Classification and risk assessment of cross-border e-commerce logistics in China's foreign trade – an empirical study based on fuzzy hierarchical analysis[J]. J Henan Normal Univ (Philos Social Sci Ed) 46(05):53–59

61. Hsiao YH, Chen MC (2016) Kansei engineering with online content mining for cross-border logistics service design[C]. 2016 5th IIAI International Congress on Advanced Applied Informatics (IIAI-AAI). IEEE, pp 138–143
62. Heng ZX (2017) Cross-border e-commerce payment representation, model and influencing factors[J]. Ent Econ 36(07):53–58
63. Dongling W (2018) Research on the development strategy of third-party cross-border payment institutions[J]. Asia-Pacific Econ (06):39–47, 147
64. Juanjuan W, Baolei S (2018) Application of blockchain technology in the field of cross-border payments in the "belt and road" region[J]. Contemp Econ Manag 40(07):84–91
65. Xuping W, Zilai S, Hongxin Z (2017) The impact of different power structures on cross-border e-commerce dual channel supply chain[J]. J Syst Eng 32(03):385–396
66. Xuanxuan Z, Guohua C (2017) Import cross-border e-commerce stocking and pricing strategy based on bertrand model[J]. Soft Sci 31(10):130–135
67. Huan H (2017) The dilemma and breakthrough of cross-border b2c e-commerce tax collection and management – based on the consideration of micro, meso and macro tax fairness[J]. Western Forum 27(05):94–101
68. Lei W (2017) China's cross-border import e-commerce model under the new customs tax policy[J]. China Circulation Econ 31(12):50–55
69. Li Z (2018) The evolution and practice of China's cross-border e-commerce tax system[J]. China Circulation Econ 32(10):48–55
70. Ruihua S, Yun T (2018) Innovation and development of cross-border import retail e-commerce model under the new customs tax policy[J]. Guizhou Soc Sci 11:129–134
71. Kreos K, Täks E, Tsap V, Pappel I, Draheim D (2019) On facilitating cross-border e-commerce through an automated vat declaration system[C]. 2019 Sixth International Conference on edemocracy & egovernment (ICEDEG). IEEE, pp 56–63
72. Shanghai Academy of Social Sciences Economic Research Institute Project Team, Liangping S, Yunyi T (2014) Research on the development and government regulation of China's cross-border e-commerce – taking small cross-border online shopping as an example[J]. Shanghai Econ Res 09:3–18
73. Lei X (2018) The impact and suggestions of customs supervision system on cross-border import e-commerce in the post-policy dividend era[J]. China Circulation Econ 32(03):52–61
74. Rong H, Xiang G, Bingzhi H (2017) Cross-border e-commerce customs risk based on bayesian network[J]. Syst Eng 35(07):115–121
75. Saprikis V (2015) An empirical investigation of internet users' perceptions towards national and international e-shops[J]. Int J E-Adoption (IJEA) 7(2):45–59
76. Han B, Kim M, Lee J (2018) Exploring consumer attitudes and purchasing intentions of cross-border online shopping in Korea[J]. J Korea Trade 22(2):86–104
77. Huang S, Chang Y (2019) Cross-border e-commerce: consumers' intention to shop on foreign websites[J]. Int Res 29(6):1256–1279
78. Han JH, Kim H-M (2019) The role of information technology use for increasing consumer informedness in cross-border electronic commerce: an empirical study[J]. Electron Commerce Res Appl 100826
79. Xiao L, Guo F, Yu F, Liu S (2019) The effects of online shopping context cues on consumers' purchase intention for cross-border e-commerce sustainability[J]. Sustainability 11(10), art. no. 2777
80. Jarvenpaa SL, Todd PA (1996) Consumer reactions to electronic shopping on the world wide web[J]. Int J Electron Commerce 1(2):59–88
81. Schaupp LC, Bélanger F (2005) A conjoint analysis of online consumer satisfaction1[J]. J Electron Commerce Res 6(2):95
82. Ha S, Stoel L (2009) Consumer e-shopping acceptance: antecedents in a technology acceptance model[J]. J Bus Res 62(5):565–571
83. Hua C (2003) Empirical study on determinants of online shopping intention[J]. Quant Econ Technol Econ Res 11:150–153

84. Heqing X, Xinhua J (2009) Research on the main influencing factors of consumer online shopping[J]. Consum Econ 25(02):38–41
85. Jie C (2012) Empirical study on the impact of consumer online shopping website experience on online purchase intention[D]. South China University of Technology
86. Lingying Z (2014) Research on the network consumer purchase decision model for the whole transaction process[D]. Harbin Institute of Technology
87. Webb GI, Pazzani MJ, Billsus D (2001) Machine learning for user modeling[J]. User Model User Adap Interact 11(1–2):19–29
88. Pavlou PA (2003) Consumer acceptance of electronic commerce: integrating trust and risk with the technology acceptance model[J]. Int J Electron Commerce 7(3):101–134
89. Baecke P, van den Poel D (2010) Improving purchasing behavior predictions by data augmentation with situational variables[J]. Int J Inform Technol Decis Mak 9(06):853–872
90. Kim HW, Xu Y, Gupta S (2012) Which is more important in internet shopping, perceived price or trust?[j]. Electron Commer Res Appl 11(3):241–252
91. Yue Z (2012) Research on the impact of trust and perceived risk on customer's online shopping intention[J]. Bus Econ (04):86–88, 91
92. Si C (2013) Consumer behavior analysis based on network integrated data in the context of big data[J]. News Commun 08:23–24
93. Chuanhong C (2013) Study on the influence of perceived website risk control on consumer behavior[J]. Indus Eng Manag 18(06):91–98
94. Zhiyan F, Xunhua G et al (2013) Several frontier topics in business management research under the background of big data[J]. J Manag Sci 01:1–9
95. Chaojun Y, Lisha C, Yali Z (2015) Constitutive-based website quality and purchase intention – cross-validation analysis of multinational and domestic e-commerce[J]. Modern Inform 35(05):41–48, 62
96. Xueqing L (2015) Research on pricing issues of cross-border import retail e-commerce – based on consumer perceived risk analysis and choice[j]. Price Theory Pract 09:79–81
97. Shuang W (2015) International comparative study on cross-border e-commerce legislation[D]. Zhejiang University
98. Mingfei Z, Jianzheng Y (2017) Preliminary exploration of the development of cross-border e-commerce policy in China[J]. E-Commerce 09:8–9
99. Weihua S, Yuying W, Lan Q, Shouzhen Z, Tomas B (2019) Creating a sustainable policy framework for cross-border e-commerce in China[J]. Sustainability 11(4):943
100. Youwei L (2016) The development trend and policy of cross-border e-commerce in China[J]. Develop Res 04:4–6
101. Yingnan X (2017) Research on the current situation and policy innovation of cross-border e-commerce development in China[J]. Inform Explor 2:85–89
102. Chunfu W (1992) On the difference between policy evaluation and policy assessment[J]. Theor Discuss 03:46–48
103. Smith TB (1973) The policy implementation process[J]. Policy Sci 4:197–209
104. Koolwal G (2010) Handbook on impact evaluation[M]. The World Bank, Washington, p 55
105. Ruiming L, Renjie Z (2015) Has the national high-tech zone promoted regional economic development? verification based on the double difference method[J]. Manag World 08:30–38
106. Cole MB, Qiuyuan Q, Sheldric RC, Morley DS, Bair-Merritt MH (2019) The effects of integrating behavioral health into primary care for low-income children[J]. Health Serv Res 54(6):1203–1213
107. Grafova IB, Freedman VA, Lurie N et al (2014) The difference-in-difference method: assessing the selection bias in the effects of neighborhood environment on health[J]. Econ Human Biol 13:20–33
108. Pippel G, Seefeld V (2015) R&D cooperation with scientific institutions: a difference-in-difference approach[J]. Econ Innov New Technol 25(5):455–469
109. Thorsten B, Ross L, Alexey L (2010) Big bad banks? The winners and losers from bank deregulation in the United States[J]. J Finance 65(5):1637–1667

110. Cerulli G (2019) Extending the difference-in-differences (did) to settings with many treated units and same intervention time: model and stata implementation[C]. 2019 stata conference. Stata users group (26)
111. Yingying Z, Yu G (2019) Study on the impact of smart city construction on the upgrading of regional manufacturing industry[J]. Soft Sci 33(09):46–52
112. Haiqiang C, Ying F, Fangzhou W (2019) The asymmetric impact of margin trading system on tail systemic risk – based on the study of extreme correlation in a-share market[j]. J Manag Sci 22(05):99–109
113. Jianzu W, Rongjuan W (2019) Has environmental conversation improved the efficiency of local government environmental governance? an empirical analysis based on the difference-in-differences method[J]. J Pub Manag 16(01):54–65,171–172
114. Jingjing Y, Yan W, Fanghao C, Yuqing W (2017) Does personal income tax reduction increase labor supply? evidence from a quasi-natural experiment[J]. Manag World (12):20–32, 187
115. Renjun C, Qinglan X, Shouqing L, Jiaqi L (2019) Can central environmental supervision improve corporate performance? taking listed industrial companies as an example[j]. Econ Rev 05:36–49
116. Yong Y, Sijie L, Yanyan C (2020) Has the "FTA strategy" improved the quality of China's export products?[J]. World Econ Res (10):63–75, 136
117. Hongyan L, Xifeng S, Xiuhui Q (2020) Institutional innovation and enterprise total factor productivity – evidence from China's free trade pilot zone[J]. Soft Sci 34(10):76–83
118. Caijing Z, Bojun W (2020) Has the construction of smart cities promoted the improvement of urban development quality? policy effect evaluation based on multi-period did method[J]. Econ Latitude 37(06):18–27
119. Hui A, Xuan H, Qianmiao Z (2021) Research on the impact of china's real estate restriction policy on housing prices - on the combined effect of restriction and purchase policies[J]. Chinese Management Sci 29(8):9
120. Arndt J (1967) Role of product-related conversations in the diffusion of a new product[J]. J Market Res 4(3):291–295
121. Westbrook RA (1987) Product/consumption-based affective responses and postpurchase processes[J]. J Market Res 24(3):258–270
122. Maru File K, Judd BB, Prince RA (1992) Interactive marketing: the influence of participation on positive word-of-mouth and referrals[J]. J Service Market 6(4):5–14
123. Bristor JM (1990) Enhanced explanations of word of mouth communications: the power of relationships[J]. Res Consum Behav 4(1):51–83
124. Brown TJ, Barry TE, Dacin PA, Gunst RF (2005) Spreading the word: investigating antecedents of consumers' positive word-of-mouth intentions and behaviors in a retailing context[J]. J Acad Market Sci 33(2):123–138
125. Xiaodong Y, Hongyan Y (2006) Enhancing corporate marketing competitiveness through word-of-mouth marketing[J]. Econ Manag 19:59–61
126. Lezhang Q (2008) How word-of-mouth marketing enhances corporate competitiveness and case study[J]. East China Econ Manag 10:98–100
127. Stauss B (1997) Global word of mouth[J]. Market Manag 6(3):28–30
128. Hennig-Thurau T, Gwinner KP, Walsh G, Gremler DD (2004) Electronic word-of-mouth via consumer-opinion platforms: what motivates consumers to articulate themselves on the internet?[J]. J Interact Market 18(1):38–52
129. Lazarus RS (1991) Emotion and adaptation[M]. Oxford University Press, New York
130. Godes D, Mayzlin D (2004) Using online conversations to study word-of-mouth communication[J]. Market Sci 23(4):545–560
131. Yafei S, Xiuqin W (2011) Analysis of the impact of negative word-of-mouth on purchase intention – a comparison of traditional word-of-mouth and online word-of-mouth[j]. Financial Issue Res 12:22–27
132. Wenyuan H, Chenfeng L (2013) Research on the impact of online word-of-mouth quality on customer perceived value and purchase intention[J]. Consum Econ 05:48–53

133. Guangming X, Daxiang J, Pei H (2018) Analysis of the impact of online word-of-mouth discrepancy based on product sales on consumer purchase behavior[J]. Nankai Manag Rev 21(06):53–66
134. Jianjun W, Lingyu W, Mengmeng W (2019) Online word-of-mouth, perceived value and consumer purchase intention: test of mediation and moderation effects[J]. J Manag Eng 33(04):80–87
135. Arndt J (1968) Selective processes in word of mouth[J]. J Advert Res 8(3):19–22
136. Anderson EW (1998) Customer satisfaction and word of mouth[J]. J Serv Res 1(1):5–17
137. Hanson WA (2000) Principles of internet marketing[D]. South-Western College
138. Chatterjee, (2001) Online review: do consumers use them?[J]. Adv Consum Res 28:133–139
139. Stephen WL, Ronald EG, Bing P (2007) Electronic word-of mouth in hospitality and tourism management[J]. Tour Manag 5(11):458–468
140. Yubo C, Jinhong X (2008) Online consumer review: word-of-mouth as a new element of marketing communication mix[J]. Manag Sci 53(3):477–491
141. Hennig-Thurau T, GWinner KP, Walsh G, et al (2004) Electronic word-of-mouth via consumer-opinion platforms: what motivates consumers to articulate themselves on the internet[J]. J Interact Market 18(1):38–52
142. Jidong B (2010) Research on the impact of negative online word-of-mouth on consumer behavioral intention[D]. Shandong University
143. Shiyang G, Xia L, Yang L, Ping Z (2012) Does online word-of-mouth determine the fate of a product? – an empirical analysis of online book reviews[J]. Nankai Manag Rev 15(04):118–128
144. Shi Wei, Wang Hongwei, He Shaoyi (2016) The impact of online word-of-mouth on market sales distribution: based on different product evaluation standards[j]. Systems engineering theory and practice 36(07):1744–1752
145. Liu Y (2006) Word-of-mouth for movies: its dynamics and impact on box office revenue[j]. J Mark 70(3):74–89
146. Chen PS, Wu S, Yoon J, et al. (2004) The impact of online recommendations and consumer feedback on sales[C]. In: International conference on information systems, pp 711–724
147. Duan W, Gu B, Whinston AB (2008) Do online reviews matter?—an empirical investigation of panel data[J]. Decis Support Syst 45(4):1007–1016
148. Wang H, Guo K (2017) The impact of online reviews on exhibitor behaviour: evidence from movie industry[J]. Enterpr Inform Syst 11(10):1518–1534
149. Qin L (2011) Word-of-blog for movies: a predictor and an outcome of box office revenue?[J]. J Electron Commerce Res 12(3):187-198
150. Singh VK, Nishant R, Kitchen PJ (2016) Self or simulacra of online reviews: an empirical perspective[J]. Psychol Market 33(12):1112–1118
151. Huang N, Hong Y, Burtch G (2017) Social network integration and user content generation: evidence from natural experiments[J]. MIS Q 41(4):1035–1058
152. Zhang X, Dellarocas C (2006) The lord of the ratings: is a movie's fate is influenced by reviews?[C]. International conference on information systems
153. Chintagunta PK, Gopinath S, Venkataraman S et al (2010) The effects of online user reviews on movie box office performance: accounting for sequential rollout and aggregation across local markets[J]. Market Sci 29(5):944–957
154. Chevalier JA, Mayzlin D (2006) The effect of word of mouth on sales: online book reviews[J]. J Market Res 43(3):345–354
155. Luca M (2011) Reviews reputation and revenue: the case of yelp[J]. Harvard Business School Working Papers
156. Baek H, Ahn JH, Choi Y (2012) Helpfulness of online consumer reviews: readers' objectives and review cues[J]. Int J Electron Commerce 17(2):99–126
157. Jeong HJ, Koo DM (2015) Combined effects of valence and attributes of e-wom on consumer judgment for message and product: the moderating effect of brand community type[J]. Int Res 25(1):2–29

158. Zhang D, Zhou L, Kehoe JL et al (2016) What online reviewer behaviors really matter? Effects of verbal and nonverbal behaviors on detection of fake online reviews[J]. J Manag Inform Syst 33(2):456–481
159. Li X (2017) Revealing or non-revealing:the impact of review disclosure policy on firm profitability[J]. Mis Quarterly 41(4):1335-+
160. Sun M (2012) How does the variance of product ratings matter[J]. Manag Sci 58(4):696–707
161. Lee J, Park J, Jung S, et al. (2015) The impact of the entropy of review text sentiments on movie box office sales[C]. International conference on electronic commerce:1-11
162. Zhao X, Wang L, Guo X et al (2015) The influence of online reviews on online hotel booking intentions[J]. Int J Contemp Hosp Manag 27(6):1343–1364
163. Pang J, Qiu L (2016) Effect of online review chunking on product attitude: the moderating role of motivation to think[J]. Int J Electron Commerce 20(3):355–383
164. Zhou W, Duan W (2016) Do professional reviews affect online user choices through user reviews? An empirical study[J]. J Manag Inform Syst 33(1):202–228
165. Keh HT, Ji WB, Wang X, et al. (2015) Online movie ratings: a cross-cultural, emerging asian markets perspective[J]. Int Market Rev 32(3-4):366–388
166. Lu X, Ba S, Huang L et al (2013) Promotional marketing or word-of-mouth? Evidence from online restaurant reviews[J]. Inform Syst Res 24(3):596–612
167. Gu B, Park J, Konana P et al (2012) The impact of external word-of-mouth sources on retailer sales of high-involvement products[J]. Inform Syst Res 23(1):182–196
168. Anderson JC, Jain DC, Chintagunta PK (1992) Customer value assessment in business markets: a state-of-practice study[J]. J Bus-Bus Market 1(1):3–29
169. Gale B, Gale BT, Wood RC (1994) Managing customer value: creating quality and service that customers can see[M]. Simon and Schuster
170. Ravald A, Grönroos C (1996) The value concept and relationship marketing[J]. Eur J Market 30(2):19–30
171. Barich H, Kotler P (1991) A framework for marketing image management[J]. MIT Sloan Manag Rev 32(2):94
172. Kotler P (2000) Marketing Management. Asian edition[M]. (trans: Ruiyun HT). Renmin University of China Press, Beijing, pp 23–25
173. Zeithaml VA (1988) Consumer perceptions of price, quality, and value: a means-end model and synthesis of evidence[J]. J Market 52:2–22
174. Monroe KB (1990) Pricing: making profitable decisions[M]. Mcgraw-Hill Companies
175. Woodruff RB (1997) Customer value: the next source for competitive advantage[J]. J Acad Market Sci 25(2):139
176. Holbrook MB (2002) Introduction to consumer value[M]//Consumer value. Routledge, pp 17–44
177. Yonghong W, Xiucheng F (2004) Analysis of the integrated model of enterprise competitiveness based on customer value[J]. China Soft Sci 11:86–92
178. Dahai D, Yi Y (2008) Theoretical analysis of consumer perceived value in the network environment[J]. J Manag 5(6):856–861
179. Hirschman EC, Holbrook MB (2010) Hedonic consumption: emerging concepts, methods and propositions[J]. J Market 46(3):92–101
180. Long Y, Yonggui W (2002) Analysis of customer value and its driving factors[J]. Manag World 06:146–147
181. Dahai D, Yufang J (2004) Customer value as an important antecedent of competitive advantage: an empirical study[J]. J Manag Sci 05:84–90
182. Yonggui W, Shunping H, Jingang X, Bin Y (2005) Value-oriented customer relationship management based on customer equity: theoretical framework and empirical analysis[J]. J Manag Sci 06:27–36
183. Chong W, Jian L, Jiabao W (2011) Construction and research of consumer perceived utility model in network environment[J]. Chinese Manag Sci 19(03):94–102
184. Ting L, Cunlin L (2012) Empirical study on the relationship between customer perceived value, customer satisfaction and customer loyalty in b2c e-commerce transaction platform[J]. Technol Innov Manag 33(6):6

185. Ruijin Z, Guoxin L, Ru W (2014) Research on the structure model of mobile data service mobile user perceived value[J]. China Soft Sci (08):138-149.
186. Baolong M, Zhenxing Z, Gao W, Jingjing B, Ying S (2015) Construction and industry analysis of brand asset index based on customer perception[J]. J Manag Sci 18(02):36–49
187. Yong D, Jinchuan X, Junhong Z (2017) Research on the influence of social media on brand preference: from the perspective of customer perceived value[J]. Oper Manag 26(06):176–184
188. Chen S, Quester PG (2006) Modeling store loyalty: perceived value in market orientation practice[J]. J Serv Market 20(20):188–198
189. Yu P, Li G, Fanghua W (2009) The influence of lifestyle and customer perceived value on chinese consumers' purchasing behavior[J]. J Syst Manag 18(06):601–607
190. Wenbo L, Rongqiu C (2009) Research on customer perceived value management strategy based on customer participation[J]. J Wuhan Univ Sci Technol (Soc Sci Ed) 11(1):49–54
191. Grisaffe D (2004) A dozen problems with applied customer measurement[J]. J Consum Satisf Dissatisfaction Complain Behav 17:1-15
192. Wei W, Haiying W (2011) Analysis of consumer behavior model based on customer value[J]. Modern Manag Sci (06):17–19, 85
193. Hongmei Z, Changyong L, Jian X, Junfeng D (2016) Research on the influence mechanism of characteristic tourism destination image on tourist behavior intention – taking helan mountain east foot grape industry tourism as an example[J]. China Soft Sci 08:50–61
194. Xin Z, Liang M, Gaoshan W (2017) Research on wechat user browsing behavior based on perceived value theory[J]. Inform Sci 35(12):136–141, 146
195. Rust TR, Olive LR (1994) Service quality: insights and managerial implications from the frontier[M]. Sage Publications, pp 1–20
196. Kotler P, Armstrong G (1998) Introduction to marketing[M]. (trans: Lijun Y). Huaxia Publishing House, Beijing, p 5
197. Sweeney LC (1999) The role of perceived risk in the quality-value relationship: a study in a retail environment[J]. J Retailing 75(1):77-105
198. Heinonen K (2004) Reconceptualizing customer perceived value: the value of time and place[J]. Manag Serv Qual: Int J 14(2/3):205–215
199. Sheth JN, Newman BI, Gross BL (1991) Why we buy what we buy: a theory of consumption values[J]. J Bus Res 22(2):159–170
200. Qingliang M, Yuqi H, Xiaojun C (2005) Research on customer value and its impact on customer relationship management performance[J]. Operat Manag 01:138–142
201. Pearl J (1986) Fusion, propagation and structuring in belief networks[J]. Artif Intell 29(3):27–30
202. Heckerman D, Geiger D, Chickering DM (1995) Learning bayesian networks: the combination of knowledge and statistical data[J]. Mach Learn 20(3):197–243
203. Chunling H (2011) Research on bayesian network structure learning and its application[D]. Hefei University of Technology
204. Xiaona Z, Jiwei L, Zhiliang W (2006) Well logging lithology prediction based on tan bayesian network classifier[J]. Microcomput Inform 25:284–286
205. Kumagai T, Akamatsu M (2006) Prediction of human driving behavior using dynamic bayesian networks[J]. IEICE Trans Inform Syst 89(2):857–860
206. Fang Z, Huiyong Z, Zhicai J (2010) Analysis of parking behavior based on bayesian network[J]. Syst Eng Theory Pract 30(05):948–955
207. Jingxin G, Zhicai J, Anning N (2015) Modeling and application of traveler's destination choice behavior based on bayesian network[J]. J Syst Manag 24(01):32–37
208. Jia R, Wencai D, Yong B (2013) UAV task decision based on bayesian network adaptive inference[J]. Syst Eng Theory Pract 33(10):2575–2582
209. García P, Amandi A, Schiaffino S et al (2007) Evaluating bayesian networks'precision for detecting students'learning styles[J]. Comput Educat 49(3):794–808
210. Acemoglu D, Ozdaglar A (2011) Opinion dynamics and learning in social networks[J]. Dyn Games Appl 1(1):3–49

211. Khong KW, Onyemeh NC, Chong AYL (2013) BSEM estimation of network effect and customer orientation empowerment on trust in social media and network environment[J]. Expert Syst Appl 40(12):4858–4870
212. Yoon JW, Cho SB (2012) An intelligent synthetic character for smartphone with bayesian networks and behavior selection networks[J]. Expert Syst Appl 39(12):11284–11292
213. Ojha R, Ghadge A, Tiwari MK, et al. (2018) Bayesian network modelling for supply chain risk propagation[J]. Int J Prod Res 56(17):5795-5819
214. Reshma V, John A (2015) Aspect based summarization of reviews using naïve bayesian classifier and fuzzy logic[c]//control communication & computing India (ICCC). 2015 international conference on IEEE, pp 617–621
215. Khopkar SS, Nikolaev AG (2017) Predicting long-term product ratings based on few early ratings and user base analysis[J]. Electron Commerce Res Appl 21:38–49
216. Chen H, Duan W, Zhou W (2017) The interplay between free sampling and word of mouth in the online software market[J]. Decis Support Syst 95:82–90
217. Guangqian Z, Xue B (2015) New product recommendation method based on consumer personality[J]. Manag Sci 28(02):60–68
218. Chamberlin E, Wen Z (2009) Theory of monopolistic competition[M].Huaxia Publishing House
219. Porter ME (1985) Competitive advantage: creating and sustaining superior performance[M]. Free Press
220. Teece DJ, Pisano G, Shuen A (1997) Dynamic capabilities and strategic management[J]. Strategic Manage J 18(7):509–533
221. Denison DR, Haaland S, Goelzer P (2004) Corporate culture and organizational effectiveness: is asia different from the rest of the world? [J]. Organ Dyn 33(1):98–109
222. Guangsheng Y (2002) Theoretical evolution of the source of corporate competitive advantage[J]. Foreign Econ Manag 10:2–7
223. Wernerfelt B (1984) A resource-based view of the firm[J]. Strategic Manage J 5(02):171–180
224. Prahalad CK, Hamel G (1990) The core competence of the corporation[J]. Harvard Bus Rev 68(03):79–91
225. Min J (2005) How to test the effectiveness of market segmentation variables[J]. Statistics Decis 24:143–144
226. Hui N, Tong L, Huan H, Mengyuan L, Huanrong S (2018) Automatic acquisition of business competitive intelligence based on online reviews[J]. J Intell 37(10):167–173, 188
227. Pang B, Lee L (2008) Opinion mining and sentiment analysis[J]. Foundations and Trends? in Information Retrieval 2(1–2):1–135
228. XiaHeng Z (2017) Types and operation modes of cross-border e-commerce[J]. China Circulation Econ 31(01):76–83
229. Dajian T, Ruiyao Y (2019) The poverty reduction effect and sustainability of poverty alleviation policies – based on the quasi-natural experiment of adjusting the list of poor counties[J]. Reform 11:126–135
230. Matthew S (2016) Firing costs and capital structure decisions[J]. J Finance 71(5):2239-2285
231. Junwei H, Guangming G (2019) Margin trading system and company's dynamic adjustment of capital structure – based on the empirical evidence of "quasi-natural experiment"[J]. Manage World 35(10):64–81
232. Baron R, Kenny D (1986) The moderator-mediator variable distinction in social psychological research: conceptual, strategic, and statistical considerations[J]. J Pers Soc Psychol 51:1173–1182
233. Pritchard A (1979) Statistical bibliography or bibliometrics[J]. J Documentation 25:348–349
234. Bikun C (2014) Research on visualization analysis of discipline knowledge[D]. Wuhan University
235. Cui H, Tao R, Jian Z (2015) Quantitative study of policy literature: a new direction for public policy research[J]. J Pub Admin 12(02):129–137, 158–159
236. Rothwell R, Zegveld W (1985) Reindustrialization and technology[M]. Longman, ME Sharpe

237. Jiang L, Yuanhao L, Cui H, Jun S (2015) Reshaping policy text data analysis with bibliometric research – the origin, migration and method innovation of policy literature measurement[J]. J Pub Admin 12(02):138–144, 159
238. Beth LN (2012) Beautiful visualization: looking at data through the eyes of experts[J]. Tech Commun 59(1):68–69
239. Xiaochun G, Petko D (2020) Bibliometrics and network analysis of cryptocurrency research[J]. J Syst Sci Complex 33(06):1933–1958
240. Vahidzadeh R, Bertanza G, Sbaffoni S et al (2021) A review based on social network analysis[J]. Region Indus Symbiosis 280:124
241. Hang L, Jianqing Z (2020) Visualization analysis of domestic and foreign innovation diffusion research based on knowledge graph[J]. Sci Res Manage 41(08):72–84
242. Xuemei X, Shenghui Y, Yonghui W (2020) Hotspots and evolutionary trends of foreign innovation ecosystem research – from the perspective of scientific knowledge map[J]. Sci Sci Manage S&T 41(10):20–42
243. Qichao Z, Zhoutao C, Chunhua C (2020) Visualization analysis of research hotspots and frontiers of team social network[J]. Sci Sci Manage S&T 41(05):54–68
244. Yuzhong L, Zengrui T, Beiquan C (2020) Visualization analysis of research hotspots and trends in international entrepreneurship investment[J]. Sci Res Manage 41(04):250–262
245. Li Z, Zili L, Yang L (2020) International science and technology policy measurement and visualization analysis[J]. Sci Res Manage 41(02):11–25
246. Xiaobin H, Baosai D (2020) Bibliometric visualization analysis of China's think tank policy literature[J]. Think Tank Theory Pract 5(03):48–57, 74
247. Xiufang X, Xiaolin Z (2017) Text mining research on technology roadmap: integrated analysis and visualization[J]. Data Anal Knowl Discov 1(01):16–25
248. Li X, Meizhi Z, Zhaoran X (2019) Research on the change of China's competition policy from the perspective of disruptive equilibrium theory[J]. Think Tank Theory Pract 4(02):14–24
249. Yanan Y, Wenhui Z, Jian Z, Shen T, Beibei Z (2019) Research on policy text visualization based on multi-view collaboration[J]. Data Anal Knowl Discov 3(06):30–41

Chapter 2
Analysis of User-Driven Factors in Cross-Border E-commerce Retail Imports

Cross-border import e-commerce is a new and common business consumption model, where consumers judge based on the "value points" mentioned in online reviews. These "value points" include customer focus and preferences for product and service attributes, such as product size, after-sales service, logistics waiting time. Therefore, key attribute indicators that consumers focus on are extracted from the displayed online review information, and existing online consumer behavior is used to predict future consumer preferences when shopping cross-border. The information data extracted through cleaning and standardization is used to quantify the overall user evaluation, clarify the perceived value driving indicators from the consumer's perspective, build a Bayesian network model for training and learning, and explore the demand points of behavior decisions including evaluation dimensions and emotional bias. This serves as a portrait of cross-border user behavior [[1]].

2.1 User Consumption Behavior Demand Analysis

In recent years, the economy of cross-border import e-commerce platforms has developed rapidly and the market share has continued to expand. Many overseas product enthusiasts purchase imported products through this platform. According to customs statistics, in 2020, 2.45 billion import and export lists were checked and released through the customs cross-border e-commerce management platform, an increase of 63.3% year-on-year. Cross-border e-commerce imports and exports reached 1.69 trillion yuan, an increase of 31.1%. In 2022, China's cross-border e-commerce imports and exports amounted to 2.1 trillion yuan, an increase of 7.1% over 2021. With the injection of market vitality and changes in consumption concepts, it is expected that the user scale of China's cross-border e-commerce will further expand and maintain a high growth rate [[2]].

L. Xiong and H. Wang, *User Driven Cross-Border E-Commerce Platform Competition and Policy Analysis*, Advanced Studies in E-Commerce,
https://doi.org/10.1007/978-981-97-3835-9_2

Before extracting consumer behavior data, through browsing websites, research reports, and related academic research, it was found that the behavior of cross-border e-commerce retail import users presents the following characteristics:

(1) the Crowd is Getting Younger, and Cross-Border Behavior is Becoming Normal

The main force of cross-border e-commerce users is concentrated on female roles, who pay more attention to product quality and shopping experience. According to the age distribution of cross-border online shopping users, it is mainly concentrated in the young group of 19–35 years old, accounting for nearly 80% of the entire consumer group. This age group of cross-border e-commerce consumers has a rich knowledge learning, stable work and income, a certain economic strength, pays attention to life quality, and has a large consumption demand. They are leaders in digging out excellent overseas products. "Face" consumption and family consumption have become the mainstream of cross-border online shopping, mainly because women of this age are in the "most beautiful" stage, and most women have already established families. In addition to improving the quality of family life, the "mother" role is willing to buy high-quality and well-reputed overseas maternal and infant products on cross-border e-commerce platforms. Beauty and personal care products and maternal and infant products have naturally become consumption hotspots [[3]].

From the age distribution of cross-border e-commerce users, it can be analyzed that the number of consumers born in the 1990s and 1995s is increasing, while the number of consumers born in the 1980s and 1985s is decreasing. This is related to age and the acceptance of new things. Faced with new consumption cultures such as "social" e-commerce and "experience" e-commerce, younger people have better pioneering abilities and curiosity, and have more time and energy than consumers born in the 1980s and 1985s. At the same time, data analysis of different age groups in cross-border consumption amounts found that the proportion of consumption amounts of those born in the 1990s and 1995s is increasing year by year. Those born in the 1990s are gradually becoming the main force of cross-border consumption, and those born in the 1995s will be the new force of cross-border consumption in the next year. Young users have become the main force of cross-border consumption [[4]].

Through data investigation and analysis, over 70% of cross-border e-commerce users are in first-tier and second-tier cities, with the proportion of cross-border consumers in first-tier cities accounting for about 40%. The proportion of cross-border consumers in second-tier cities is increasing year by year. These are the main cities for cross-border consumption, indicating that cross-border consumption is mainly reflected in areas with higher levels of economic development. This regional group has higher demands for living consumption levels and quality of life. At the same time, the data found that the largest contribution to the proportion of cross-border consumption amounts comes from second-tier cities. This may be somewhat contrary to people's subconscious understanding. First-tier cities have more exposure to new consumption, but they lag behind second-tier cities in terms of consumption amounts. However, the per-customer transaction value in first-tier cities is much higher than in other cities. One of the main reasons for this is believed to be the significantly fewer number of first-tier cities compared to second-tier cities.

However, by looking at the proportion of consumption amounts each year, it is found that the consumption proportions of first-tier and second-tier cities remain basically unchanged, with a slight decrease. The cross-border consumption amounts of third-tier and fourth-tier cities are increasing year by year, from less than 20% in 2016 to over 40% in 2020. In the first half of 2023, China's cross-border e-commerce import and export volume reached 1.1 trillion yuan, a year-on-year increase of 16%, achieving double-digit rapid growth. Among cities of different tiers, the per-customer transaction value of consumers in first-tier cities far exceeds that of third-tier, fourth-tier cities, and other cities. Undoubtedly, the cross-border consumption capacity and the ability to afford overseas product prices in first-tier and second-tier cities are greater than in other cities. However, the year-on-year growth rate of the per-customer transaction value in third-tier and fourth-tier cities is much higher than in first-tier cities. It is predicted that most consumers are young people, and third-tier and fourth-tier cities will be the must-compete areas for cross-border import e-commerce platforms in the future. This also indicates that cross-border consumption is further sinking in city distribution and becoming normalized and popularized.

(2) Diversification of Consumption Regions, Refinement of Category Demand

To cater to and stimulate the consumption upgrade of overseas product enthusiasts, cross-border e-commerce retail import platforms are constantly expanding the types and countries of imported products on the platform. In recent years, there have been some changes in the mainstream cross-border import retail e-commerce platforms. The top three in the proportion of cross-border e-commerce transaction volume on the platform are: NetEase Koala, Tmall International, and Vipshop International. Specifically, NetEase Koala ranks first with a market share of 21.4%; Tmall International ranks second with a market share of 17.7%; Vipshop International ranks third with a market share of 16.1%; JD Global ranks fourth with a market share of 15.2%. In recent years, the market share rankings of cross-border e-commerce platforms are: Tmall International, NetEase Koala, and JD Global. Specifically, Tmall International ranks first with a market share of 25.1%; NetEase Koala ranks second with a market share of 18.2%; JD Global ranks third with a market share of 15.7%; Vipshop International ranks fourth with a market share of 9.2%. Platforms like Tmall International, JD Global, and Vipshop International are cross-border import e-commerce channels under relatively large retail e-commerce platforms [[1]], backed by their own high-traffic platforms, they occupy a considerable market share; NetEase Koala is an independent cross-border import shopping platform, with its extremely selective operation mode and the support of NetEase Group behind it, it has already occupied a considerable market share in the industry, and the oligopoly effect has appeared.

Looking at the penetration of consumers from various regions, the consumer groups of cross-border e-commerce in places like Beijing, Shanghai, and Hong Kong are the most active. Looking at the geographical distribution of cross-border consumer users corresponding to the cross-border consumption penetration rate, cross-border e-commerce users are mainly concentrated in Guangdong, accounting for 14.1%, Shanghai accounting for 13.2%, and Beijing accounting for 12.2%.

Among the remaining provinces, Jiangsu accounts for 9.2%, Shandong accounts for 7.2%, Zhejiang accounts for 5.2%, Fujian accounts for 4.9%, and Hebei accounts for 3.7%. The ranking of the geographical distribution of cross-border consumer users is as follows: Guangdong, Beijing, Shanghai, Jiangsu, Zhejiang, Shandong, Sichuan, Fujian, and Hubei. The penetration rates in the chart are roughly divided into four levels. Hong Kong, Shanghai, and Beijing have the highest penetration rates. The second level is mainly composed of Guangdong, Jiangsu, Zhejiang, and other coastal eastern regions. The third level includes Shandong, Hebei, and Sichuan, which are emerging central regions. The fourth level includes Liaoning, Heilongjiang, and Jilin, which are northern heavy industry regions. The fifth level includes Ningxia and Qinghai, which are less developed western regions. It is worth noting that the penetration rates in Xinjiang and Tibet are in the middle and upper levels, and the reason for the small population base in these areas cannot be ignored.

The data shows that cross-border e-commerce users are mainly concentrated and still concentrated in the eastern coastal areas. This is due to the early support of national policies in the eastern regions, the developed economy, the early start of cross-border import e-commerce, superior conditions, strong consumption capacity, and consumers pursuing a quality life. This coincides with the cross-border consumption penetration rate in various regions, among which the growth of the consumer population in the central region is prominent. In terms of import countries, the top five countries for import consumption in recent years are Japan, the United States, Australia, South Korea, and Germany. Different countries have different preferences for cross-border product selection [5], as shown in Fig. 2.1. Cross-border e-commerce consumers tend to buy categories such as masks, diapers, and beauty cleaning tools from Japan; dietary nutritional supplements, infant nutrition, and ladies' bags from the United States; masks, facial care sets, and sunscreens from South Korea; dietary nutritional supplements, infant nutrition, and adult milk powder from Australia; dietary nutritional supplements, infant milk powder, and cups/water cups/water bottles from Germany. The enthusiasm of cross-border e-commerce users for these countries remains high.

Fig. 2.1 Top five countries and categories of cross-border imports in recent years

Fig. 2.2 Regional preferences of some product categories

Major cross-border e-commerce retail platforms cover a wide range of products with a wide vertical depth. Beauty, daily use, maternal and child, clothing, and other hot-selling categories display thousands of brands on the platform. The platform actively collaborates with thousands of top international brands and well-known suppliers [6]. By cross-comparing consumer regional data with category preference data, it is found that different categories have different consumption regions. Overall, Shanghai, Beijing, and Guangzhou basically occupy the top three in all categories. Figure 2.2 shows the regional preferences for some product categories. It is found that users in Shanghai and Beijing have higher health awareness and quality of life requirements. Families in economically developed areas pay more attention to the health and product quality of their babies. Foodies and beauty experts are concentrated in Beijing, Shanghai, and Guangzhou.

(3) Quality Attention Upgrade, Consumer Interaction Content

With the vigorous development of cross-border e-commerce, various cross-border e-commerce platforms have emerged. There are many platforms, and the quality of products varies. At the same time, with the further expansion of product categories, cross-border e-commerce consumers have higher requirements for product quality [7]. According to a survey by the China E-commerce Research Center, the sensitivity of cross-border e-commerce has shifted from price to quality. In the past, the focus of cross-border online shopping was mostly on the price of overseas products. With the improvement of domestic consumers' quality of life, consumers are paying more attention to high-quality and cost-effective products. Only 15% of cross-border online shopping users prefer low-priced products, as shown in Fig. 2.3. When choosing an e-commerce platform, more than 60% of users prefer platforms that offer carefully selected products, as shown in Fig. 2.4.

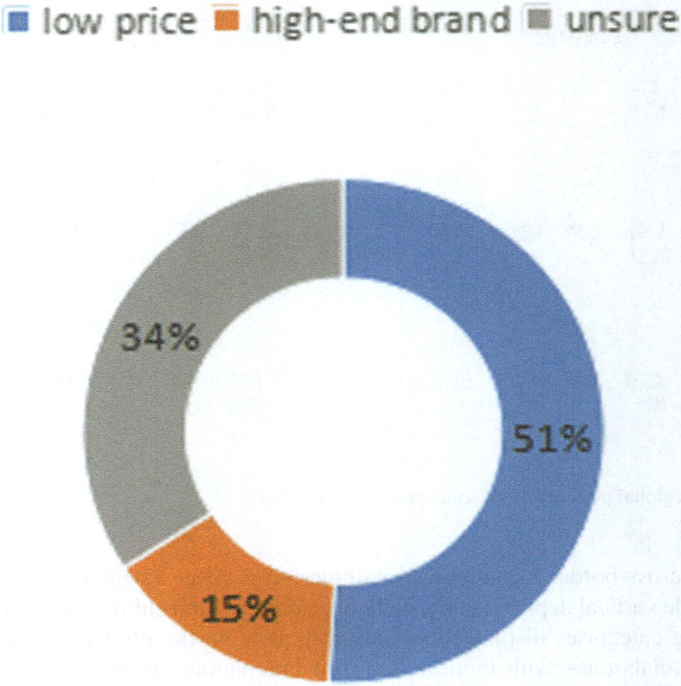

Fig. 2.3 Distribution of demand preference of cross-border e-commerce consumers

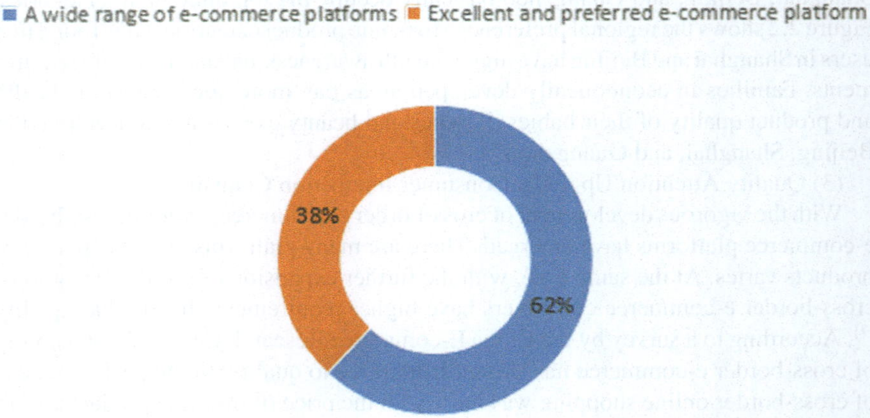

Fig. 2.4 Cross-border e-commerce platform preference

According to research data, more than 60% of cross-border e-commerce consumers believe that they are pursuing more personalized, high-quality, and diverse products and services than before. As people's consumption levels continue to improve, the consumption of products has evolved from simply satisfying material needs to pursuing high-quality products, and the concept of focusing on brands is becoming increasingly prominent.

The change in the consumption concept of cross-border e-commerce users is obvious, leaning more toward the pursuit of high-quality products and services. One reason for this is the good development of the domestic economy, which has improved the economic strength of cross-border consumers. Another reason is that the cross-border consumer group is mostly concentrated among young people, whose consumption habits are becoming more rational and stable. This requires cross-border e-commerce platforms to adapt to changes in people's consumption concepts, grasp the quality control of the platform, provide high-quality products, and offer a good development opportunity for cross-border e-commerce platforms that have better product quality guarantees. Further improving the quality of user services, meeting consumers' rigid needs, adding service highlights, increasing user stickiness, increasing the frequency and unit price of repeat purchases, and optimizing personalized high-quality products have become the main competitive elements of cross-border e-commerce platforms. At the same time, content interaction has also become an indispensable part of cross-border import consumption.

2.2 Data Capture and Cleaning

By analyzing cross-border e-commerce retail materials, papers, and other related reports, we selected the most representative three types of products and the ten hottest products in Tmall International and Tmall Mall as research objects [[1]]. The ten hottest products were selected based on the highest customer purchase volume and the fastest rising popularity. We used Python language algorithms, PyCharm, and Navicat software to capture online comment data, selectively remove, desensitize, etc., and summarize the user names, transaction time, popularity, transaction quantity, comment text, and pictures in the online comment data into a unified standardized format for further keyword extraction and analysis.

Through the impurity cleaning, dehumidification, desensitization, and sorting of 30 kinds of product online comment data, we refined, collected, and summarized the index attributes that consumers focus on in online comments, further determined the attribute mechanism characteristics of consumers' attention to the "value point" of the index, classified and summarized the same type of "value points", and determined the secondary driving indicators. At the same time, the evaluation dimensions and emotional bias in the online comment text were classified into five emotional dimensions, and the corresponding emotional database was constructed. Strictly according to the database, each secondary driving indicator was scored and quantified. Based on the Likert scale's 5-level scoring standard, the text content in the online comments was standardized and converted into digital data, becoming the basic input data for constructing the Bayesian network.

2.2.1 Source of Online Comment Data

The captured online comment data mainly includes displayUserNick (user nickname), auctionSku (product attributes), cmsSource (source), rateDate (transaction date), and rateContent (comment content) on the imported B2C cross-border e-commerce platform website.

Firstly, according to the previous analysis, Tmall International, NetEase Kaola, and JD Global Purchase hold the major market shares in the cross-border import market. Through consumer research and comparison of the penetration and authenticity perception of the main platforms, it is found that Tmall International ranks first in penetration among all cross-border platforms, followed by JD Global Purchase and NetEase Kaola. Tmall International and JD Global Purchase, as cross-border channel models under comprehensive e-commerce platforms, have the advantages of existing brand culture and penetration. As a comprehensive retail e-commerce platform, Tmall International is conducive to the innovation and quality comparison of product varieties, with a high degree of product quality assurance, establishing a good reputation among consumers. At the same time, in the era of new retail thinking, consumer concepts are changing, and consumers are increasingly focusing on high-quality products or services. Intellectual property and brand culture are becoming the trend, and authenticity trust is gradually becoming the primary factor considered by cross-border e-commerce consumers, with high user breadth and penetration. Tmall Mall, as a shopping platform for domestic users, is independent of each other, has users within the same range, and the quality and level of users are consistent. Therefore, Tmall International is chosen as the import B2C cross-border e-commerce user platform. Correspondingly, Tmall Mall is a platform website for purchasing overseas retail products domestically.

Secondly, at present, users of cross-border e-commerce generally prefer to consume beauty, maternal and child, food and other brand products. The product categories preferred by cross-border e-commerce consumers include beauty care, maternal and child, shoes and clothing, food, jewelry, and luggage. Customs data shows that in recent years, the beauty and makeup category accounts for 43.2% of the total cross-border imports, ranking first; beauty care product orders have been the first for a long time, so this article studies the beauty care category.

Furthermore, because there are many subcategories and brands under beauty care, such as masks, facial essences, facial care sets, it is necessary to choose the product that best represents this category as the research object. According to the "Tmall International Annual Consumption Trend Report", under the beauty and makeup category, foundation liquid/cream, perfume, lip balm/lipstick are the top three categories with rising popularity. The top 10 sales on Tmall International are used as the research samples for each category, see Figs. 2.5–2.7.

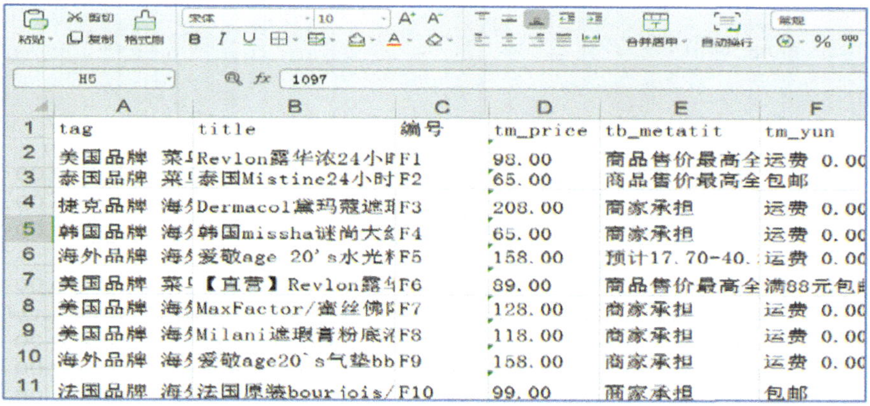

	A	B	C	D	E	F
1	tag	title	编号	tm_price	tb_metatit	tm_yun
2	美国品牌 菜	Revlon露华浓24小	F1	98.00	商品售价最高全	运费 0.0
3	泰国品牌 菜	泰国Mistine24小时	F2	65.00	商品售价最高全	包邮
4	捷克品牌 海	Dermacol黛玛蔻遮	F3	208.00	商家承担	运费 0.0
5	韩国品牌 海	韩国missha谜尚大	F4	65.00	商家承担	运费 0.0
6	海外品牌 海	爱敬age 20's水光	F5	158.00	预计17.70-40.	运费 0.0
7	美国品牌 菜	【直营】Revlon露	F6	89.00	商品售价最高全	满88元包
8	美国品牌 海	MaxFactor/蜜丝佛	F7	128.00	商家承担	运费 0.0
9	美国品牌 海	Milani遮瑕膏粉底	F8	118.00	商家承担	运费 0.0
10	海外品牌 海	爱敬age20`s气垫bb	F9	158.00	商家承担	运费 0.0
11	法国品牌 海	法国原装bourjois/	F10	99.00	商家承担	包邮

Fig. 2.5 Top ten sales of liquid foundation/cream on Tmall Global

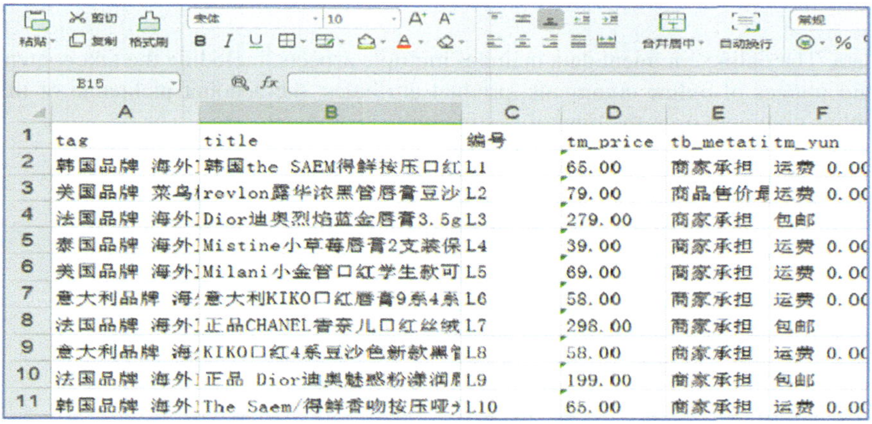

	A	B	C	D	E	F
1	tag	title	编号	tm_price	tb_metati	tm_yun
2	韩国品牌 海外	韩国the SAEM得鲜按压口红	L1	65.00	商家承担	运费 0.0
3	美国品牌 菜鸟	revlon露华浓黑管唇膏豆沙	L2	79.00	商品售价	运费 0.0
4	法国品牌 海外	Dior迪奥烈焰蓝金唇膏3.5g	L3	279.00	商家承担	包邮
5	泰国品牌 海外	Mistine小草莓唇膏2支装保	L4	39.00	商家承担	运费 0.0
6	美国品牌 海外	Milani小金管口红学生款可	L5	69.00	商家承担	运费 0.0
7	意大利品牌 海	意大利KIKO口红唇膏9系4系	L6	58.00	商家承担	运费 0.0
8	法国品牌 海外	正品CHANEL香奈儿口红丝绒	L7	298.00	商家承担	包邮
9	意大利品牌 海	KIKO口红4系豆沙色新款黑	L8	58.00	商家承担	运费 0.0
10	法国品牌 海外	正品 Dior迪奥魅惑粉漾润	L9	199.00	商家承担	包邮
11	韩国品牌 海外	The Saem/得鲜香吻按压哑	L10	65.00	商家承担	运费 0.0

Fig. 2.6 Top ten lipstick/lipstick sales on Tmall International

2.2.2 Data Capture and Information Analysis

After determining the research object and individual, the implementation of capturing online comments for 30 hot-selling products begins, with the following specific steps: Firstly, study the characteristics of the Tmall International platform website comment system and the expression form of comment content, determine the text information, image information, and format layout information of the online comments to be captured, use Python + Mysql to collect data, and use Scrapy's URL parsing and recursive crawling method to implement the loop capture of online comment system page data, the architecture process is shown in Fig. 2.8. The captured data content mainly includes specific product brand data, platform sales data, and online comment

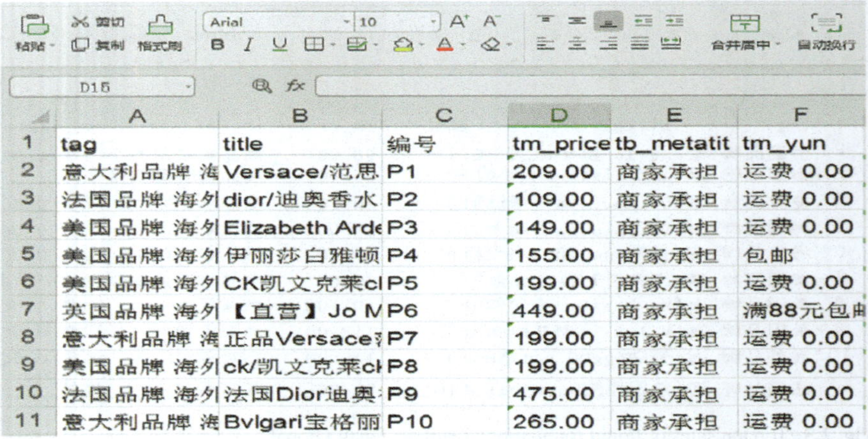

	A	B	C	D	E	F
1	tag	title	编号	tm_price	tb_metatit	tm_yun
2	意大利品牌 海	Versace/范思	P1	209.00	商家承担	运费 0.00
3	法国品牌 海外	dior/迪奥香水	P2	109.00	商家承担	运费 0.00
4	美国品牌 海外	Elizabeth Ard	P3	149.00	商家承担	运费 0.00
5	美国品牌 海外	伊丽莎白雅顿	P4	155.00	商家承担	包邮
6	美国品牌 海外	CK凯文克莱cl	P5	199.00	商家承担	运费 0.00
7	英国品牌 海外	【直营】Jo M	P6	449.00	商家承担	满88元包由
8	意大利品牌 海	正品Versace	P7	199.00	商家承担	运费 0.00
9	美国品牌 海外	ck/凯文克莱c	P8	199.00	商家承担	运费 0.00
10	法国品牌 海外	法国Dior迪奥	P9	475.00	商家承担	运费 0.00
11	意大利品牌 海	Bvlgari宝格丽	P10	265.00	商家承担	运费 0.00

Fig. 2.7 Screenshot of top ten perfume sales on Tmall International

data. The online comment data includes multiple aspects, including the text content and images of online comments, product attributes, the account nickname of the online comment user, the time of posting online comments, etc.

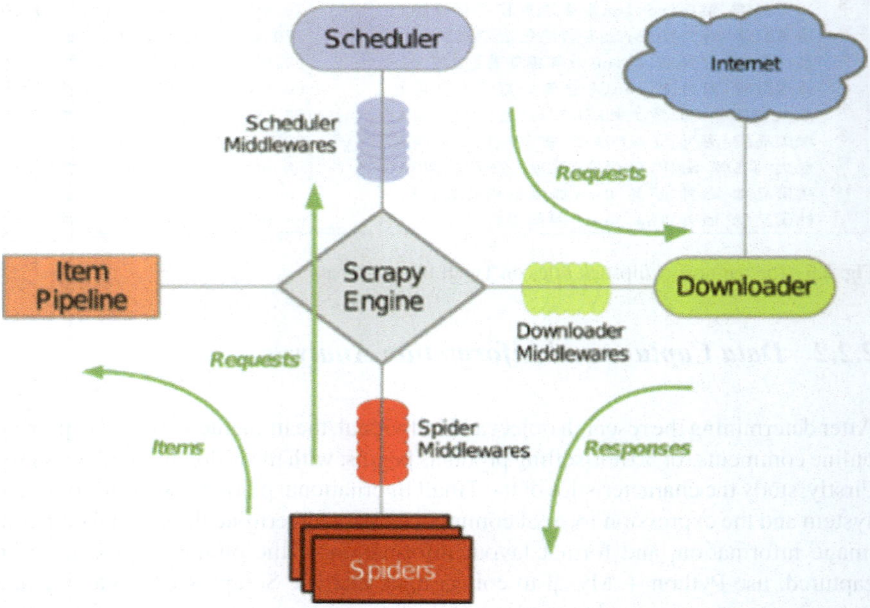

Fig. 2.8 Scrapy architecture flowchart

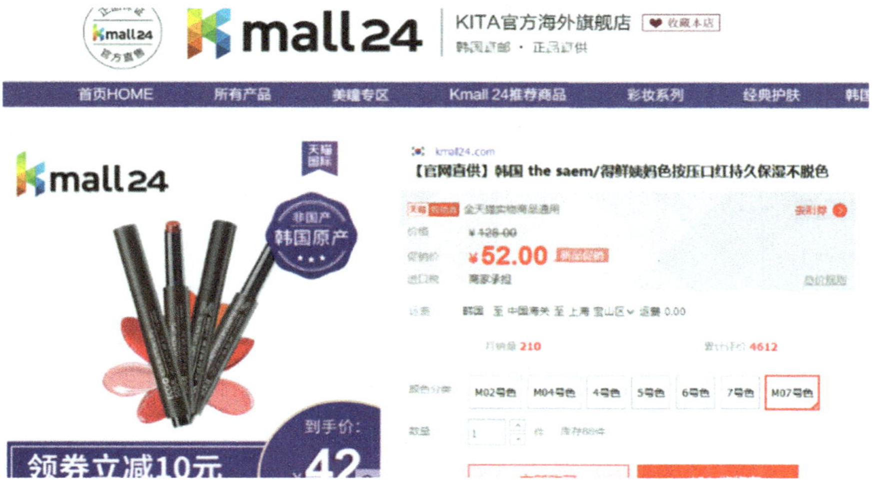

Fig. 2.9 Fresh product information grab page example

After determining the individual products according to the rules, the top 10 in sales of foundation liquid/paste are: F1: Revlon, F2: Mistine from Thailand, F3: Dermacol, F4: Missha from Korea, F5: Age20's, F6: Revlon, F7: MaxFactor, F8: Milani from the United States, F9: Age20's, F10: Bourjois from France, marked with F (Foundation), F1 to F10 represent the descending order of sales; similarly, lipstick is marked with L (Lipstick), L1 to L10 represent the descending order of sales; perfume is marked with P (Perfume), P1 to P10 represent the descending order of sales.

After determining the time range, Python + Mysql is used to collect data, and the URL parsing and recursive crawling method of Scrapy is used to implement the automatic data crawling loop. Figure 2.9 is an example of the fresh product information crawling page, and Fig. 2.10 is an example of online comment crawling.

After completing the selection, crawling, and sorting of specific representative product online reputation data, Tables 2.1–2.3 are the page statistics of specific products in the research category displayed on the cross-border import retail platform, including price (yuan), import tax (yuan), freight (yuan), sales (pieces), cumulative online reviews (articles), collection times (popularity), etc., which to some extent reflect the consumer's trust and recognition of the product and the activity level.

For the online comment information obtained by crawling, preliminary screening is carried out to exclude invalid comments, duplicate reviews, advertisements, irrelevant reviews, etc., and the remaining online comment data is de-noised, desensitized, and unified, leaving only effective, complete, and unified online comments. By mining and counting the highly concerned attributes in the online comment content, and referring to the high-frequency comment content extracted from the Tmall International comment system, the key content of the comments is further identified, and the indicators that consumers focus on are refined and classified.

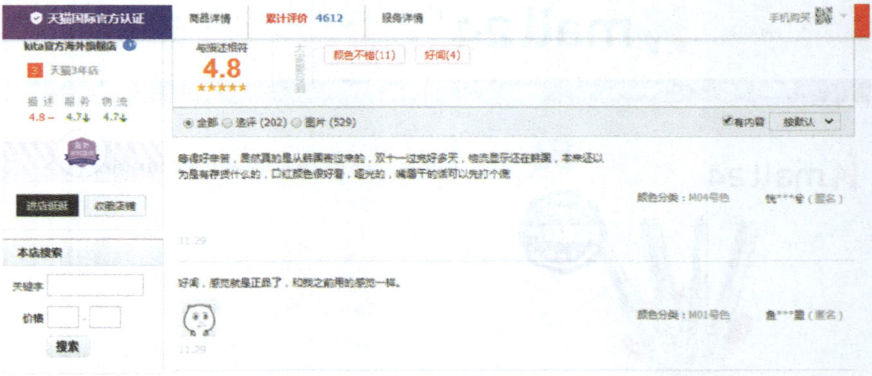

Fig. 2.10 Sample grab page for fresh product online reviews

Table 2.1 Product information of liquid foundation and cream1

No	Price (Yuan)	Import duty (Yuan)	Freight (Yuan)	Monthly volume (pieces)	Cumulative reviews (pieces)	Number of favorites (popularity)
F1	98.00	Products sold up to full tax included	0.00	16,736	94,105	247,048
F2	65.00	Products sold for the highest price Full tax inclusive	Exempt from postage	15,633	88,985	291,001
F3	208.00	Merchant borne	0.00	14,923	18,005	136,488
F4	65.00	Merchant undertake	0.00	10,842	10,975	3,077
F5	158.00	Expect $17.70–40.34	0.00	9,876	9,065	532
F6	89.00	Products sold for the highest price Full tax inclusive	Free shipping over 88 yuan	5,952	11,569	77,140
F7	128.00	Merchant borne	0.00	5,718	3,515	13,931
F8	118.00	Merchant borne	0.00	5,274	19,221	93,335
F9	158.00	Merchant borne	Shipping fee 0.00	3,743	4,460	16,251
F10	99.00	Merchant borne	Free shipping	2,569	5,898	69,141

Table 2.2 Lip balm/lipstick product information2

No	Price (Yuan)	Import duty (Yuan)	Freight (Yuan)	Monthly volume (pieces)	Cumulative reviews (pieces)	Number of favorites (popularity)
L1	65.00	Merchant undertake	Shipping fee 0.00	24,657	45,505	15,726
L2	79.00	Full tax package	Freight 0.00	17,961	99,895	264,354
L3	279.00	Merchant borne	Free shipping	15,050	27,954	98,882
L4	39.00	Merchant undertake	Shipping fee 0.00	10,804	5,924	11,644
L5	69.00	Merchant undertake	Shipping fee 0.00	9,880	187,286	306,677
L6	58.00	Merchant undertake	Shipping fee 0.00	7,710	37,345	209,864
L7	298.00	Merchant borne	Free shipping	5,640	16,473	80,978
L8	58.00	Merchant undertake	Shipping fee 0.00	4,052	29,717	111,617
L9	199.00	Merchant bear	Free shipping	2,831	33,539	127,186
L10	65.00	Merchant undertake	Shipping fee 0.00	1,682	72,455	161,299

Finally, based on the above summary, the words with high weight and frequency in online comments are classified into the customer perceived value driving model, determining the secondary driving indicators that consumers focus on and affect their behavioral preferences, building an empirical test model based on the theoretical concept model, and determining the scoring scale of the secondary driving indicators under different product categories, standardizing the effective, complete, and unified online comments into numerical information.

2.3 Data Secondary Driving Indicator Quantitative Scoring

2.3.1 Comment Data Preprocessing Cleaning

Python + Mysql is used to collect data, and the URL parsing and recursive crawling method of Scrapy is used to automatically collect data. Some of the code is as follows, and the calculation part is shown in Fig. 2.11:

```
#Foundation.py.....
data = driver.page_source.
```

Table 2.3 Perfume product information3

No	Price (Yuan)	Import duty (Yuan)	Freight (Yuan)	Monthly volume (pieces)	Cumulative reviews (pieces)	Number of favorites (popularity)
P1	209.00	Merchant borne	Shipping fee 0.00	6,761	14,378	50,574
P2	109.00	Merchant borne	Shipping fee 0.00	5,724	2,697	17,556
P3	149.00	Merchant borne	Shipping fee 0.00	3,724	4,351	28,127
P4	155.00	Merchant borne	Free shipping	2,867	18,769	49,333
P5	199.00	Merchant undertake	Shipping fee 0.00	2,812	35,460	115,103
P6	449.00	Merchant borne	Free shipping over 88 yuan	2,731	5,887	78,585
P7	199.00	Merchant undertake	Shipping fee 0.00	2,184	6,665	25,513
P8	199.00	Merchant undertake	Shipping fee 0.00	1,365	24,814	81,871
P9	475.00	Merchant borne	Freight 0.00	1,291	1,577	12,342
P10	265.00	Merchant borne	Shipping fee 0.00	698	7,861	31,884

```
headersParameters = {
    'Connection': 'Keep-Alive',
    'Accept': 'text/html, application/xhtml+xml, */*',
    'Accept-Language': 'en-US, en; q=0.8, zh-Hans-CN; q=0.5, zh-Hans; q=0.3',
    'Accept-Encoding': 'gzip, deflate'.
    'User-Agent': 'Mozilla/6.1 (Windows NT 6.3; WOW64; Trident/7.0; rv:11.0) like Gecko'
    }
page = 0
while page<99:
    page += 1
    urlparams = {'itemId':'43487174504','sellerId':'2298016439','currentPage':str(page)}
    repones = requests.get('https://rate.tmall.com/list_detail_rate.htm',params=urlparams,headers=he

    jsondata = repones.text[15:]
    data = json.loads(jsondata)
    for list in data['rateList']:
```

Fig. 2.11 Python data scraping page

driver.quit.
html = etree.HTML(data).
tags = html.xpath("//div[@class = 'fromName']/text()").
tag = list_func(tags).

print tag.
title_pre = html.xpath("//div[@class = 'tb-detail-hd']/h1/text()").
title = list_func(title_pre).........

The captured data is stored in SQL file, converted into Excel file by effective editing using navicat.exe, and preprocessed. The data result is shown in Fig. 2.12 and Fig. 2.13:

This time, 56,885 pieces of data were crawled from Tmall International, about 2,000 pieces for each product, and nearly 20,000 online comments for the same brand products overseas in Tmall Mall. Due to the display rules of online comments in Tmall International and Tmall Mall, the data crawled this time is part of the data displayed under this condition. Therefore, the source data during this period is far greater than the visible data. This paper uses these 56,885 pieces of data as the source data for cleaning, excluding invalid comments, duplicate reviews, advertisements, irrelevant reviews, etc., and the remaining data for each variety is shown in Table 2.4:

The specific cleaning rules are as follows:

lipstick_1.xls	2018/12/2 15:05	XLS worksheet
lipstick_2.xls	2018/12/2 15:53	XLS worksheet
2lipstick_3.xls	2018/12/2 16:13	XLS worksheet
National lipstick_4.xls	2018/12/2 16:40	
lipstick_5.xls lipstick_6.xls lipstick_7.xls lipstick_8.xls lipstick_9.xls	2018/12/2 17:092018/12/2 18:162018/12/2 22:022018/12/2 22:302018/12/2 22:43	XLS worksheet XLS worksheet XLS worksheet XLS worksheet XLS
lipstick_10.xls	2018/12/2 23:05	XLS worksheet
lipstick-brand.xls	2018/12/2 22:43	XLS worksheet

Fig. 2.12 Screenshot of source data of lip balm/lipstick

displayUse	auctionSku	cmsS	rateDa sellerId	rateContent
Lost the tree	Color category: Mixed oily skin 0-1: Tmall		2018-02949540698	Very good, do not take off makeup, very good stuff
x***9	Color classification: Mixed oily skin 0-11 days		2018-02949540698	I am mixed oil skin, but the moisturizing is not done
Snow ***5	Color category: Mixed oily skin 0-11 Day cat		2018-02949540698	works well, really doesn't take off makeup
a***j	Color category: mixed oily skin 0-1 day cat		2018-02949540698	Bought for my classmates, Taobao flagship store than other
A *** ah	Color Category: Medium-dry skin D-110	Tmall	2018-02949540 698	Tried on the hand, the color is like the face
x***a	Color category: Mixed oily skin 0-11 Day cat		2018-02949540 698	Fair enough
Go ***	Color category: mixed oily skin 0-11 day cat		2018-02949540 698	It's not working yet. I've used catch-up reviews
Constant *** hum	Color category: Mixed Oily Skin 0-11 Day Cat		2018-02949540 698	Classic products Remember I used this six or seven years ago
g***9	Color category: Medium dry skin D-150	Tmall	2018-0 2949540698	Liquid foundation will look white on your face naturally.
a*** Ming	Color category: Mixed Oily Skin 0-11 Day Cat		2018-029495406982018-0	Concealer is good, cheeks don't take off easily, that is
Yellow ***0	Color category: Mixed Oily Skin 0-1 Tmall		2949540698	Baby received the same delivery as before
You *** Yu	Color classification: Mixed Oily Skin 0-11 Tmall		2018-02949540 698	B: I think it's a good feeling
Han *** brother	Color category: Mixed oily skin 0-1 Tmall		2018-02949540 698	Concealer is good, will not die white, Zhitu recommended
9**e	Color category: 200	Tmall	2018-0 2949540698	Useless

Fig. 2.13 Screenshot of partial source data of foundation/cream

Table 2.4 Comparison of individual source data of Tmall international samples before and after cleaning4

No	Source data (strips)	Cleaning data (bar)
F1	2000	1933
F2	1980	1933
F3	1980	1931
F4	2168	1542
F5	1978	1966
F6	1980	1923
F7	1806	1674
F8	1980	1919
F9	1980	1812
F10	1980	1898
L1	1980	1812
L2	1980	1879
L3	1980	1880
L4	1980	1872
L5	1980	1871
L6	1980	1809
L7	1980	1841
L8	1980	1774
L9	2000	1875
L10	2000	1838
P1	1980	1894
P2	1393	1358
P3	1980	1910
P4	1980	1898
P5	1980	1931
P6	1980	1891
P7	1980	1916
P8	1980	1854
P9	1230	1184
P10	730	685

Irrelevant Review: The content of the review is irrelevant to the product, for example: "This clothing….";

Invalid Review: The content of the review consists of invalid behaviors such as punctuation marks, emojis, padding words, or stacking of tone words, for example: "Padding words below~…";

Advertisement: Using the review section to advertise or promote commission for their own products;

Repeated Review: If the same review content appears in the review section due to multiple orders at the same time or simultaneous purchase of multiple products, only one valid review will be retained;

Stacked Word Review: If the review content is copied and pasted to form a multi-word review, the stacked word review will be deleted, and only one valid review will be retained, similar to repeated review behavior.

As can be seen from Table 2.4, a total of 53,503 valid reviews were collected for 30 products, with the earliest review time being the start time of data collection, i.e., November. Almost every representative product's online review system shows a time span of 6 months, with some months having more online reviews and some months having fewer. For example, February is the period with the fewest reviews for the 30 products, but it is still found that there are online reviews from purchased users almost every day. The overall online review data has a large time span, is evenly distributed, and has a large total number, providing a good experimental basis. Therefore, based on the above conditions, relevant secondary driving indicators can be extracted from consumer online review information for Bayesian network modeling analysis.

2.3.2 *Comment Data Keyword Extraction*

Before using the NLPIR-Parser software to extract keywords and count frequencies from text information, refer to the keyword features refined by the Tmall International online review system. This system has already counted the corresponding frequencies, providing official reference value, and providing direction and basis for this paper to refine keywords, and can be compared. The high-frequency comment information of the 30 product online review systems is shown in Table 2.5:

It shows the high-frequency review text of some products, "1736" and other numbers represent the frequency of the word or phrase in the displayed online review system. This frequency will change with the increase of reviews, folding, etc., but the high-frequency words refined by the reference system can assist this paper in further determining high-attention features. In the analysis and summary process of high-frequency text, first zero the information indicating emotional bias, in other words, personal color modifiers such as: quite, should, still, refine the core expression feature indicators in online reviews, that is, the attribute words that consumers perceive in the process of cross-border online shopping that highlight product and service competitiveness. Due to the differences among purchased users in online reviews, the expressions are different, including words that express similar or the same meanings, such as "really" and "genuine", so they are, respectively, retained in the review information for summary, and finally summarized.

Use NLPIR-Parser software to extract keywords and count frequencies from text information. Keyword extraction can extract several representative words or phrases from a single paper or collection of papers, as shown in Fig. 2.14, which is the result of keyword extraction from a collection of ten foundation liquids/creams, refining semantic queries, and quick matching.

Table 2.5 High-frequency information of Tmall International online review system5

ID	High-frequency information	Match the description (points)
F1	The emphasis is on cheap (1736) effect can also be (1479) quite watery (1430) very Natural (1427) Quick to handle (1104) Good concealer strength (999) Not much concealer (460)	4.8
F2	Very Natural (2689) Good Stuff (2622) Cost Effective (2505) Light Through Concealer (1822) Very moisturizing (1770) Fast Logistics (1733) Average concealer (638)	4.8
F3	The concealer is OK (2106) works just fine (674) Not at all (427) Great customer service Patient (272) Very fast (234) Very malleable (224) A little chunky (213)	4.8
…		
L1	Nice color (11) Nice smell (4)	4.8
L2	Color like (13,680) Very wet (10,577) Fast (3644) and so cheap (3204) The stuff is good (2718) The color is good (1354) The color is wrong (1170)	4.8
L3	The color is also good (611) The scan code is genuine (551) The quality is good (270) very moist (231) The logistics is fast (212) Very fragrant (93) The packaging is very bad (205)	4.7
…		
P1	The fragrance lasts (127) is genuine (56) It's cheaper (38) and it lasts (35) fast Pass fast (17) Bottle looks good (12) But doesn't last (14)	4.8
P2	Sweet feeling (8) Good seller (3) Logistics also give strength (3)	4.8
P3	Flower scent (258) Cheap price (53) Genuine (46) Well packed (45) Leave fragrance to return Can (44) Baby very good (28) Very good value for money (3) pungent taste (60) Lasting Degree average (39) Poor quality (5)	4.8
…		

After the keyword extraction of the selected file is completed, the system automatically opens the result file keylist, as shown in Fig. 2.15. The keyword analysis content includes: words, word properties, weights, and frequency statistics. The system defaults to sorting words by weight. The data is imported into EXCEL for further classification and screening, initially determining whether similar words are from the same text based on word properties, and then manually reviewing; weight serves as the initial basis for classifying and summarizing high-frequency words.

After screening and determining the keywords with characteristic value, they are summarized one by one in the EXCEL database to count their frequency of occurrence, and some of the statistical results are shown in Table 2.6:

Present the word cloud in a more visual form, as shown in Fig. 2.16

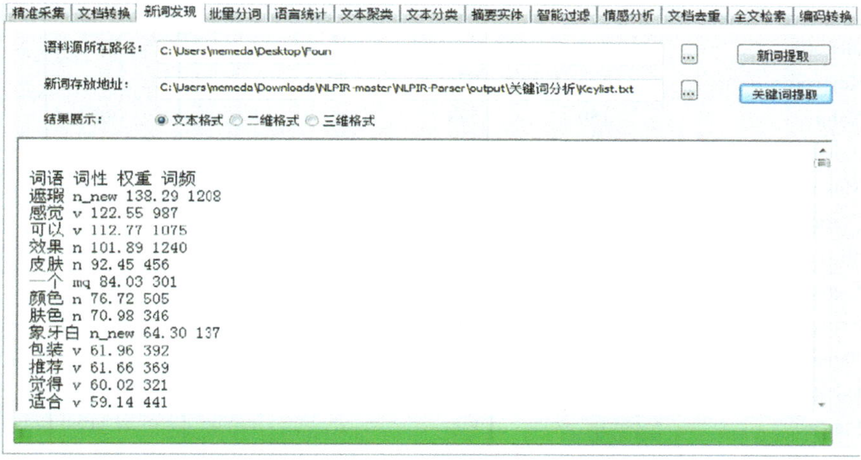

Fig. 2.14 Keyword extraction

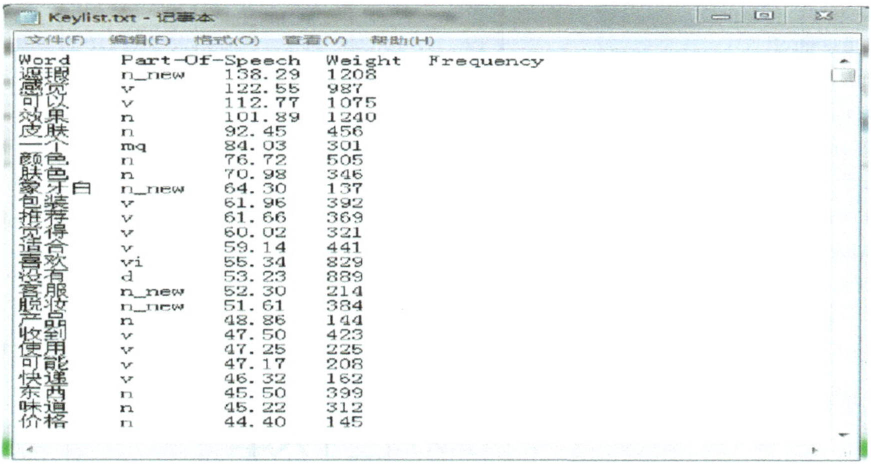

Fig. 2.15 F1–F10 Keyword extraction (keylist)

Under the category of foundation liquid/paste, according to statistical results, the most frequently appearing terms are "natural", "powdery white", "concealer", "makeup removal", etc. This indicates that in the online reviews captured, cross-border e-commerce retail import users pay more attention to the makeup effect, product quality (texture, oil control, etc.), durability, and authenticity guarantee when evaluating foundation liquid/paste. At the same time, related keywords have similarities, which requires further summarization and generalization.

Table 2.6 Frequency statistics of ten product review keywords for some foundation liquid/cream categories

Keywords	F1	F2	F3	…	F
Nature	159	193	51	…	965
Pinky white	119	122	74		586
Makeup off	71	99	32		384
Color	61	57	52		505
oil	55	35	20		310
Logistics	51	55	19		334
Express	39	12	12		162
Floating powder	39	25	15		238
Docile	39	33	12		225
Flavor	38	8	8		312
Wrapping	37	33	60		392
Genuine	35	21	13		657
Card powder	31	36	19		240
Delicate	29	20	2	…	170
Oil control	27	19	1		116
embellish	27	29	19		223
Customer service	25	14	38		214
Moistening	20	16	10		223
Service attitude	20	12	5		90
Price	19	15	11		145
Makeup sense	18	8	30		115
Allergies	6	11	6		62
…					

Fig. 2.16 Partial foundation liquid/cream category ten product review keywords cloud map

2.3.3 Comment Data Secondary Driving Indicators

The secondary driving indicators of the makeup product model are selected for empirical testing. The specific secondary driving indicators are shown in Table 2.7. The value driving indicators found in the table are more detailed, and the merchant's focus is more complex, so they are measured in detail; packaging reflects consumers' acceptance and praise of the product brand, so authenticity guarantee and packaging are used as secondary indicators of brand driving factors; service driving mainly involves merchant services in online reviews; technology driving is reflected in the logistics delivery and feedback system of the platform and merchants.

The keyword frequency data information after statistics is large and difficult to operate conveniently. It is scattered and similar, lacks summarization and representativeness. The keywords with similar meanings and expressing the same perceptual attributes in the cleaned online review keywords are classified and summarized based on customer perception driving factors to determine the frequency and weight of the secondary driving indicators affecting the consumption preferences of import B2C cross-border e-commerce users. The secondary driving indicators of each product are summarized in frequency, and the next step is to score the secondary driving indicators under each comment to get the "total score" analogous to customer perceived value, further standardizing the source data of the predictive variables for Bayesian network modeling.

Based on expert opinions and experimental staff analysis, the keywords corresponding to the secondary indicators of specific research product objects under different categories are statistically summarized, and the classification results are shown in Tables 2.8–2.10.

Through the analysis of the product and service features of the foundation liquid/ paste purchased by users, and the summarization of related keywords, the keywords are classified into ten secondary driving indicators, namely: makeup effect, concealer effect, duration, skin type, logistics, authenticity guarantee, product quality, merchant service, packaging, and price. These are the product or service attribute features that

Table 2.7 Four-dimensional driving factors and second-level driving indicators6

Driving Factors	Secondary driving Indicators		
	Liquid foundation/ cream (F)	**Lip balm/lipstick (L)**	**Perfume (P)**
Brand driven	Authentic guarantee, packaging	Genuine guarantee, packaging	Genuine guarantee, packaging
Service driven	Merchant services	Merchant services	Merchant services
Value driven	Duration, makeup effect, concealer effect, skin type, price, product quality	Duration, makeup effect, lip type, price, color, product quality	Duration, taste, price, product quality, mechanical features
Technology driven	Logistics	Logistics	Logistics

Table 2.8 Characteristic variables of keyword classification of liquid foundation/paste7

Keyword summary	Secondary driving indicator variable	Variable represents
Natural, makeup, nude makeup, makeup effect, conforming, fit, smooth, gloss, false white, white face, mask, etc	Makeup effects	X1
Concealer, concealer strength, concealer strength, etc	Concealer effect	X2
Makeup removal, lasting, holding, staying power, etc	Duration	X3
Mixed oil, oil skin, oiliness, dry, etc	Skin type	X4
Price, parity, etc	Price	X5
Logistics, express delivery, speed of delivery, etc	Logistics	X6
Genuine, real, official, etc	Genuine guarantee	X7
Light, moisturizing, waterproof, allergic, itchy face, fragrance, smell, powder tone, etc	Product quality	X8
Customer service, service, etc	Merchant services	X9
Packaging, boxes, bins, etc	Packing	X10

Table 2.9 Lipstick/lipstick keyword classification characteristic variables8

Summary of keywords	Secondary driving indicator variable	Variable represents
Matte, lip bite, hued, etc	Makeup effects	Y1
Fading, lasting, dip cups, etc	Duration	Y2
Yellow skin, lip color, lip lines, etc	Lip texture categories	Y3
Color, brick red, chromatic aberration, Aunt, rust red, chroma Bean paste, color, etc	Colors	Y4
Price, parity, etc	Price	Y5
Logistics, express delivery, speed of delivery, etc	Logistics	Y6
Genuine, real, official, etc	Genuine guarantee	Y7
Light, moisturizing, waterproof, odor, etc	Product quality	Y8
Customer service, service, etc	Merchant service	Y9
Packaging, boxes, bins, etc	Packing	Y10

Table 2.10 Characteristic variables of perfume keywords classification9

Keyword summary	Secondary driving indicator variable	Variable represents
Retention time, duration, lingering fragrance, etc	Duration	Z1
Logistics, express delivery, speed of delivery, etc	Logistics	Z2
Authentic, real, official, etc	Genuine guarantee	Z3
Tail note, essence, full-bodied, etc	Product quality	Z4
Customer service, service, etc	Merchant services	Z5
Packaging, boxes, bins, etc	Packing	Z6
Price, parity, etc	Price	Z7
Fragrance, smell, taste, etc	Taste	Z8
Sprinkler heads, nozzles, watering cans, etc	Mechanical functions	Z9

cross-border retail import users pay more attention to, reflecting the comprehensive competitiveness of products and services, and to a certain extent expressing the behavioral preferences of cross-border retail import consumers. Based on the model, this paper will analyze consumer behavior from these ten indicators, set them as ten secondary driving indicator variables, form the basis variables for constructing the Bayesian network, and represent them with X1–X10.

Through the analysis of the product and service features of lipstick/lipstick user needs, and the classification of related keywords, the keywords are summarized into ten secondary driving indicators, namely: makeup effect, duration, lip type, color, price, logistics, authenticity guarantee, product quality, merchant service, and packaging. This paper uses the source data under these ten secondary driving indicators as the basis variables for constructing the lipstick/lipstick Bayesian network, and represents them with Y1–Y10.

Similarly, through the analysis of the product and service features of perfume purchased by users, and the summarization of related keywords, the keywords are classified into nine secondary driving indicators, namely: duration, logistics, authenticity guarantee, product quality, merchant service, packaging, price, scent, and mechanical function. These are the product or service attribute features that cross-border retail import users pay more attention to, reflecting the comprehensive competitiveness of products and services. This paper will analyze user needs from these nine secondary driving indicators, construct a Bayesian network model, and represent them with Z1–Z9.

2.3.4 Standardization Scoring of Secondary Driving Indicators

Based on the research above, we conducted frequency statistics of key information for ten products under three categories. Taking liquid foundation/cream as an example, as shown in Table 2.11, user preferences can be observed from the high-frequency secondary driving indicators: a higher frequency indicates more online reviews from users, and thus we can determine the focus of users.

Combining the scoring system of Tmall International online reviews (total score of 5) and the Likert scale five-point system to judge the degree of recognition of secondary driving indicators, a certain scoring standard is set for the secondary driving indicators of ten products under three categories. These details help researchers quantify the evaluation of product or service attributes perceived by consumers. This method is often used in survey research, and with its objective, fair, and standardized rules, it has become the most commonly used scale in experimental demonstrations. When converting the text data of online reviews from cross-border e-commerce retail users into numerical data, the Likert scale five-point scoring system is used, as shown in Table 2.12.

Table 2.11 Summary of secondary driving index frequency of ten products of liquid foundation/paste10

No	X1	X2	X3	X4	X5	X6	X7	X8	X9	X10
F1	284	392	200	43	100	351	108	130	110	353
F2	291	400	178	21	105	431	587	142	89	265
F3	265	409	276	34	168	276	398	110	102	276
F4	284	453	254	25	128	338	465	109	65	409
F5	247	379	231	46	180	457	231	217	115	402
F6	297	489	188	63	153	289	343	221	83	297
F7	198	437	163	58	109	398	392	231	77	284
F8	234	461	199	59	114	198	569	207	91	356
F9	276	395	208	37	149	451	341	156	125	279
F10	256	387	311	21	98	254	274	187	104	399

Table 2.12 Five-point scoring rule of Likert Scale11

Scoring Criteria	Score
Very good/excellent/exceptionally good	5
good	4
Average/good	3
Not good	2
Very bad/especially bad/extremely bad	1

Based on the adjectives expressing emotional attitudes appearing in the online review text, combined with the differences and connections of different secondary driving indicator variables, different scoring details are set for different variables. For independent secondary driving indicators, there are differences in the specific forms of scoring details. In online review information, users in different consumption areas have language or dialect differences, so the behavior habits of expressing emotions also differ. However, the intensity of emotional color is usually expressed with certain adjectives, such as using "very" or "extremely" to modify, or expressing with internet slang, such as "naisi" = "nice". On this basis, specific scoring details are set, as shown in Table 2.13. This article will strictly convert text data into standardized numerical data according to the scoring details.

Table 2.13 Variable scoring rules12

Variable	5 points	4 points	3 points	2 points	1 point
Makeup effects	Extra natural/ perfect nude makeup	Nice looking/ natural	Average/good	A bit of float powder/oil out	Not good/very poor
Concealer effect	Very concealer/ especially	Very good	Average/good	Somewhat not	Particularly not
Duration	Long lasting, super	nice	Average/good	Not much	Extremely not
Skin/lip texture	Extra fit/ perfect match	Fit	Average/good	Not recommended	Very poor
Color	So pretty, love it	Look good, like	Average/good	Not good looking	Very unattractive
Logistics	Fast and especially timely	In time, fast	Normal	A little slow	Slow
Genuine guarantee	Absolute genuine/ counter goods	Genuine	Don't know the real thing	There is a difference with the real thing	Fake and inferior
Product quality	Good	nice	Average/good	Somewhat poor	Extremely bad
Merchant service	Warm/ excellent service	nice	Average/good	Bad attitude	Bad attitude
Packaging	Perfect packaging	No breakage	Normal	Simple packing	Particularly poor
Price	Super deal	Affordable/ Affordable	Average/good	It's expensive, a bit much	It's not a good deal
Taste	Nice smell	Nice smell	Average/good	Bad smell	Pungent
Mechanical features	Very easy to use/convenient	expediency	Average/good	Not working well	Extremely difficult to use

Following the differences in the expression forms of indicator scoring, the results of previous research experiments are comprehensively used to standardize and score them. During the data sorting and analysis process, the phenomenon of synonym assimilation occurs, such as the degree of emotional color bias "naisi" can be equivalent to "great". For secondary driving indicators not mentioned in the user's review content, this article defaults to the median, that is, 3 points, representing approval and acceptance. The standardized numerical data serves as the model data for each secondary driving indicator, and the source data for the overall score of cross-border e-commerce retail import behavior preferences is calculated based on its own weight. For the same variable, different users perceive different emotions. For such characteristic variables with overlapping review emotions, scoring needs to be based on user satisfaction, such as the scent of the same perfume, users have different sensitivities and acceptances for this product.

Finally, the scoring of the user's overall comprehensive evaluation needs to be based on two processes: (1) Users may summarize after evaluating the indicators of each dimension, such as texts like "In summary, it's not bad" or "Give 5 stars for the product", then the overall score is directly determined by these statements; (2) When users do not explicitly explain the overall score after evaluating the indicators of each dimension, the average of the scores of each secondary driving indicator can be calculated to determine the overall comprehensive evaluation score.

References

1. Guo Y, Bao Y, Stuart BJ et al (2018) To sell or not to sell: Exploring sellers' trust and risk of chargeback fraud in cross-border electronic commerce[J]. Inform Syst J 28(2):359–383
2. Wang Y, Lee S H (2017) The effect of cross-border e-commerce on china's international trade: An empirical study based on transaction cost analysis[J]. Sustainability 9(11): 2028
3. Wang H, Xiao M, Huo Y (2017) Research on the construction strategy of cross-border e-commerce comprehensive pilot area based on salop mode [J]. Int J Innov Comput Inform Contr 13(5):1563–1577
4. Wei S, Hongwei W, Shaoyi H (2016) The impact of online word-of-mouth on market sales distribution: Based on different product evaluation standards[J]. Syst Eng Theory Pract 36(07):1744–1752

Chapter 3
Construction and Analysis of Cross-Border E-commerce Retail Import User Preference Model

Cross-border import e-commerce has developed into a new and common consumption habit for consumers, who generally judge the "value points" mentioned in the online reviews of products. "Value points" include the focus points and preferences of consumers for product and service attributes, such as the size of the product, after-sales service, logistics waiting time, and also contain the emotional preferences of consumers for the product. Emotional interactions between consumers will infect and spread to each other, and this diffusion behavior will also accelerate emotional fluctuations and contagion, such as sudden high-intensity emotional outbreaks, sudden increases in the number of reviews. In a complete time series, the emotional tendency, emotional intensity, and diffusion speed corresponding to the emotional energy can clearly describe the changes in consumer emotional preferences, corresponding to the emotional performance of each time period.

3.1 Construction of Bayesian Network Model of Cross-Border E-commerce Retail Import User Preference

The Bayesian classification method fully draws on the prior information of the sample data while analyzing the data information in statistics. Using the Bayesian network, the historical online review data and "common sense" can be combined to establish a probability model network diagram, explore the potential causal relationship between sample variables, and make predictions. The software used for modeling in this article is Clementine developed by IBM. Clementine software is used to import data, filter, set types, and construct a Bayesian network for analysis and prediction.

By importing and filtering online review data of the ten hottest products under three categories, a Bayesian network is generated for a total of 14 secondary driving

L. Xiong and H. Wang, *User Driven Cross-Border E-Commerce Platform Competition and Policy Analysis*, Advanced Studies in E-Commerce,
https://doi.org/10.1007/978-981-97-3835-9_3

indicators. The conditional occurrence probabilities and importance rankings of each secondary driving indicator in the network model are analyzed. The cross-border retail import consumer behavior preferences are analyzed from four directions: Bayesian network accuracy, model structure, conditional probability, and indicator importance level.

By converting the standardized scores of each secondary driving indicator into a structure recognizable by Clementine software, they are classified, summarized, and loaded into the software. A Bayesian network probability graph composed of secondary driving indicators with different probability distributions and a total goal is constructed through a series of collaborative operations. The importance comparison of each driving indicator in the network graph is also made [[1]].

3.1.1 Introduction to Clementine Software

Data mining is the process of refining information and knowledge of potential value that is hidden and unknown to people in advance from large data that is incomplete, noisy, fuzzy, and randomly produced, using knowledge from multiple disciplines such as statistics, computer science, and software science. It is a data analysis method that includes depth and breadth.

Clementine software simplifies the algorithm process, includes data sources in various formats, provides many commonly used mathematical statistics and business intelligence models, and finally provides an analysis structure with a visual interface for easy learning and understanding, such as: neural networks, principal component analysis, association rule analysis. Its data mining idea facilitates the work. At the same time, Clementine software performs operations through a series of nodes and flows between nodes to complete data analysis. This process is called data flow, which is implemented on the data flow area interface. Each node corresponds to different collaborations of data files, representing different goal achievements. The directed arrow between nodes represents the direction of the next step of the flow and finally realizes the modeling results based on graphic analysis, which serves as the basis for judging the feasibility of the model. The data flow is similar to script code, which can be used in the process of mining different data files, and it is convenient for data storage and calling [[2]].

3.1.2 Bayesian Network Model Construction Process

This article uses the Bayesian network model in Clementine software to model and analyze the user consumption behavior preference model of the imported B2C cross-border e-commerce platform website based on online reviews. The individual sample data of the ten hottest selling products under the selected three categories, that is, the secondary driving indicator data of user online review information is loaded into the

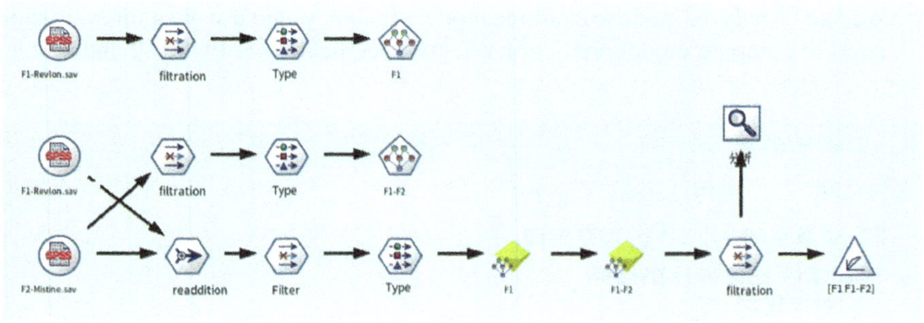

Fig. 3.1 Clementine software Bayesian network modeling data flow

software to build a Bayesian network model with its secondary driving indicators after data format conversion. Then, the conditional probability distribution of each variable (secondary driving indicator) in the network structure diagram is calculated separately, and the relative importance of each factor node is analyzed. After the model is accurately evaluated, the judgment and prediction of user purchase demand preferences for various products are obtained [[3]].

Due to the similarity of sample product features and sufficient sample data, the training and comparison of the Bayesian network model are carried out, and then the appropriate samples and models are selected. The specific operation process is demonstrated with the sample data of foundation liquid/cream.

First, use the first sample F1 data under the foundation liquid/cream category to train the first Bayesian network model, then use the second sample F2 combined with F1 to train the second Bayesian network, and so on, until it is combined to the tenth sample F10, that is, the total sample volume of foundation liquid/cream FUN. Finally, the constructed Bayesian networks are compared, and the sample data with better results are preferentially selected for the next step of analysis and prediction work, as shown in Fig. 3.1 [[4]].

The specific steps are as follows:

1. Import the standardized F1 data samples into the data flow area, preprocess in advance, filter out secondary driving indicators unrelated to the target variable to increase model efficiency, and set input/output types and other corresponding secondary driving indicator formats. Establish a TAN Bayesian network. Since the initial modeling includes the probability relationship between all variables (secondary driving indicators), the modeling scale is large, so choose the parameter learning method of "Bayesian adjustment for small cell counts";
2. Loop this process, keep the above operation process unchanged, check "Continue training existing model" during modeling to get the results of F1-F2 data training;
3. Add an "Append" node, merge F1 and F2 data to check their respective training results, repeat the loop of "Filter" and "Type" nodes and add the F1 Bayesian network and F1-F2 Bayesian network into the next process in turn, filter and rename the output variables for easy identification and memory;

4. Add an "Analysis" node to examine model efficiency, and use the gain evaluation chart to compare model prediction effects, specifically see Figs. 3.2 and 3.3.

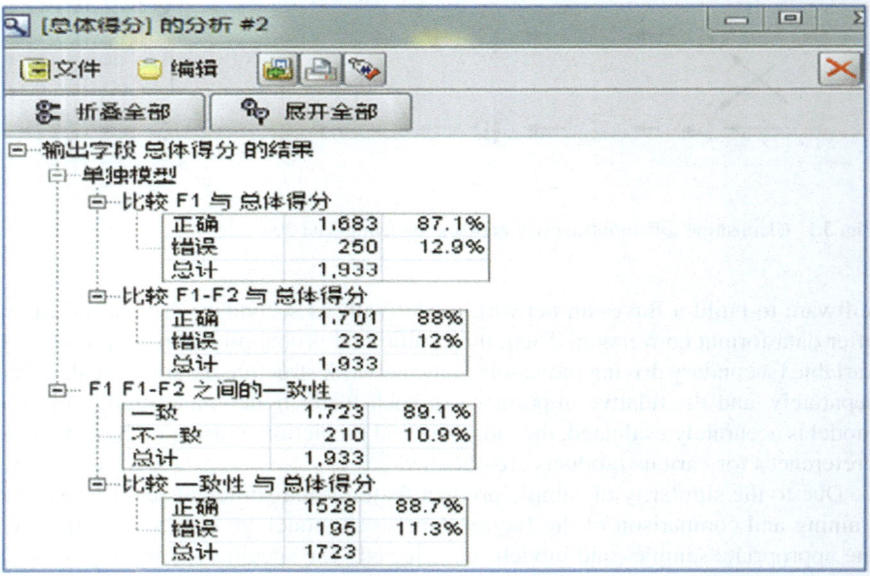

Fig. 3.2 Efficiency analysis of F1 and F1-F2 models

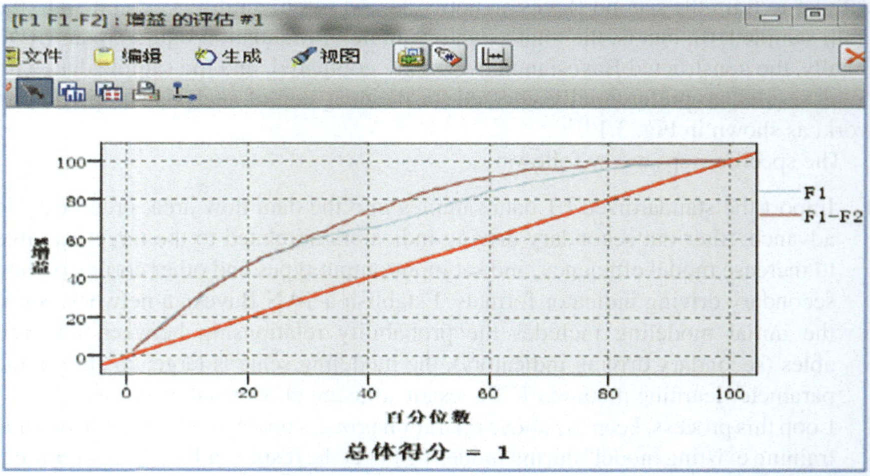

Fig. 3.3 Gain evaluation of F1 versus F1-F2

It is found from Fig. 3.2 that the accuracy of the F1 Bayesian model and the F1-F2 Bayesian model is basically the same, and the F1-F2 Bayesian model is slightly better than the F1 Bayesian model, so the F1-F2 Bayesian network model is preferred.

In the gain evaluation chart, the larger the arc of the arc, the better the gain of the corresponding Bayesian model. In other words, when achieving the same effect, this model uses less sample data. Figure 3.3 finds that the gain of the F1-F2 model is slightly higher than that of the F1 model, and the models built with the data of the two products have better credibility and better prediction effects. Therefore, the F1-F2 Bayesian model should be preferred. By analogy, the construction of the Bayesian network model of the foundation/cream should be based on all sample data for continuous iterative training and learning to build the model; the same is true for lipstick/lipstick and perfume.

3.1.2.1 Bayesian Network Model Construction

During the data capture and preprocessing, considering the "value points", functions, services, and many other factors of the product, the foundation/cream with the highest popularity TOP1 is selected as the research target. Products with high sales have many online reviews. Summarizing many analogous words will help the completeness of information and improve the accuracy of standardized data. This article summarizes the keywords in the online review text information into ten secondary driving indicator variables and a target variable representing the overall score [[5]].

As known from the previous text, iterative modeling of online review data samples of ten products under foundation/cream will be carried out. The preprocessed, cleaned, and standardized variable data will be imported into Clementine software. After loading, filtering, and setting types, it enters the Bayesian network modeling process. The ten secondary driving indicators are used as independent variables, that is, input variables. Relatively speaking, the overall score is used as the dependent variable, that is, the output variable for training and modeling. TAN is selected to build the network structure, and the parameter learning method of "Bayesian adjustment for small cell counts" is selected. Generate the Bayesian network diagram and calculate the conditional probability of each node in the network and the importance of each node (secondary driving indicator), to judge the consumer preference factors of B2C cross-border e-commerce users for products. The Bayesian network diagram of foundation/cream is shown in Fig. 3.4:

In Fig. 3.4, the overall score is the output variable, and the other ten secondary driving indicators jointly affect the output variable. They are linked up and down in a directed but acyclic structure, and each secondary driving indicator vector directly or indirectly affects each other. Figure 3.4 shows: there is a correlation between the overall score and the ten secondary driving indicators, and there is a strong correlation between the overall score and the concealing effect, duration, makeup effect, etc. The concealing effect is significantly related to the duration and packaging, and the product quality is related to the price and merchant service, etc. At the same time, the Bayesian network diagram automatically calculates the occurrence probability

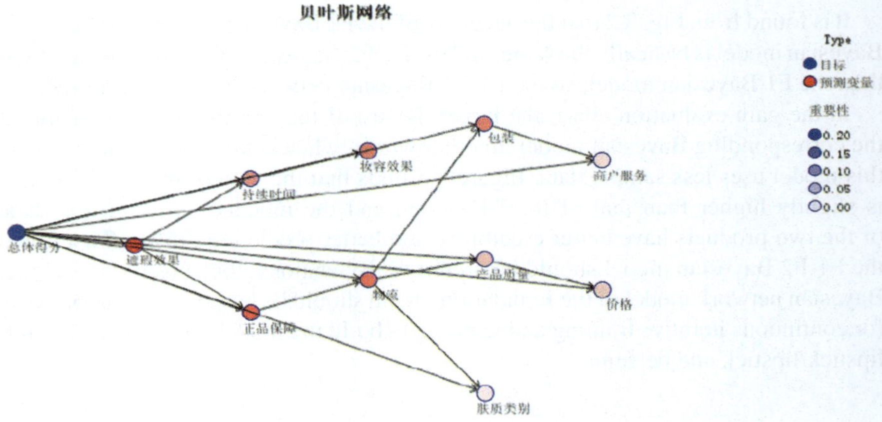

Fig. 3.4 Liquid foundation/Paste FUN Bayesian network

of each node under the condition of its parent node [[6]]. Figure 3.5 is the conditional probability distribution diagram of the output of foundation liquid/paste; from the figure, we can more intuitively observe the relationship between each secondary driving indicator, they may have a strong influence on each other, each node may be the parent node of other nodes, or it may be the child node of other nodes.

According to the constructed Bayesian network, the conditional probability of each node (secondary driving indicator) under the action of its parent node is obtained, and the distribution probability of some nodes is shown in Tables 3.1–3.4.

From the conditional probability of the overall score of the output variable and the concealing effect of the input variable, the probability of the overall score node being rated as 3 points or above is 0.72, of which the probability of 3 points is larger

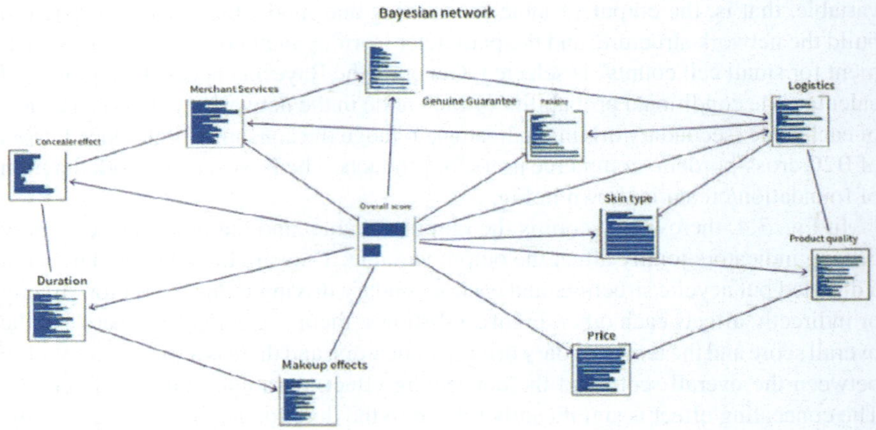

Fig. 3.5 Conditional probability distribution for liquid foundation/paste FUN

Table 3.1 Conditional probability of overall score1

Probabilities				
1	2	3	4	5
0.013	0.264	0.587	0.124	0.009

Table 3.2 Conditional probability of concealer effect2

Parent Level	Probability				
Overall Score	1	2	3	4	5
1	1	0	0	0	0
2	0.899	0.099	0	0	0
3	0	0	0.543	0.21	0.245
4	0	0	0.187	0.1	0.701
5	0	0	0	0	1

Table 3.3 Conditional probability of makeup effect3

Parent Level		Probability				
Duration	Overall Score	1	2	3	4	5
1	**1**	1	0	0	0	0
2	**3**	0	0.124	0.873	0	0
3	**3**	0.002	0.023	0.817	0.141	0.003
3	**4**	0	0.002	0.747	0.228	0.003
4	**4**	0	0	0.849	0.139	0
4	**5**	0	0	0	0.305	0.693
5	**4**	0	0	0.919	0.079	0
5	**5**	0	0	0	0	1
…						

at 0.587. This shows that most users accept the comprehensive score of this type of product, and at the same time, under the overall evaluation of 2 points, 3 points, 4 points, and 5 points, the probabilities of the concealing effect being 1 point, 3 points, 5 points, and 5 points are 0.899, 0.543, 0.701, and 1 respectively.

The parent nodes of the makeup effect are the overall score and duration, which show different probability distributions when the duration score is within the range of 1~5 points, most of which are concentrated at 3 points or above, indicating that users generally accept the duration of this type of product. Among them, the maximum probability of getting one point is 1, and the maximum probability of getting 5 points is also 1. The parent nodes of duration and genuine guarantee are both concealing effect and overall score. The two nodes have a larger probability of getting 3 points or above in the range of 1~5 points of concealing effect, some even get a larger

Table 3.4 Duration and packing condition probabilities4

Parent Level		Duration Conditional Probability					Genuine Guarantee probability				
Concealer Effect	Overall Score	1	2	3	4	5	1	2	3	4	5
1	**1**	1	0	0	0	0	1	0	0	0	0
1	**2**	0	0.116	0.876	0.006	0	0.058	0.67	0.27	0	0
2	**2**	0.067	0.778	0.208	0.011	0.003	0.195	0.514	0.245	0.044	0
2	**4**	0	0.033	0.031	0.718	0.216	0	0	0.147	0.649	0.201
3	**3**	0	0.064	0.763	0.17	0	0	0.049	0.704	0.197	0.097
3	**4**	0	0.032	0.311	0.527	0.125	0	0	0.277	0.522	0.199
4	**4**	0	0	0.561	0.368	0.065	0	0.093	0.368	0.536	0.001
4	**5**	0	0	0.193	0.269	0.536	0	0	0.341	0.358	0.559
5	**5**	0	0	0	0	1	0	0	0	0	1
…											

probability at 4 points and 5 points, indicating that users have a higher acceptance of duration and genuine guarantee based on the perception of concealing effect and overall score of this type of product, and other nodes are inferred by analogy [[7]].

The following Fig. 3.6 is a histogram of the importance of foundation liquid/paste product variables (secondary driving indicators), from top to bottom, the importance is relatively weakened. This paper finds that when purchasing this type of product, users prefer to pay attention to some secondary driving indicators of product value driving factors, such as concealing effect, makeup effect, duration, which is significantly different from other products, reflecting the preference of users of this type of product, followed by genuine guarantee, logistics, packaging, the weakest points of attention are price, customer service and user's own skin type.

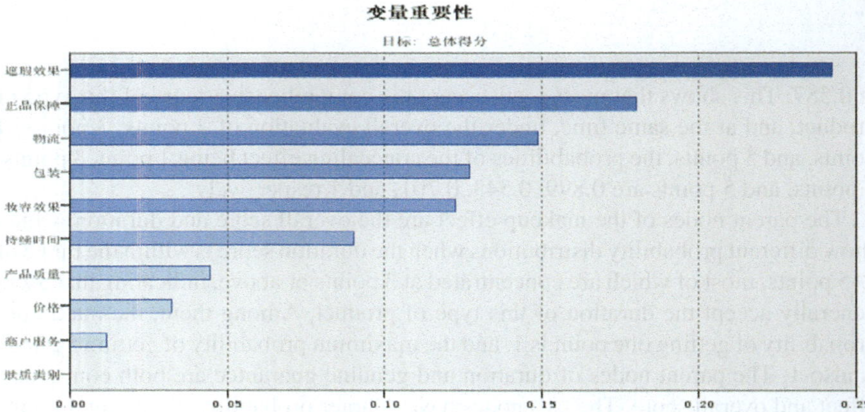

Fig. 3.6 Importance of liquid foundation/cream FUN variable

Choosing the TOP2 lipstick/lipstick as the research target, this paper summarizes the keywords in the online comment text information into ten secondary driving indicator variables, that is, input variables, and an output variable representing the overall score.

From the previous text, it is known that iterative modeling of online review data samples for ten products under the lipstick category will be carried out. The preprocessed, cleaned, and standardized variable data will be imported into Clementine software. After loading, filtering, and setting types, it will enter the Bayesian network modeling process. The ten secondary driving indicators will be used as independent variables, i.e., input variables. Conversely, the overall score will be used as the dependent variable, i.e., output variable for training and modeling. The TAN is selected to construct the network structure, and the parameter learning method of "Bayesian adjustment for small cell counts" is chosen. The Bayesian network diagram is generated and the conditional probabilities and importance levels of each node (secondary driving indicators) in the network are calculated. This helps to determine the consumer preference factors of imported B2C cross-border e-commerce users for products. The lipstick Bayesian network diagram is shown in Fig. 3.7.

In Fig. 3.7, the overall score is the output variable, and the other ten secondary driving indicator variables collectively affect the output variable. They are linked in a directed but acyclic structure, and each secondary driving indicator vector directly or indirectly affects each other. Figure 3.8 shows that there is a correlation between the overall score and the ten secondary driving indicators, and there is a strong correlation between the overall score and color, duration, logistics, and genuine product guarantee. The genuine product guarantee is directly related to lip quality category, makeup effect, and merchant service, and product quality is related to price and packaging.

At the same time, the Bayesian network diagram automatically calculates the occurrence probability of each node under the condition of its parent node. Fig. 3.8

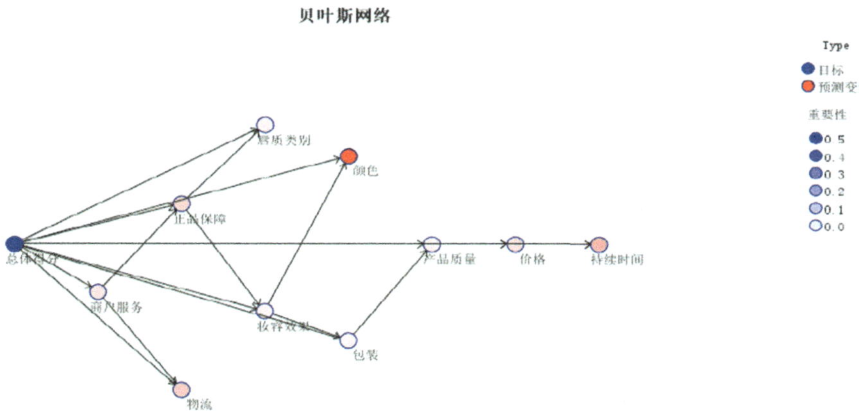

Fig. 3.7 LIP balm/lipstick Lip Bayesian network

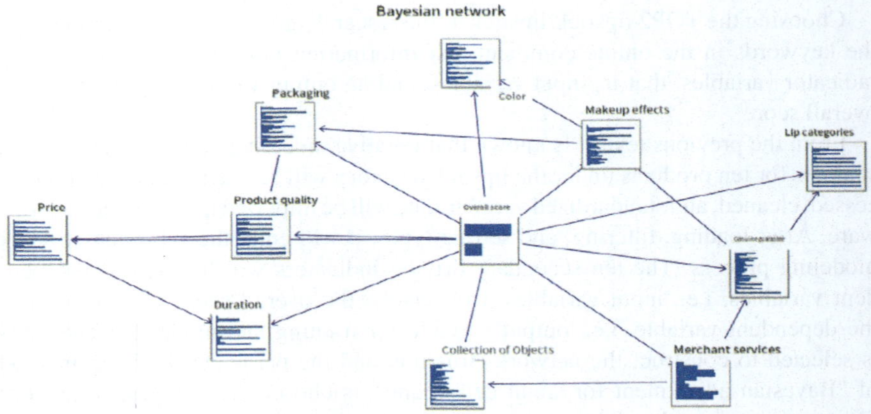

Fig. 3.8 LIP balm/lipstick LIP conditional probability distribution

is the conditional probability distribution diagram of lipstick output; from the figure, we can more intuitively observe the relationship between each secondary driving indicator, which may have a strong influence on each other. Each node could be the parent node of other nodes or the child node of other nodes. According to the constructed Bayesian network, the conditional probability of each node (secondary driving indicator) under the action of its parent node is obtained. Randomly selected nodes (secondary driving indicators) are shown in Tables 3.5–3.8.

From the conditional probability of the output variable overall score and the input variable merchant service, the probability of the overall score node being rated as 3 points or above is 0.737, of which the probability of 3 points is relatively large at 0.612. This indicates that most users accept the comprehensive score of this type

Table 3.5 Conditional probability of overall score5

Probabilities				
1	2	3	4	5
0.008	0.253	0.612	0.120	0.005

Table 3.6 Merchant Condition of Service probabilities6

Parent Level	Probability				
Overall score	1	2	3	4	5
1	0.294	0.332	0.218	0.093	0.06
2	0.16	0.315	0.307	0.164	0.052
3	0.037	0.261	0.336	0.261	0.102
4	0.005	0.144	0.005	0.283	0.561
5	0	0	0	0.1	0.898

Table 3.7 color conditional probabilities7

Parent Level		Probability				
Overall Score	Makeup Effect	1	2	3	4	5
2	3	0.001	0.001	0.726	0.039	0.23
3	3	0	0	0.072	0.735	0.19
4	3	0.001	0.301	0.545	0.151	0
5	3	0	0.001	0.19	0.736	0.072
1	4	0.244	0.611	0.112	0.03	0
2	4	0.162	0.394	0.417	0.024	0
3	4	0.003	0.154	0.23	0.381	0.23
4	5	0.001	0.001	0.883	0.111	0.001
5	4	0	0	0	0.06	0.939
5	5	0	0	0	0	1
…						

of product. Meanwhile, under the overall evaluation of 1 point, 2 points, 3 points, 4 points, and 5 points, the probabilities of merchant service being 2 points, 2 points, 3 points, 5 points, and 5 points are 0.332, 0.315, 0.336, 0.561, and 0.898 respectively. As shown in Fig. 3.8 and Table 3.7, the parent nodes of color are the overall score and makeup effect. When the makeup effect and overall score are within the range of 1~5 points, they show different probability distributions. The distribution shows uniformity, indicating that users have a universal preference for the color variable of this type of product. Among them, the maximum probability of getting 2 points is 0.611, the maximum probability of getting 3 points is 0.883, the maximum probability of getting 4 points is 0.736, and the maximum probability of getting 5 points is 1.

The parent nodes of genuine product guarantee and logistics are both merchant service and overall score. The two nodes get extreme values in the probability distribution within the range of 1~5 points of concealing effect, and there are individual cases, such as the maximum probability of genuine product guarantee score being 1 is 0.923. This indicates that the changes brought about by the long-tail effect should be paid attention to. In general, users have a high acceptance of genuine product guarantee and logistics based on the merchant service and overall score of this type of product. Other secondary driving indicators can be inferred by analogy [[8]].

Figure 3.9 shows a histogram of the importance of variables (secondary driving indicators) under the category of lipstick products, with the importance decreasing from top to bottom. This study found that users of this type of product prefer to focus on the value points of the product itself (value driving factors) when purchasing, especially the color. This is related to the characteristics of lipstick and is significantly different from other products, reflecting the preferences of users of this type of product. At the same time, attention is paid to the duration, logistics, and authenticity guarantee, followed by price, merchant service, and product quality. The weakest focus is on packaging, lip quality category, and makeup effect.

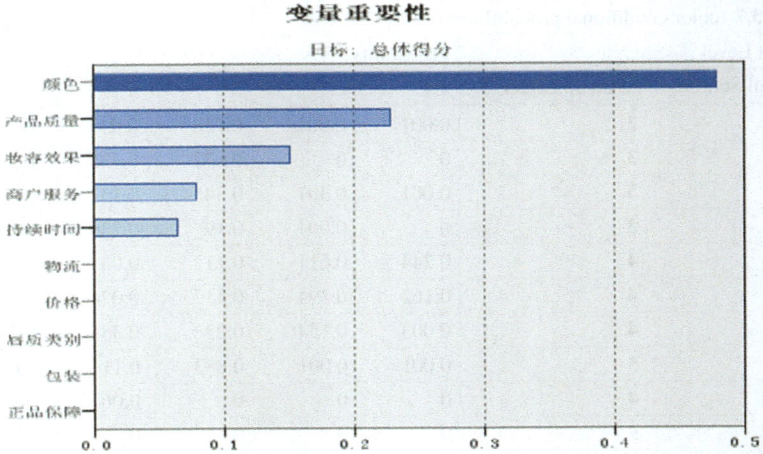

Fig. 3.9 Importance of LIP balm/lipstick LIP variables

The top three popular perfumes were chosen as the research target. This study summarized the keywords in the online comment text information into nine secondary driving indicator variables, i.e., input variables, and one output variable representing the overall score.

As known from the previous text, iterative modeling of online comment data samples of ten products under the perfume category will be carried out. The preprocessed, cleaned, and standardized variable data will be imported into Clementine software. After loading, filtering, and setting types, it will enter the Bayesian network modeling process. The nine secondary driving indicators are used as independent variables, i.e., input variables. Relatively speaking, the overall score is used as the dependent variable, i.e., output variable for training modeling. The TAN is selected to build the network structure, and the "Bayesian adjustment of small cell count" parameter learning method is selected to generate the Bayesian network diagram and calculate the conditional probability and importance of each node (secondary driving indicator) in the network. This helps to judge the consumer preference factors of imported B2C cross-border e-commerce users for products. The perfume Bayesian network diagram is shown in Fig. 3.10:

In Fig. 3.10, the overall score is the output variable, and the other nine secondary driving indicator variables jointly affect the output variable. They are linked in a directed but acyclic structure, and each secondary driving indicator vector directly or indirectly affects each other. Figure 3.10 shows: there is a correlation between the overall score and the nine secondary driving indicators, and there is a strong correlation between the overall score and the taste, duration, packaging, authenticity guarantee, etc. The authenticity guarantee is directly related to the taste and packaging, and the merchant service is related to the price, taste, logistics, etc. At the same time, the Bayesian network diagram automatically calculates the occurrence probability of each node under the condition of its parent node [[9]]. Figure 3.11 is the

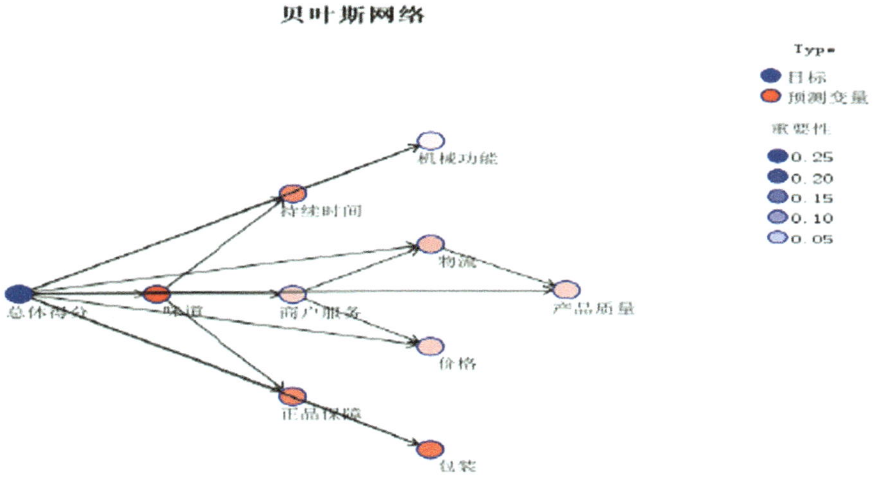

Fig. 3.10 PER Bayesian network for perfume

conditional probability distribution diagram of the perfume category output; from the figure, you can more intuitively observe the relationship between each secondary driving indicator, they may have a strong influence on each other, each node may be the parent node of other nodes, or it may be the child node of other nodes.

According to the constructed Bayesian network, the conditional probability of each node (secondary driving indicator) under the action of its parent node is obtained, and nodes (secondary driving indicators) are randomly selected as shown in Tables 3.9–3.12.

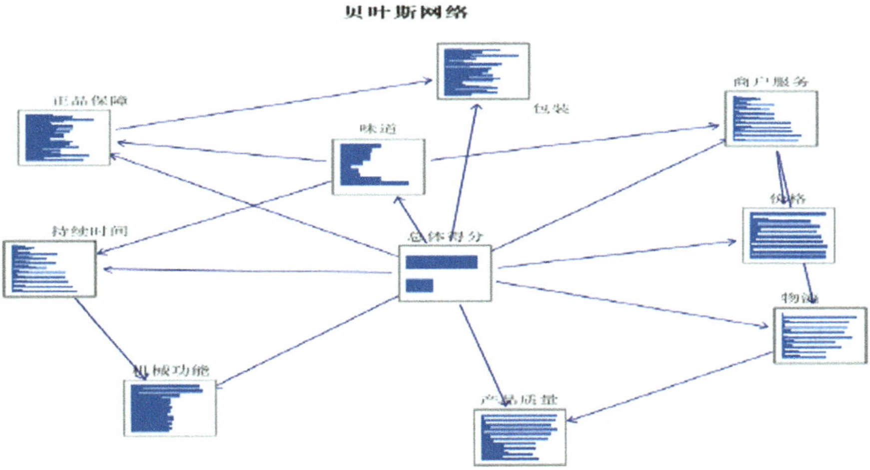

Fig. 3.11 PER conditional probability distribution of perfume

Table 3.8 Genuine product guarantee and logistics conditional probability8

Parent Level		Genuine Guarantee Conditional Probability					Logistics Conditional Probability				
Merchant Services	Overall Score	1	2	3	4	5	1	2	3	4	5
1	**1**	0.923	0.056	0.019	0	0	0.96	0.037	0	0	0
1	**2**	0.553	0.349	0.096	0	0	0.901	0.096	0	0	0
1	**3**	0.556	0.213	0.164	0.066	0	0.719	0.262	0.016	0	0
2	**3**	0.276	0.294	0.3	0.11	0.018	0.416	0.551	0.03	0	0
2	**4**	0.423	0.274	0.1	0.125	0.075	0.349	0.324	0.299	0.024	0
2	**5**	0.169	0.194	0.188	0.22	0.226	0.211	0.282	0.223	0.282	0
3	**4**	0.176	0.176	0.118	0.351	0.176	0.038	0.222	0.295	0.332	0.111
4	**5**	0.2	0.106	0.188	0.129	0.376	0	0.05	0.314	0.282	0.352
5	**5**	00.75	0.075	0.222	0.222	0.405	0.092	0.092	0.092	0.45	0.271
...											

Table 3.9 Conditional probability of total score9

Probabilities				
1	2	3	4	5
0.005	0.269	0.610	0.114	0.001

Table 3.10 Flavor conditional probabilities10

Parent Level	Probability				
Overall Score	1	2	3	4	5
1	0.444	0.262	0.12	0.109	0.062
2	0.144	0.19	0.261	0.206	0.196
3	0	0.058	0.072	0.173	0.694
4	0	0.014	0.055	0.194	0.734
5	0	0.009	0.028	0.171	0.789

From the conditional probability of the output variable overall score and the input variable taste, it can be seen that the probability of the overall score node being rated as 3 points or above is 0.725, of which the probability of 3 points is the largest at 0.610. This indicates that over 60% of users rate this type of product as 3 points or above. At the same time, under the conditions of the overall evaluation being 1 point, 2 points, 3 points, 4 points, and 5 points, the probabilities of the taste being 1 point, 3 points, 5 points, 5 points, and 5 points are 0.444, 0.261, 0.694, 0.734, and 0.789 respectively.

Table 3.11 Logistics conditional probabilities11

Parent Level		Probability				
Merchant Services	Overall Score	1	2	3	4	5
1	**3**	0	0.13	0.69	0.149	0.029
3	**3**	0.01	0.039	0.566	0.219	0.164
4	**3**	0.229	0.167	0.573	0.024	0.004
5	**3**	0.777	0.04	0.12	0.01	0.02
2	**4**	0.003	0.003	0.003	0.073	0.917
3	**4**	0.036	0.036	0.036	0.036	0.854
5	**4**	0.07	0.818	0.1	0.001	0
2	**5**	0	0.016	0.192	0.734	0.055
4	**5**	0.001	0.001	0.033	0.097	0.866
5	**5**	0.008	0.008	0.008	0.008	0.965
...						

The parent node of logistics is the overall score and merchant service, which shows different probability distributions when the overall score and merchant service are within the range of 1~5 points. The distribution is relatively scattered, indicating that users have differences in the acceptance of logistics for this type of product. Among them, the maximum probability of getting 1 point is 0.777, the maximum probability of getting 2 points is 0.818, the maximum probability of getting 3 points is 0.69, the maximum probability of getting 4 points is 0.734, and the maximum probability of getting 5 points is 0.965. The parent nodes of genuine guarantee and duration are both taste and overall score. The two nodes have a relatively high probability of getting 3 points or above within the range of 1~5 points for taste and overall score. There are also individual cases, such as the maximum probability of getting 1 point for genuine guarantee is 0.45.

Overall, users have a high acceptance of genuine guarantee and duration based on the taste and overall score of this type of product, and other secondary driving indicators can be inferred by analogy.

The above Fig. 3.12 is a histogram of the importance of variables (secondary driving indicators) under the category of perfume products. The importance decreases from top to bottom. This article finds that users pay attention to the prominent product feature attribute variables when purchasing this type of product, represented by taste. This is related to the characteristics of the perfume category and has obvious exclusivity. At the same time, due to the high average price of this category, users pay more attention to packaging, reflecting the preferences of users of this type of product, and the focus is on duration and genuine guarantee, followed by price, merchant service and product quality. The weakest focus is on the mechanical function of the perfume, such as the fogging of the nozzle.

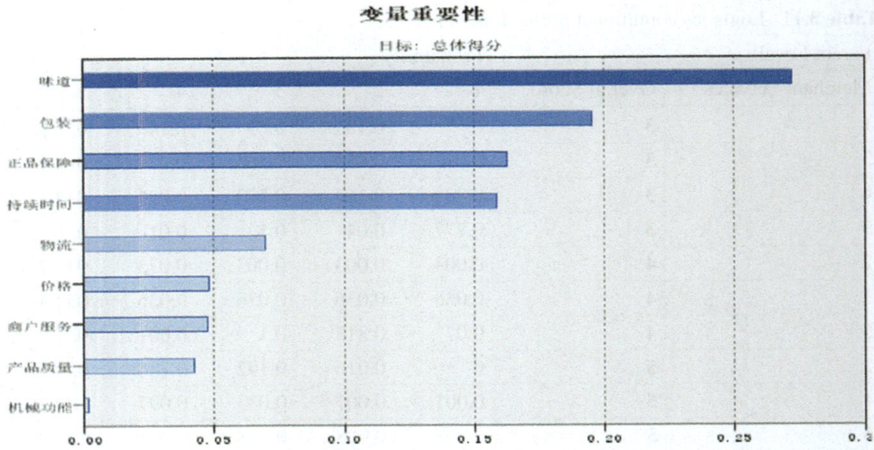

Fig. 3.12 Importance of PER variable for perfumes

3.2 Cross-Border E-commerce Retail Import User Preference Bayesian Network Model Analysis

3.2.1 Cross-Border E-commerce Retail Import User Shopping Preference and Probability Analysis

As can be seen from the Bayesian network model structure diagram constructed in the previous text, there is a clear correlation between the output variable, i.e., the overall score, and each secondary driving indicator in the Bayesian network of the three categories of products.

In the FUN Bayesian network structure of foundation liquid/paste, the concealing effect is related to duration and genuine guarantee, the makeup effect is related to duration, logistics is related to packaging, genuine guarantee and skin type, product quality is related to logistics and price, and merchant service is related to packaging.

In the LIP Bayesian network structure of lipstick/lipstick, color is related to makeup effect, genuine guarantee is related to lip type, makeup effect and merchant service, merchant service is also related to logistics, product quality is related to packaging, and price is related to product quality and duration.

In the PER Bayesian network structure of perfume, taste is related to duration, genuine guarantee and merchant service, packaging is related to genuine guarantee, price is related to merchant service, logistics is related to merchant service and product quality, and mechanical function is related to duration.

Looking at the network structure diagram, each node may be a parent node or a child node. According to the node conditional probability table calculated in the structure diagram, the probability of the judged node event occurring under the parent node event is shown. From the overall view of each category of products, the conditional probability distribution of the shown node (secondary driving indicator) under the influence of its parent node is similar for scores from 1 to 5. Among them, the probability of online evaluation score of 3 points is relatively more, and then more evaluation scores are 4~5 points. There are differences in the probability of online evaluation scores of 1 point and 2 points, but overall it shows that most users basically approve of the evaluation of the secondary driving indicators of the product, and some users may have differences in evaluation. The evaluation related to the secondary driving indicators of the child node will be affected by the synergistic effect of the parent node, so when mining business potential, merchants need to clearly understand user consumption preferences and consider the consequences of being affected by the parent node.

3.2.2 *Analysis of the Importance of Cross-Border E-commerce Retail Import User Shopping Preferences*

By constructing models for ten secondary driving indicators of foundation liquid/ cream, ten secondary driving indicators of lipstick, and nine secondary driving indicators of perfume, and calculating the importance of each secondary driving indicator based on the trained models, we can intuitively predict users' perceived experience of each secondary driving indicator after purchasing the product and thus predict the shopping preferences of cross-border e-commerce retail import users for different types of products. Table 3.13 summarizes the importance of secondary driving indicators for the three types of products:

Table 3.12 Genuine guarantee and duration conditions12

Parent Level		Genuine Guarantee Conditional Probability					Duration Conditional Probability				
Taste	Overall score	1	2	3	4	5	1	2	3	4	5
1	1	0.45	0.139	0.139	0.25	0.02	0.851	0.131	0.016	0	0
1	3	0.052	0.082	0.302	0.362	0.2	0.002	0.006	0.234	0.118	0.583
1	4	0.053	0.181	0.494	0.266	0.004	0.001	0.001	0.091	0.212	0.693
2	1	0.293	0.195	0.286	0.22	0.003	0.2	0.242	0.299	0.178	0.079
2	3	0.089	0.247	0.357	0.205	0.1	0.001	0.034	0.166	0.233	0.564
2	5	0.002	0.177	0.173	0.12	0.526	0	0.058	0.072	0.173	0.694
3	4	0.067	0.122	0.21	0.233	0.365	0	0.06	0.206	0.279	0.452
4	3	0.346	0.186	0.188	0.129	0.149	0.734	0.194	0.055	0.1	0.044
4	5	0.055	0.075	0.244	0.218	0.406	0	0.009	0.028	0.171	0.789
...											

Table 3.13 Summary and summary of the importance of second-level driving indicators13

Secondary Drive Index Product Category	Liquid Foundation/Cream	Lip Balm/Lipstick	Perfume
Makeup effects	0.123	0.000	-
Concealer effect	0.243	-	-
duration	0.090	0.166	0.159
Skin Type category	0.000	-	-
Labial categories	-	0.000	-
Colors	-	0.564	-
Price	0.033	0.048	0.048
Logistics	0.149	0.104	0.070
Genuine guarantee	0.18	0.073	0.162
Product quality	0.045	0.010	0.043
Merchant service	0.012	0.035	0.048
Wrapping	0.127	0.000	0.196
Flavor	-	-	0.272
Mechanical features	-	-	0.002

In the table, the more important secondary driving indicators are bolded. It can be seen that in foundation liquid/cream, the concealment effect and authenticity guarantee are the most important secondary driving indicators, with values of 0.243 and 0.18 respectively, followed by logistics, packaging, and makeup effect, with values of 0.149, 0.127, and 0.123 respectively. Therefore, it is speculated that users prefer these factors when purchasing foundation liquid/cream; in lipstick, color and duration are the most important secondary driving indicators, with values of 0.564 and 0.166 respectively, indicating that users prefer the shopping perception experience of color and duration when purchasing this type of product, followed by logistics and authenticity guarantee, with importance values of 0.104 and 0.073 respectively; in perfume, scent and packaging are the most important secondary driving indicators, with values of 0.272 and 0.196 respectively, indicating that users prefer the shopping perception experience of scent and packaging when purchasing this type of product, which is predicted to be mostly for gift giving, followed by authenticity guarantee and duration, with importance values of 0.162 and 0.159 respectively. By observing the importance of each secondary driving indicator, it can be seen that the importance of secondary driving indicators for the three types of products varies, but overall, value driving is the most important factor for users, and authenticity guarantee also occupies a relatively high position, indicating that when purchasing overseas products, in addition to the characteristics of the product itself, authenticity guarantee is an important guarantee for the success of the transaction. Secondly, due to the long distance and time span of overseas products, users also pay more attention to logistics and packaging.

3.3 Comparison of Bayesian Network Models of User Preferences on Cross-Border and Non-Cross-Border Platforms

The demand for quality consumption is driving the rapid development of cross-border e-commerce, quality e-commerce, and luxury e-commerce. According to publicly available online data, Fig. 3.13 shows that cross-border online shopping users focus more on the authenticity guarantee during the shopping process (54.6%), in addition to the reputation of the e-commerce platform, the richness of the products, whether they are carefully selected, etc., while they pay less attention to price factors such as promotional discounts and price advantages. The concept of cross-border online shopping users is shifting from pursuing cost-effectiveness to pursuing quality. Cross-border e-commerce platforms need to pay attention to the source channels of products, quality, and reputation building in order to win the favor of cross-border online shopping users.

However, are there differences in preferences among users who make purchases on the platform?

The same overseas retail product will occur on both cross-border and non-cross-border platforms. This article uses Tmall International as the cross-border platform, and Tmall Mall/Taobao as the domestic non-cross-border platform (without considering the source of the product, only considering the transaction channel) to construct the Bayesian network model of the same product and conduct a comparative analysis.

Firstly, referring to the existing categories and individual research objects, online user reviews from the same time were collected from Tmall. Due to the incomplete variety of overseas products on domestic platforms and the uncertainty of the stores, this paper randomly selected single items from stores with many online reviews.

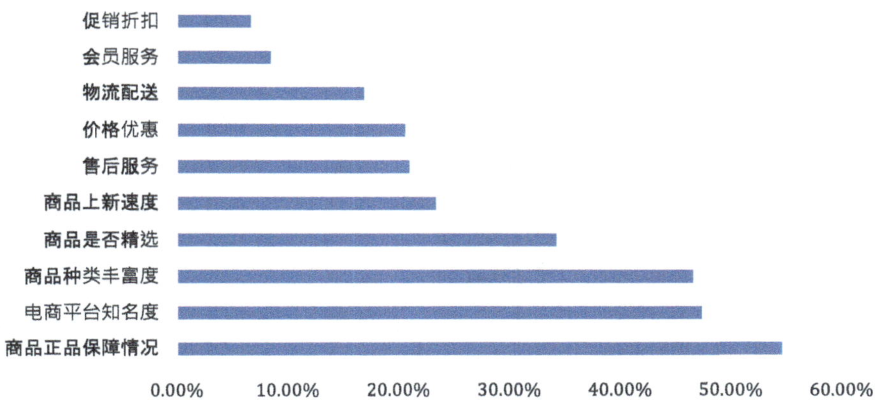

Fig. 3.13 Distribution of factors that cross-border e-commerce consumers pay attention to e-commerce platforms

The most popular TOP1 foundation liquid/paste was finally chosen as the comparative research object category. A total of ten foundation liquid/paste products were collected from non-cross-border platforms, with a total of 17,694 online review data. After data preprocessing, cleaning, and filtering, keywords were summarized into secondary driving indicators (the same secondary driving indicators as F). After standardizing the sample data, it was converted into a format suitable for importing into the Clementine software to build a Bayesian network model with its secondary driving indicators, named FUN1, resulting in Fig. 3.14. This was then compared with the cross-border platform foundation liquid/paste FUN (Fig. 3.15):

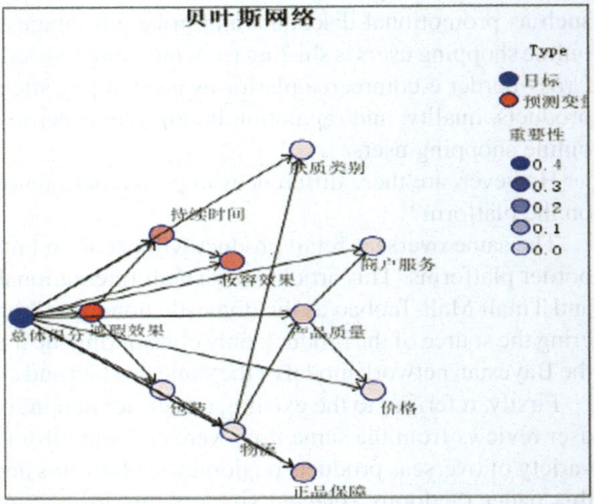

Fig. 3.14 non-cross-border platform FUN1 Bayesian network

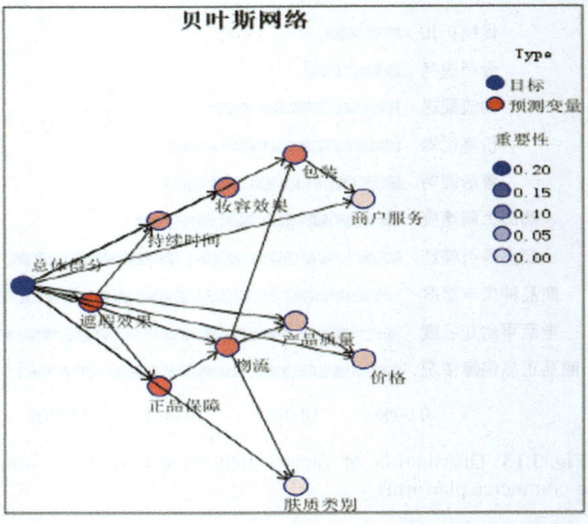

Fig. 3.15 Cross-border platform FUN Bayesian Network

Comparative analysis of the FUN Bayesian model and the FUN1 Bayesian model found that the network structure diagrams of the two are very consistent, and the interactions between each secondary driving indicator are further confirmed. However, after evaluating the accuracy of the model, it was found that there are differences in the contribution of predictive variables to the target in the FUN Bayesian model and the FUN1 Bayesian model. This was followed by a further examination of the variable importance in the FUN model and the FUN1 model;

As seen in Figs. 3.16 and 3.17, the importance of variables in the FUN1 model are in the following order: concealing effect, makeup effect, duration, genuine guarantee, merchant service, price, etc., and there is a large gap in the importance between each variable; while the importance of variables in the FUN model are in the following order: concealing effect, genuine guarantee, logistics, packaging, makeup effect, duration, product quality, price, merchant service, skin type category, there are step differences between different variable categories, among which the most obvious are concealing effect, genuine guarantee, and logistics;

From the model structure and charts, we can consider: (1) The importance ranking of secondary indicators for both non-cross-border platforms and cross-border platforms shows a stepwise distribution, but there are significant differences in the numerical values. The values of each indicator in cross-border platforms are more uniform, while the values of each indicator in non-cross-border platforms fluctuate more, showing a "moon-holding" phenomenon, where some indicators can almost be omitted; (2) Value-driven factors are the focus of user attention in online reviews on both platforms. The importance ranking of secondary indicators of value-driven

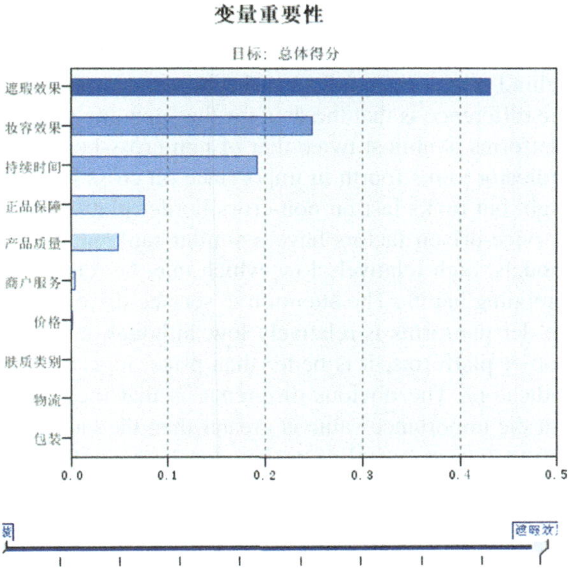

Fig. 3.16 Importance of FUN1 variable for non-cross-border platforms

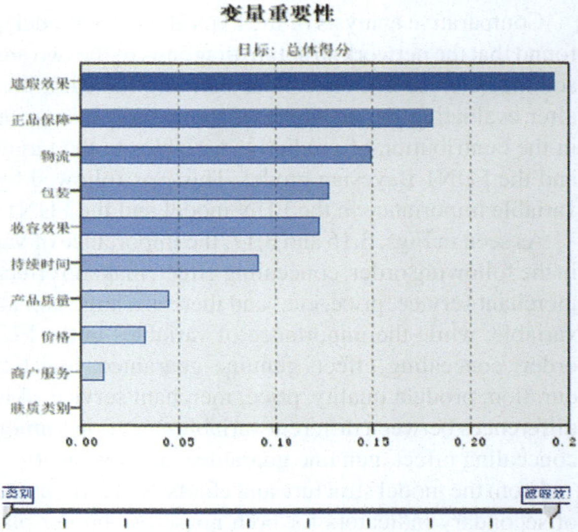

Fig. 3.17 Importance of FUN variable for cross-border platforms

factors on both platforms is in the order of concealing effect, makeup effect, and duration, in decreasing order. The difference lies in the fact that the secondary indicators of value-driven factors are different on different platforms. In the online reviews of cross-border platforms, the secondary indicators of value-driven factors are interspersed with brand-driven factors and technology-driven factors, while there is no such phenomenon in cross-border platforms. In addition, the importance values of each secondary indicator under the non-cross-border platform are almost twice those of the same indicators on the cross-border platform; (3) Brand-driven factors rank behind value-driven factors in the importance of online reviews on both platforms, but the difference is that the data for the "genuine guarantee" indicator on cross-border platforms is almost twice that of non-cross-border platforms, and the "packaging" indicator ranks fourth in importance on cross-border platforms, which is relatively high, but ranks last on non-cross-border platforms and can almost be ignored; (4) Service-driven factors have a similar ranking structure in the importance of both models, both relatively low, which may be related to the increasingly autonomous shopping habits. The attention to service-driven factors in online reviews on cross-border platforms is relatively low, although it is also relatively low on non-cross-border platforms, it is better than price, logistics, packaging, and other secondary indicators. The obvious difference is that the former ranks lower than the latter, but the importance value is greater than the latter; (5) The attention to technology-driven factors in online reviews on both platforms is quite different. The importance ranking in online reviews on cross-border platforms is third, indicating that consumers pay more attention to technology-driven factors. The importance ranking in online reviews on non-cross-border platforms is second to last, which can almost be ignored. This phenomenon indicates that the cost of cross-border logistics is high, the time span is large, the packaging handling methods of cross-border platforms are not consistent with the "secondary processing" packaging of non-cross-border platforms, and thus the importance of technology-driven factors is inconsistent; (6) The inconsistency of knowledge acquisition channels and the convenience of customer service communication lead to different perceived shopping experiences, the specific reasons need further analysis and empirical verification, which will be the goal of the next step of research.

In addition, the importance of the variable "genuine guarantee", which is the focus of this observation, is less sensitive to the purchase behavior that occurs on non-cross-border platforms. Users care more about product features, which also explains the relevance of this user to platform selection, while users on cross-border platforms are more sensitive to the "genuine guarantee" secondary driving indicator. In terms of actual importance values, the FUN model and the FUN1 model are close, but the FUN model pays more attention to quality. From this, we can find and speculate: users on cross-border platforms are more sensitive to "genuine guarantee", fully demonstrating the importance and necessity of cross-border platforms; under the same circumstances, users on non-cross-border platforms are more sensitive to value-driven factors (product characteristics), which needs further academic research in the future.

References

1. Matthew S (2016) Firing costs and capital structure decisions[J]. J Finance 71(5):2239–2286
2. Pritchard A (1979) Statistical bibliography or bibliometrics[J]. J Doc 25:348–349
3. Rothwell, R., Zegveld, W. (1985). Reindustrialization and Technology[M]. London: Longman.
4. Zahra SA, George G (2002) International entrepreneurship: The current status of the field and future research agenda In: Hitt M, Ireland D, Sexton D, Camp M (eds) Strategic entrepreneurship: Creating an integrated mindset. Blackwell, Cambridge[J], MA, pp 255−288
5. Corbitt BJ, Thanasankit T, Yi H (2003) Trust and e-commerce: A study of consumer perceptions[J]. Electron commer Res Appl 2(3):203–215
6. Li X, Mingming L, Zhaoran L (2018) Research on the pricing mechanism of data products in China—An analysis based on the theory of customer perceived value[J]. Price Theory Pract 04:147–150
7. Koufaris M, Hampton-Sosa W (2004) The development of initial trust in an online company by new customers[J]. Inform Manag 41(3):377–397
8. Caruana A, Ewing MT (2010) How corporate reputation, quality, and value influence online loyalty[J]. J Bus Res 63(9–10):1103–1110
9. Guo Y, Bao Y, Stuart BJ et al (2018) To sell or not to sell: Exploring sellers' trust and risk of chargeback fraud in cross-border electronic commerce[J]. Inform Syst J 28(2):359–383

Chapter 4
Analysis of Competitive Advantage of Cross-Border E-commerce Platforms from the Perspective of Platform Enterprises

Cross-border e-commerce platforms are important means for consumers to make cross-border purchases. From the perspective of platform enterprises, different types of transaction subjects and import modes adopted by import cross-border e-commerce platforms represent different self-positioning, operation modes, and regulatory modes of the platform. This means that different types of platforms will have different competitive advantages, and the competitive advantage of the platform is a key factor for consumers to choose different platforms for purchase. This chapter will start from the perspective of import cross-border e-commerce platforms and combine their characteristics, take 50 import cross-border e-commerce platform enterprises as research objects, build a research model of platform competitive advantage based on the two dimensions of transaction subject and import mode, and analyze the relationship between different factors under the two dimensions and the matching between factors and website traffic, and explore the key factors that can promote its competitive advantage from the perspective of the platform itself.

4.1 Import Cross-Border E-commerce Platform

4.1.1 Import Cross-Border E-commerce Transaction Subject

The import cross-border e-commerce market involves multiple transaction subjects, including cross-border e-commerce import operators (i.e., cross-border e-commerce enterprises), cross-border e-commerce third-party platform operators (i.e., import cross-border e-commerce platforms), domestic service providers, and consumers. Among them, the import cross-border e-commerce platform is one of the transaction subjects in the e-commerce market. In the dimension of transaction subjects, this

L. Xiong and H. Wang, *User Driven Cross-Border E-Commerce Platform Competition and Policy Analysis*, Advanced Studies in E-Commerce,
https://doi.org/10.1007/978-981-97-3835-9_4

article mainly analyzes the development and operation subjects of B2C import cross-border e-commerce platforms, the categories of operated goods, and the popularity of operated goods.

Based on the classification of the platform's development and operation entities, it can be divided into platform-based cross-border e-commerce for imports (referred to as "platform-based e-commerce") and self-operated cross-border e-commerce for imports (referred to as "self-operated e-commerce"). Platform-based e-commerce is mainly responsible for developing and operating third-party e-commerce websites, some of which also provide warehousing and distribution, payment, marketing, and other supporting services; self-operated e-commerce not only needs to build and maintain the website's daily operations, but also needs to solve the problems of product procurement, marketing, warehousing and distribution, customer service, payment, etc., such as Kaola. Based on the classification of the product categories operated by the platform, it can be divided into vertical cross-border e-commerce for imports (referred to as "vertical e-commerce") and comprehensive cross-border e-commerce for imports (referred to as "comprehensive e-commerce") [[1]]. Vertical e-commerce sells relatively concentrated product categories and mainly provides consumer products for specific groups or fields, such as Baby Grid; comprehensive e-commerce sells a more complete range of product categories and is not targeted at specific groups or fields, such as Xiaohongshu. Finally, based on the classification of the popularity of the products operated by the platform, it can be divided into explosive cross-border e-commerce for imports (referred to as "explosive e-commerce") and long-tail cross-border e-commerce for imports (referred to as "long-tail e-commerce"). Explosive e-commerce focuses on selling products that are in short supply, have a good reputation, and have high sales, such as Darling; while long-tail e-commerce is a concept opposite to explosive e-commerce, it not only sells explosive products but also sells long-tail products with individuality but small demand, such as Haituncun.

4.1.2 Cross-Border E-commerce Import Model

Different import models imply different operation models and regulatory models. The cross-border e-commerce import model can be divided into bonded import model (customs supervision code 1210) and direct mail import model (customs supervision code 9610) [[2]], the process of these two import models is shown in Fig. 4.1.

The bonded import model refers to the advance transportation of imported goods to the customs special supervision area, and the import declaration is made according to the general trade import with the property of the goods, and the customs establish an electronic account book, and then the goods are released according to the property of the goods based on the consumer order and enter the domestic market, and the relevant account book is written off. The direct mail import model refers to the import of goods in the form of mail, express, etc., from abroad to the domestic market, and

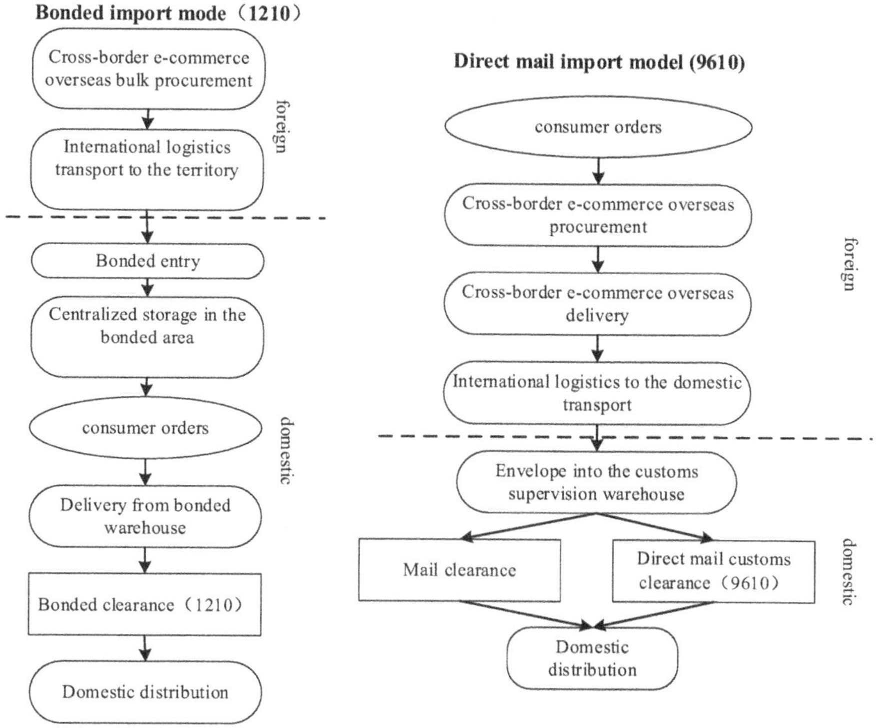

Fig. 4.1 Cross-border e-commerce import mode

the customs clearance is defined by the property of the goods, applicable to the postal tax rate.

The bonded import model can meet the needs of sellers for bulk stock, shorten the delivery time for consumers, and reduce the probability of transportation damage, but the quantity and variety of cross-border goods for bulk stock are limited. The direct mail import model can reduce the input of stock funds and reduce investment risks, but its delivery time is often very long, the logistics speed is slow, the probability of transportation damage is greater, the probability of non-returnable goods is greater, and the tax rates used by these two import models are different. Different cross-border e-commerce platforms have their own considerations when choosing import models, either choosing one of the import models (referred to as "single import model") or choosing both import models (referred to as "mixed import model").

4.2 Research Hypothesis on the Competitive Advantage of Import Cross-Border E-commerce Platforms

The choice of different transaction entities by import cross-border e-commerce platforms represents its positioning in different target markets, and to a certain extent determines the quality, variety, price, and logistics timeliness of overseas goods that consumers can purchase on the platform, and affects consumers' willingness to use different platforms. At the same time, the matching method of different transaction entities and import models chosen by import cross-border e-commerce platforms will further affect the competitive advantage of the platform.

Based on the classification of the development and operation entities of the platform, the trading entities can be divided into platform-based e-commerce and self-operated e-commerce. Among them, platform-based e-commerce has many merchants and the goods sold on the platform are provided by the merchants, while self-operated e-commerce purchases goods for sale by the platform itself. In comparison, platform-based e-commerce has a wider and more abundant source of goods and a more diverse range of goods, and this type of platform belongs to a light asset model, therefore it has a competitive advantage. From this, we get Hypothesis 1 (H_1). Secondly, from the perspective of import models, the diversity of merchants makes platform-based e-commerce need diverse import models, and platform-based e-commerce is more compatible with mixed import models. The original platform-based e-commerce already has a greater competitive advantage, and the mixed import model will increase this competitive advantage, from which we can get Hypothesis 1a (H_{1a}); however, under the single import model, the merchants of platform-based e-commerce cannot choose according to their own situation, reducing the efficiency of customs clearance and logistics, while the types of goods of self-operated e-commerce are relatively limited, choosing a single import model suitable for themselves can unify sales and distribution, lower costs and higher efficiency, thus making it more competitive, hence we get Hypothesis 1b (H_{1b}). Based on this, the following hypotheses are proposed:

H_1: Platform-based e-commerce has a greater competitive advantage than self-operated e-commerce

H_{1a}: Under the mixed import model, platform-based e-commerce has a greater competitive advantage than self-operated e-commerce

H_{1b}: Under the single import model, self-operated e-commerce has a greater competitive advantage than platform-based e-commerce

Based on the classification of the types of goods operated by the platform, the trading entities can be divided into comprehensive e-commerce and vertical e-commerce. Among them, the goods sold by comprehensive e-commerce cover multiple aspects of consumer demand, while vertical e-commerce provides consumer products in specific areas. In comparison, comprehensive e-commerce offers a more diverse range of goods, a wider target consumer group, and has a competitive advantage, hence we get Hypothesis 2 (H_2). Secondly, in combination with the import model, the diversity of goods categories makes comprehensive e-commerce also need diverse import models to meet the sales needs of the platform, therefore comprehensive e-commerce and mixed import models are more compatible, and the mixed import model will increase the competitive advantage of comprehensive e-commerce, hence we get Hypothesis 2a (H_{2a}); under the single import model, because the product categories of vertical e-commerce are limited, choosing the best single import model can achieve efficient logistics distribution and save corporate capital costs, thus making it more competitive, hence we get Hypothesis 2b (H_{2b}). Based on this, the following hypotheses are proposed:

H_2: Comprehensive e-commerce has a greater competitive advantage than vertical e-commerce
H_{2a}: Under the mixed import model, comprehensive e-commerce has a greater competitive advantage than vertical e-commerce
H_{2b}: Under the single import model, vertical e-commerce has a greater competitive advantage than comprehensive e-commerce

Based on the classification of the best-selling degree of goods on the platform, the trading entities can be divided into long-tail e-commerce and explosive e-commerce. Among them, long-tail e-commerce not only sells explosive goods but also increases the sales of long-tail goods, while explosive e-commerce mainly sells explosive goods. Compared with the latter, the goods sold by long-tail e-commerce are more diversified and personalized and have more competitive advantages, hence hypothesis 3 (H_3). Next, discussing the import mode, the more dispersed sources of long-tail goods make long-tail e-commerce also need diversified import modes. Long-tail e-commerce and mixed import modes are more matched, and this match will increase the competitive advantage of long-tail e-commerce, hence hypothesis 3a (H_{3a}). Under the single import mode, the goods sold by explosive e-commerce often have high popularity and large sales volume. Choosing a single import mode that suits their own situation can achieve efficient customs clearance and logistics efficiency and achieve sales, thus making it more competitive, hence hypothesis 3b (H_{3b}). Based on this, the following hypotheses are proposed:

H_3: Long-tail e-commerce has more competitive advantages than explosive e-commerce
H_{3a}: Under the mixed import mode, long-tail e-commerce has more competitive advantages than explosive e-commerce
H_{3b}: Under the single import mode, explosive e-commerce has more competitive advantages than long-tail e-commerce

Combining the above hypotheses, the model of competitive advantage research of import cross-border e-commerce platform from the platform perspective is constructed as shown in Fig. 4.2, mainly including two aspects: one is the impact of different types of trading entities on platform competitive advantage, and the other is the impact of the match between different types of trading entities and import modes on platform competitive advantage.

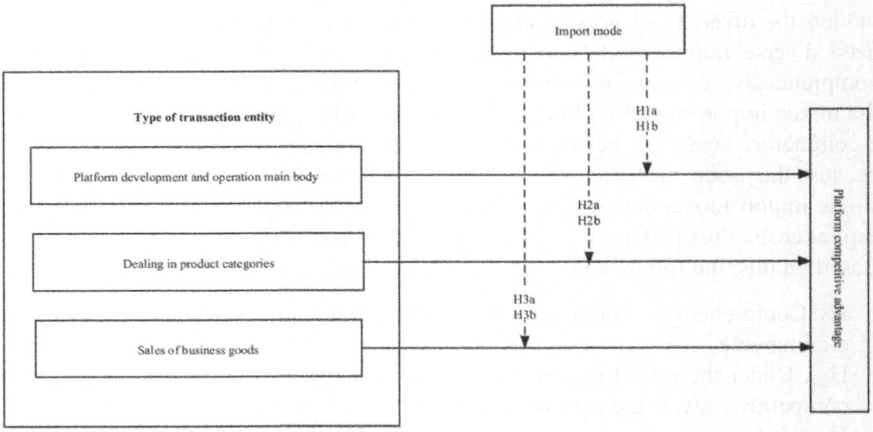

Fig. 4.2 Research model of competitive advantage of cross-border import E-commerce platform from the perspective of platform enterprises

4.3 Collection and Measurement of Import Cross-Border E-commerce Platform Data

4.3.1 Collection of Platform Data

This chapter takes the small and medium-sized B2C import cross-border e-commerce platforms in our country as the research object. According to the scale of the platform website and its activity, 50 small and medium-sized import cross-border e-commerce platform companies that are still actively operating and do not have the background of Internet giants were randomly selected as research samples, and these platforms include both platforms that are only responsible for website operation and companies that are responsible for both website operation and product sales.

For the qualitative data collection of the 50 small and medium-sized B2C import cross-border e-commerce platform companies in the dimensions of trading entity type and import mode, it mainly includes two processes: first, by collecting the platform's public materials, viewing the platform's introduction and other processes to obtain the platform's-related raw data, and by three experts to judge the trading entity type and platform import mode of different platforms under different classification dimensions and reach a unified opinion; second, through a combination of field research and online consultation, adjust the preliminary judgment results, and finally determine the trading entity type and import mode of each platform.

4.3.2 Measurement of Variables in the Platform Competitive Advantage Research Model

The measurement basis for each variable in the research model is shown in Table 4.1. For platform competitive advantage, the website traffic is quantified from the platform perspective, and the ranking results of the third-party evaluation agency Alexa are used to measure website traffic. The Alexa comprehensive ranking is considered relatively authoritative and can be used to evaluate the website traffic index, which includes "million user clicks" and "number of pages browsed per user". Alexa only records websites ranked in the top 10 million, and its results can to some extent show the traffic and popularity of a website. The range of website rankings recorded by Alexa is too wide, so in order to more accurately reflect the competitive situation of the website, this chapter considers websites ranked within 1 million as having high traffic, and those ranked outside 1 million and those without rankings as having low traffic. The Alexa comprehensive rankings for the research samples in December 2018 were collected to measure the competitive advantage of cross-border e-commerce platforms for imports from the platform perspective.

Table 4.1 Measurement of variables1

Variables	Measurements
Platform development and operation body (platform/self-operated)	Platform type import cross-border e-commerce is recorded as 1, self-operated import cross-border e-commerce is recorded as 0
Product category (integrated/vertical)	Integrated import cross-border e-commerce is recorded as 1, vertical import cross-border e-commerce is recorded as 0
Sales of goods (explosive type/long-tail type)	Explosive import cross-border e-commerce is recorded as 1, long-tail import cross-border e-commerce is recorded as 0
Import mode (mixed import mode/single import mode)	The mixed import mode is denoted as 1 and the single import mode is denoted as 0
Number of website views (large/small)	A site with a large number of views is recorded as 1, and a site with a small number of views is recorded as 0

4.4 Analysis of Competitive Advantage of Cross-Border E-commerce Platforms for Imports

4.4.1 Descriptive Statistical Analysis

This chapter conducts a descriptive statistical analysis of platform data (as shown in Fig. 4.3) and finds that firstly, there are differences in the choice of transaction subjects and import modes among cross-border e-commerce platforms for imports: in terms of transaction subjects, platform-based e-commerce accounts for 36% (18/50), comprehensive e-commerce accounts for 36% (18/50), and explosive e-commerce accounts for 54% (27/50); in terms of import modes, platforms choosing mixed import modes account for 48% (24/50). Secondly, among the 50 platforms surveyed, 27 have high website traffic, and there are differences in the proportion of platforms with high website traffic under the dimensions of transaction subjects and import modes. In addition, while many cross-border e-commerce platforms for imports have been established, some poorly developed platforms have ceased operations. In April 2018, 34 cross-border e-commerce platform samples for imports were collected. By December 2018, 8.82% of the platforms (such as Cross-Border Bonded Shopping, etc.) had ceased operations, indicating that the competition among the platforms is very fierce.

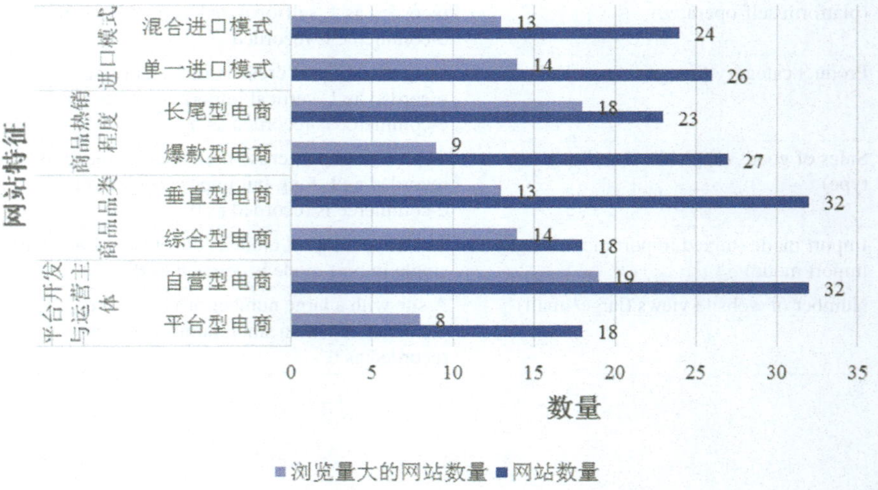

Fig. 4.3 Characteristics of 50 cross-border import e-commerce platforms

4.4.2 Contingency Table Analysis

The nine hypotheses proposed in the previous section are verified through contingency table analysis, and the relevant data results are shown in Table 4.2.

(1) Platform Development and Operation Subjects and Their Matching with Import Modes

As shown in Table 4.2, the platform development and operation subjects are independent of the website traffic, the significance of the chi-square test is 0.309, H_1 is not established, that is, the development and operation subjects of the platform do not significantly affect the users' use of the platform. At the same time, under the mixed import mode and single import mode, the platform development and operation subjects are still independent of the website traffic, so H_{1a} and H_{1b} are not established. The reason for the above results may be: when different platforms choose import modes, they mainly depend on the type of goods operated by the platform, the economic situation of the platform, the situation of the merchants themselves, etc., and most consumers are not very sensitive to the factors of platform development and operation subjects and their matching with import modes. Regardless of the type of transaction subject and import mode chosen by the platform, if it can meet consumers' requirements for overseas goods in terms of variety, quality, price, authenticity, and logistics timeliness, it can promote consumers' use of such platforms.

(2) Product Categories and Their Matching with Import Modes

As shown in Tables 4.2 and 4.3, there is a significant correlation between product categories and website traffic, with a chi-square test significance of 0.011. In comprehensive e-commerce, the proportion of websites with high traffic reaches 77.78% (14/18), while in vertical e-commerce, the proportion of websites with high traffic is 40.63% (13/32). The ratio of website traffic (small/large) for these two types of platforms is 5.115, with a 95% confidence interval of 1.372 to 19.077. The website traffic of comprehensive e-commerce is larger, thus H_2 is established.

Under the mixed import model, the exact significance of the Fisher's test is 0.240, rejecting H_{2a}, that is, the match between product categories and the mixed import model does not significantly affect users' use of the platform. Under the single import model, there is a significant correlation between product categories and website traffic, with an exact significance of the Fisher's test of 0.036. The proportion of comprehensive e-commerce websites with high traffic reaches 87.5% (7/8), and the proportion of vertical e-commerce websites with high traffic is only 38.89% (7/18). The ratio of website traffic (small/large) for these two types of platforms is 11.000, with a 95% confidence interval of 1.103 to 109.674. Under the single import model, the website traffic of comprehensive e-commerce is larger, that is, the match between the single import model and comprehensive e-commerce is better, but the above analysis results are exactly the opposite of hypothesis 2b, so H_{2b} is still not established. Further analysis of these data results shows that under the single import model, only 8 are comprehensive e-commerce, of which 7 are platforms with high website traffic, but 5 of these 7 platforms also belong to long-tail e-commerce. The contingency table analysis cannot prove which feature affects the website traffic. The

Table 4.2 Influence of characteristics of import cross-border e-commerce platforms on their competitive advantages2

Variables	Import Patterns	Pearson Chi-Square Values	Degree of Freedom	Progressive Significance of Pearson Chi-Square Test (Two-Sided)	Exact Significance of Fisher Test (Two-Sided)	The Ratio of Website Views (Small/Large)		
						value	95%Confidence Interval	
							Upper Limit	Lower Limit
Main body of platform development and operation	In total	1.034	1	0.309	0.382	0.547	0.170	1.758
	Mixed Import pattern	0.011a	1	0.916	1.000	1.094	0.208	5.756
	Single import mode	2.331a	1	0.127	0.218	0.273	0.050	1.502
Category of goods	Total	6.402	1	0.011 *	0.018 *	5.115	1.372	19.077
	Mixed Import Mode	1.731a	1	0.188	0.240	3.111	0.559	17.330
	Single import mode	5.266a	1	0.022 *	0.036 *	11.000	1.103	109.674
Merchandise sells like hot cakes Degree	Total	10.092	1	0.001 **	0.002 **	0.139	0.039	0.496
	Mixed import mode	8.866a	1	0.003 **	0.005 **	0.044	0.004	0.475
	Single import mode	2.476	1	0.116	0.238	0.278	0.055	1.409

Note: * $p < 0.05$, ** $p < 0.01$, *** $p < 0.001$

Table 4.3 Influences of product categories on website page views under different import modes3

Import Patterns			Product Category		Total
			Vertical	Comprehensive	
Hybrid import model	Website views	small	8	3	11
		big	6	7	13
	Total		14	10	24
Single import mode	Site views	small	11	1	12
		big	7	7	14
	Total		18	8	26
Total	Website views	small	19	4	23
		big	13	14	27
	Total		32	18	50

test results of the popularity of products will be further analyzed in the following text. In summary, the factor of product category has a significant impact on the competitive advantage of the platform, and comprehensive e-commerce has more competitive advantages, but the competitive advantage reflected by the factor of product category is not related to the import model.

(3)Popularity of Products and Their Match with Import Models

As shown in Tables 4.2 and 4.4, there is a significant correlation between the popularity of products and website traffic, with a chi-square test significance of 0.001. In long-tail e-commerce, the proportion of websites with high traffic reaches 78.26% (18/23), while in explosive e-commerce, the proportion of websites with high traffic is only 33.33% (9/27). The ratio of website traffic (small/large) for these two types of platforms is 0.139, with a 95% confidence interval of 0.039 to 0.496. The website traffic of long-tail e-commerce is larger, thus H_3 is established.

Table 4.4 Influence of the degree of hot selling of goods on the number of website page views under different import modes

Import Mode			Popularity of Goods		Total
			Long-tail Type	Pop Style	
Hybrid import model	Website views	small	1	10	11
		big	9	4	13
	Total			10	14
Single import mode	Site views	small	4	8	12
		big	9	5	14
	Total			13	13
Total	Website views	small	5	18	23
		big	18	9	27
	Total			23	27

Under the mixed import model, the exact significance of the Fisher's test is 0.005, and the proportion of long-tail e-commerce websites with high traffic reaches 90% (9/10), while the proportion of vertical import cross-border e-commerce platform websites with high traffic is only 28.57% (4/14). The ratio of website traffic (small/large) for these two types of platforms is 0.044, with a 95% confidence interval of 0.004 to 0.475. Therefore, under the mixed import model, the website traffic of long-tail e-commerce is larger, that is, the match between the mixed import model and long-tail e-commerce is better, thus H 3a is established. Under the single import model, the significance of the chi-square test is 0.116, rejecting H 3b, that is, the impact of the popularity of products and the match with the single import model on the competitive advantage of the platform is not significant.

References

1. Xiong L, Dai Q, Xu Z (2019) A study on the matching of cross-border e-commerce transaction subjects and import models: Based on data from 50 small and micro cross-border e-commerce platforms. Price Monthly (09):46-52. doi:10.14076/j.issn.1006-2025.2019.09.07
2. Xiangyang L (2017) Evaluation of the effectiveness of the new policy on customs supervision of cross-border import e-commerce[J]. Shanghai Econ Res 07:117–127

Chapter 5
Analysis of Competitive Advantage of Cross-Border E-commerce Platforms from the User Perspective

In the previous chapter, this article analyzed the influencing factors of the competitive advantage of import cross-border e-commerce platforms from the perspective of platform companies in terms of transaction modes and import modes and found that the development and operation of the main body of import cross-border e-commerce platforms did not have a significant impact on the platform's competitive advantage. That is, from an overall analysis, there is no significant difference in the competitive advantage between platform-based e-commerce and self-operated e-commerce. Nevertheless, from the perspective of platform characteristics, there are still significant differences in the competitive advantages of platform-based e-commerce and self-operated e-commerce in terms of products, procurement channels, prices, logistics, and customer service, which need further analysis.

Import cross-border e-commerce APP (referred to in this article as "import cross-border e-commerce platform") is an important way for users to make cross-border purchases through mobile clients. From the user's perspective, the products owned by the import cross-border e-commerce platform, the services provided, and the functions of the platform itself all affect the user's willingness to use the platform, thereby affecting the platform's competitive advantage. Therefore, this chapter will continue to explore the competitive advantage of import cross-border e-commerce platforms from the user's perspective.

5.1 Cross-Border E-commerce Consumer Emotional Preference Evolution Model Construction

Cross-border imported e-commerce has developed into a new and common consumption habit of consumers, who generally judge the "value points" mentioned in online reviews of products. "Value points" include consumers' focus on product and service attributes and consumption preferences, such as product size, after-sales service,

L. Xiong and H. Wang, *User Driven Cross-Border E-Commerce Platform Competition and Policy Analysis*, Advanced Studies in E-Commerce,
https://doi.org/10.1007/978-981-97-3835-9_5

logistics waiting time, and contain consumers' emotional preferences for products. Emotional interactions among consumers will infect and spread each other, and this diffusion behavior will also accelerate emotional fluctuations and contagion, such as sudden high-intensity emotional outburst and sudden increase in the number of comments. In a complete time series, the emotional energy corresponding to the emotional tendency, emotional intensity and diffusion speed can clearly describe the change of consumers' emotional preference and correspond to the emotional performance in each time interval. Therefore, analyzing the evolution rule of consumers' emotion in online reviews and analyzing the characteristics of consumers' emotional tendency under time series can provide decision support for the sales guidance of cross-border imported products in a specific time interval and make effective strategies.

Since the outbreak of COVID-19, the number of news and comments on various related news media has continued to increase, and many Internet users have strong emotional reactions to the epidemic, and their normal life has been significantly affected. In terms of cross-border imports, Dalian Customs found the first imported fresh products whose outer packaging samples tested positive for COVID-19 nucleic acid. In the past two months, there have been many positive cases of imported fresh products' outer packaging. Sentiment analysis research on consumers' comments on imported fresh products can not only reflect the impact of the outbreak environment on people's emotions, but also help businesses and platforms to judge-related products, to make timely and effective responses. Therefore, this chapter takes the positive test event of imported fresh products' outer packaging related to the novel coronavirus outbreak as the entry point, builds the evolution model of cross-border e-commerce consumers' emotional preferences, analyzes and studies the review data of imported fresh products on cross-border e-commerce platforms, and provides reference ideas and application value for cross-border e-commerce platforms and merchants. The specific model is shown in Fig. 5.1.

5.2 Review Data Collection and Cleaning of Cross-Border Import E-commerce Platforms

Through the analysis of relevant data and reports of cross-border e-commerce import retail fresh products, the review data of Jingdong Fresh (https://fresh.jd.com/) e-commerce platform is taken as the data source of the research sample, and popular imported products among the most representative four categories of products are selected as the research object. Octopus software was used to capture the relevant online review data, and then the Python language algorithm and PyCharm were used to selectively remove and desensitize the captured data, etc. The user's name, comment time, comment content, comment star rating, product name and picture data content in the online review data were summarized and unified in standardized formats. Convenient for further keyword extraction and analysis.

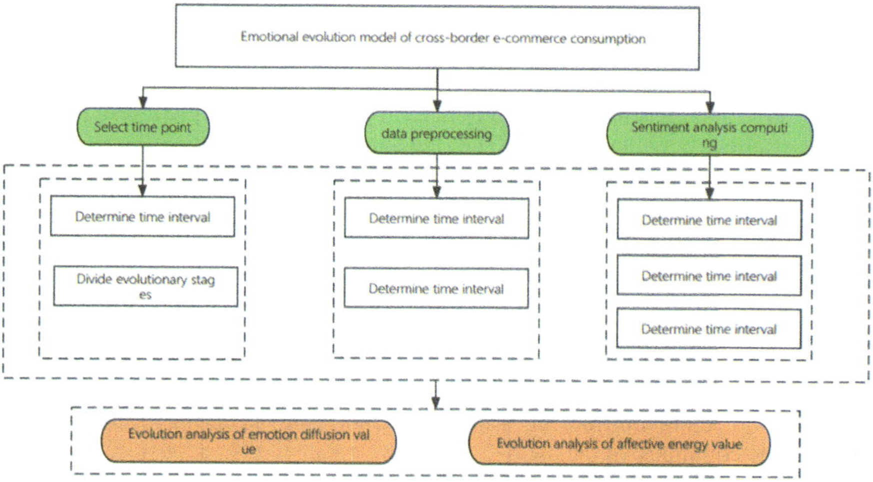

Fig. 5.1 Evolution model of cross-border e-commerce consumers' emotional preferences

Through the impurity cleaning, dedryness, desensitization and sorting of the online review data of 50 kinds of products, the emotion dictionary of the online review of imported fresh products of cross-border e-commerce was constructed, the affective bias dimension was divided .Standardizing and converting the textual content of online reviews into numerical data is used to construct a visual path that showcases the evolution of consumer sentiment in the context of the pandemic when positive cases are detected on the packaging of imported fresh products. This numerical data will serve as input to help analyze and visualize the changes and evolution of consumer sentiment over different time periods. This analysis is based on specific time slices (such as the time point when a positive case is detected).

5.2.1 Source of Online Review Data

The research data of this article uses the review data in the JD Fresh (https://fresh.jd.com/) e-commerce platform as the data source for the research sample for content analysis. In terms of sample selection, according to the product classification method of JD Fresh platform, imported fresh products are divided into fresh fruits, seafood, selected meats, and cold drinks and frozen foods. The online review data of these four types of products are selected as the research objects, covering a wide range of imported fresh product types, with high universality and significant research significance. In terms of platform selection, JD Fresh is the fresh brand of JD Group, a leading e-commerce company. Its business scope covers a wide range, and its products are delivered by JD Logistics' fresh cold chain. It has full-temperature cold storage in core cities across the country and has become the most important global new season fresh product launch platform. It has a stable market share in the fresh e-commerce industry. The number of reviews posted by consumers on this platform is huge, providing extremely important data support for this article.

The top 15 products in terms of sales in each category of imported fresh products were used as data crawling samples. The crawled product review data was used as the data source to build a product review corpus. The fields include usernames, review times, review content, review star ratings, product names, etc., with a total of 20,284 data crawled. Among them, there are 5,305 pieces of seafood, 5,218 pieces of fresh fruit, 5,085 pieces of selected meats, and 4,676 pieces of cold drinks and frozen foods. Due to the restrictions of the online review display rules of the JD Fresh platform, the data captured this time is part of the data displayed under this condition. Therefore, the source data for this time period is far greater than the visible data. The crawling review time interval is from January 2019 to December 2020. The products crawled were all listed before this time interval and were not removed during the time period, ensuring the continuity of the data.

5.2.2 Pre-Norms of Online Comments

The online comments on e-commerce platforms are arbitrary, leading to some comments with non-standard language, chaotic syntax, and even some with irrelevant content, typos, repetitive content, and other comments of no or low value. Therefore, before analyzing online comments for word segmentation, feature dictionary construction, sentiment dictionary construction, etc., the original comments crawled need to be de-noised, duplicate and worthless comments removed, to obtain online comments that are available for analysis and have research value. The main cleaning rules are as follows:

(1) Delete irrelevant comments: Comments unrelated to imported fresh produce, mainly divided into two categories: one is comments that only express simple emotional attitudes and have no evaluation object, such as "good good good good good good good good good good good good good good good good good good good" which is just to make up 15 words; the other is junk comments completely unrelated to the relevant fresh produce features, such as "the changeable end of the class class class stimulates i oh stock and v not lack two hundred". For this, this article manually identifies and deletes comments that are obviously unrelated to imported fresh produce.

(2) Delete repetitive comments and advertising comments: Repetitive comments refer to some users copying and pasting other users' comments for certain rewards, or ordering the same product multiple times at the same time resulting in two comments that are almost identical, for these comments this article only retains one; there are also some users who repeat a word or phrase multiple times in the comments to make up the word count, such as "good good good good good good good good good good good good good good good good good good good", for these comments this article compresses and removes words, only retaining non-repetitive content to replace the

Table 5.1 Data volume distribution of reviews before and after preprocessing

Reviews of Imported Fresh Products	Seafood and Aquatic Products	Fresh Fruit	Choice Meat	Cold Drinks and Frozen Food	Total
Raw review data (bar)	5,305	5,218	5,085	4,676	20,284
Preprocessed data (bar)	3,562	3,535	4,045	3,448	14,591

original content. Advertising comments refer to comments that obviously use the comment area to advertise or promote commissions for their own products, such as "I have always been a loyal customer of Guoying Fresh! Trust Guoying Fresh, support Guoying Fresh! Good service, good things, whether big or small, if you like it, you must buy it and try it!", delete comments that are obviously advertising and brushing orders.

(3) Non-standard comments. Online comments are often expressed in a popular and colloquial way by users, so the original comment data crawled will have some rather casual expressions, such as "The logistics is quite fast, I opened it with joy, but the quality... the skin has started to turn black, the whole fruit is just dying". For ease of analysis, these comments are standardized and unified by manually adding punctuation marks, replacing typos, etc.

After preprocessing the original data of imported fresh produce comments crawled, this article finally retains 14,591 valid user online comments. The distribution of comment data in the original online comment database and the preprocessed database is shown in Table 5.1.

5.3 Calculation of Consumer Emotion Recognition in Cross-Border E-commerce

5.3.1 Word Segmentation and Part-Of-Speech Tagging of Online Review Data

Before sentiment analysis of online comments, word segmentation and part-of-speech tagging of online comments are required. The accuracy of word segmentation results of online comments affects the subsequent sentiment analysis results of online comments. Therefore, word segmentation tools with higher accuracy should be selected to achieve word segmentation of online comments.

In this paper, a Jieba word segmentation tool is used to perform word segmentation and part-of-speech tagging on the preprocessed review text, and finally the stop words are removed by referring to the stop word table.

Since online reviews have no fixed format, there are many new words on the Internet, and there are many proper terms in the field of cross-border e-commerce,

Table 5.2 Partial custom user dictionary table

Category	New User Dictionary
Common expressions of online shopping	Box horse, good reviews, medium reviews, bad reviews, rookie, buyback, selling, direct sales
Fresh product-related nouns	Insulated bag, cold chain, foam box, fish roe, raw cut, traceable, expanded bag

Table 5.3 Part of the stop list content

Source	Stop Words
Hit stop word list	Uh, hey, or, just, that, also, and then, however, so, rather, which way, this, these, here…

fresh products also have more unique and distinct review characteristics, and therefore, user-defined user dictionaries should be defined before the review data is divided into words. In the user-defined user dictionary, this paper mainly adds common expressions of online shopping and proper nouns related to cross-border e-commerce and fresh products. Table 5.2 lists some contents of the customized user dictionary.

After word segmentation of the text, there will be many words that have nothing to do with sentiment analysis, such as "this", "from", etc. In order to improve the accuracy of feature extraction and sentiment analysis, this paper uses the Hit stop word list to eliminate these words. Table 5.3 shows some contents of the Hit stop word list used in this paper.

Call the word segmentation tool kit jieba through Python language, and add the user-defined user dictionary and Hit stop word list to segment and part-of-speech tagging the preprocessed online comments, as shown in Fig. 5.2.

The results of part-of-speech tagging are shown in Table 5.4.

5.3.2 *Emotion Dictionary Construction*

Emotion words refer to the words that can express emotion color in the text, and the types of speech include nouns, adjectives, verbs, adverbs, etc. In the existing text emotion analysis, emotion words are usually divided into positive emotion words and negative emotion words.

At present, there have been some domestic scholars sorted out several strong universal emotion words set, for example, HowNet Emotion Dictionary (HowNet), Chinese Emotion Dictionary (NTUSD), etc. However, because these commonly used Chinese emotion dictionaries are more general and have a wide coverage, the analysis effect of domain-specific viewpoint text is not good, so this paper is based on the word set used in HowNet emotion analysis, combined with Soochow University ECSD e-commerce field emotion dictionary, Select the positive emotion word set, negative emotion word set and degree level word set to build the emotion dictionary

	A	B
1	原数据	分词数据
2	味道不错，比较新鲜，下次还会继续	味道 不错 比较 新鲜 下次 继续
3	三文鱼还可以，下次还是自己切，切好的感觉不太顺	三文鱼 可以 下次 自己 切 切 好 感觉 不 太 顺口
4	物流很快，原本担心物流，看来多余了；包装的很好，	物流 很快 原本 担心 物流 看来 多余 包装 很 好 冰袋
5	以前经常买，很新鲜。可能因为怕新冠污染，这次没	以前 经常 买 很 新鲜 可能 因为 怕 新冠 污染 这次 没
6	新鲜，便宜，很久没有吃这么痛快了	新鲜 便宜 很 久 没有 吃 痛快
7	东西很新鲜，口感真的不错，速度也很快，一百个赞	东西 很 新鲜 口感 真的 不错 速度 很快 一百 个 赞
8	不错，包装非常结实，送货速度很快，满意	不错 包装 非常 结实 送货 速度 很快 满意
9	包装很好，拆开都还是冰冻的，这种天气能做到这样	包装 很 好 拆开 冰冻 天气 能 做到 商家 物流 点赞
10	物流快，包装严实，质量很好	物流 快 包装 严实 质量 很 好
11	送货上门速度快，干净新鲜	送货 上门 速度 快 干净 新鲜
12	口感不错，顺丰发货速度没的说	口感 不错 顺丰 发货 速度
13	鱼肉很新鲜，价格也很划算，下次继续购买哦	鱼肉 很 新鲜 价格 很 划算 下次 继续 购买
14	缺点没有按我的备注要求来：1、没切成片2、没有多	缺点 没有 按 备注 要求 来 没 切 成 片 没有 多 给 冰袋
15	顺丰邮寄了四天彻底不新鲜了。。很失望 以前明明隔	顺丰 邮寄 天 彻底 不 新鲜 很 失望 以前 明明 隔 天 味
16	物流的速度很快，快递小哥也很负责任，因为是冷藏	物流 速度 很快 快递 小哥 很 负责任 因为 冷藏 送过来
17	泡沫箱外包装，内有为三文鱼保鲜的两包干冰，今天	泡沫箱 外包装 内 三文鱼 保鲜 包 干冰 下单 下午 收到
18	包装很好，快递员工作认真负责，点个赞。	包装 很 好 快递员 工作 认真 负责 点 个 赞
19	商品收到咯，特别喜欢，一收到就迫不及待地打开了，	商品 收到 特别 喜欢 收到 迫不及待 打开 家人 很 满意

Fig. 5.2 Screenshot of the word segmentation results of some online reviews of imported fresh products

Table 5.4 Statistics of part-of-speech tagging and word frequency of some online comments of imported fresh products

Tag Word	Word Frequency	Part-of-speech	Tag Word	Word Frequency	Part-of-speech
very	3612	adverb	flavor	980	noun
good	2796	adjective	don't	938	adverb
nice	2295	adjective	fresh	817	adjective
buy	1606	verb	steak	782	noun
eat	1460	verb	drink	668	verb

of cross-border import e-commerce platform fresh product online review. To increase the accuracy and usability of the emotion dictionary, this paper adds some emotion network words combined with the characteristics of the imported fresh industry in the construction process of the emotion dictionary. The contents of some emotion network words are shown in Table 5.5. At the same time, this paper assigns simple weights to the basic emotion words without adverb modification. The weights of positive emotion words are set to 1, and those of negative emotion words are set to − 1.

In online comments, users often use adverbs to express emotional intensity and polarity, that is, to modify the opinions expressed by different adverbs. Among them,

Table 5.5 Contents of some network emotion words

Emotion Word Set Name	Emotion Words
Positive network emotion words	Fresh, affordable, cost-effective, delicious, awesome
Negative network emotion words	Broken, routine, speechless, garbage, chicken ribs

Table 5.6 Contents of partial degree adverbs table

Adverb of Degree	Level	Weight
The most; Completely; Extremely; Absolutely; Very much...	"Most"	5
Very; Too; Particularly; Far; Not a few; Special; In particular...	"Very"	4
Quite; Also; Even more; Still; More and more; Better...	"More"	3
Slightly; A bit; Pretty; Some; Quite; A little; Somewhat...	"Slightly"	2
Super; Excessive; Too...	"Super"	1

Table 5.7 Contents of the negative word list

Negative Words	Weights
No, don't, not, nothing, not necessarily, can't, never, not yet, difficult, not quite	− 1

adverbs of degree are a kind of adverbs, which mainly play the role of limiting and modifying, and are used to express the degree of emotion. In online comments, users often use adverbs of degree to modify their opinions, and using different adverbs of degree to modify opinions will convey different intensity of emotion. Therefore, it is necessary to set the weights of degree adverbs in the sentiment dictionary. According to the intensity of the positive and negative emotion words given, this paper divides the degree thesaurus into five levels. The content of part of the degree adverbs set is shown in Table 5.6.

Negative words are words that have a negative meaning and are also a kind of adverb. The number of negative words modified by emotion words affects the emotional polarity of online comments. When there are an odd number of negative words modified emotion words, the polarity of emotion words remains unchanged, and when there are an even number of negative words, the polarity of emotion words will be reversed. Combining the online reviews of fresh products and common negative words in this paper, the negative word set constructed in this paper is shown in Table 5.7, and the weight of these negative words is set to − 1.

5.3.3 Calculation Method of Affective Energy Value

The calculation of affective energy value of online comments mainly involves the affective tendency and affective intensity of the comments. The polarity of affective tendency depends not only on the affective words in the sentence, but also on the degree of adverbs and negative words that modify the affective words. In this chapter, when constructing the basic emotion dictionary, the degree adverb table and the negative emotion table, the corresponding weights are given to different emotion words. Therefore, when calculating the emotional value of different feature attributes, the calculation is mainly based on the weight of various emotional words. The specific formula for calculating the emotional intensity value is as follows:

$$F_i = M_{w_{ai}} * (-1)^n W_{w_{bi}} * W_i \tag{5.1}$$

$$Score_d = \sum_{i=1}^{m} F_i \tag{5.2}$$

In the formula, F_i refers to the emotional intensity of a certain evaluation phrase, W_i refers to the polarity of emotion words, $M_{w_{ai}}$ refers to the weight of degree adverbs, $W_{w_{bi}}$ refers to the weight of negative words, n refers to the number of negative words modifying feature words. The total emotional intensity value of the final comment d is expressed as $Score_d$.

The emotional polarity of comment d is judged,

$$T_d = \begin{cases} 1, \text{Score}_d > 0 \\ 0, \text{Score}_d = 0 \\ -1, \text{Score}_d < 0 \end{cases} \tag{5.3}$$

$T_d = 1$ indicates that the emotional polarity of comment d is generally positive, $T_d = 0$ indicates that the emotional polarity of comment d is generally neutral, and $T_d = 1$ indicates that the emotional polarity of comment d is generally negative.

5.4 Analysis on the Emotional Evolution of Cross-Border E-commerce Consumers Under the Epidemic Environment

5.4.1 Time Series Evolution Stage Division

According to the press conference of the Joint Prevention and Control Mechanism of the State Council, on July 3, 2020, Dalian Customs for the first time tested positive for COVID-19 nucleic acid from a sample inside a container of frozen South American white shrimp produced by an Ecuadorian company. Within two months after that, the outer packaging of imported fresh products was frequently breached, and more than 10-related incidents occurred in China (see Table 5.8).

And on August 16, CCTV News reported that the World Health Organization pointed out that "there is no evidence that the novel coronavirus can be transmitted through food, and there is no case of human infection from eating certain food, so there is no need to be overly alarmed". Therefore, in combination with the announcement of the official press conference, news and the number of events, four-time Windows were divided to analyze the impact of the epidemic environment on the emotional evolution of cross-border e-commerce consumers buying imported fresh products: Normal control period S1, epidemic outbreak period S2, imported fresh incident outbreak peak S3 (referred to as outbreak peak), imported fresh incident spread control period S4 (referred to as spread control period).

Table 5.8 Statistics of positive cases in the outer packaging of imported fresh products

Time	A Positive Test on the Outer Packaging of Imported Fresh Products Involved Products	Product Category
2020–07-03	Frozen South American white shrimp imported from Ecuador (Xiamen, Dalian)	Seafood and aquatic products
2020–07-14	Frozen South American white shrimp imported from Ecuador (Pingxiang, Jiangxi Province)	Seafood and aquatic products
2020–07-15	Frozen South American white shrimp imported from Ecuador (Chongqing)	Seafood and aquatic products
2020–07-16	Frozen South American white shrimp imported from Ecuador (Yunnan)	Seafood and aquatic products
2020–07-23	Imported cold storage food from Kaiyang Seafood in Dalian	Seafood and Aquatic Products
2020–08-09	Imported frozen seafood products (Yantai)	Frozen meat
2020–08-11	Brazil imports frozen chicken wings	Frozen meat
2020–08-12	Frozen South American white shrimp imported from Ecuador (Wuhu)	Seafood and aquatic products
2020–08-13	Frozen South American white shrimp imported from Ecuador (Xi 'an)	Seafood and aquatic products
2020–08-14	Brazil imports frozen chicken wings	Frozen meat

5.4.2 Temporal Evolution Characteristics of Emotional Diffusion Value

Starting from the dimension of emotion diffusion and taking monthly as the time statistical unit, the area diagram of the change in the number of comments on Jingdong fresh imported products is drawn, and the area size represents the size of emotion diffusion, as shown in Fig. 5.3.

1. During normal control period S1 (January – November 2019), product sales were approximately replaced by the number of reviews, and the increase in emotional diffusion value was replaced by the decrease in the number of ratings. Consumers' emotional diffusion value of imported fresh products from Jingdong was in a normal state of fluctuation, changing and spreading at any time.
2. In the outbreak period S2 (January – June 2020), the novel coronavirus outbreak occurred. In the initial outbreak environment, in January 2020, the whole country entered the epidemic prevention and control stage, and the city was closed and quarantined at home, and the number of comments on imported fresh products on Jingdong dropped sharply; The trend of consumer sentiment diffusion value from February to June was basically consistent with that in the normal control period, with no significant change in sentiment diffusion.
3. During the outbreak peak period S3 (July – August 2020), the imported fresh packaging samples were tested positive for COVID-19 nucleic acid for the first time. Within 40 days, ten similar incidents occurred nationwide, which aroused

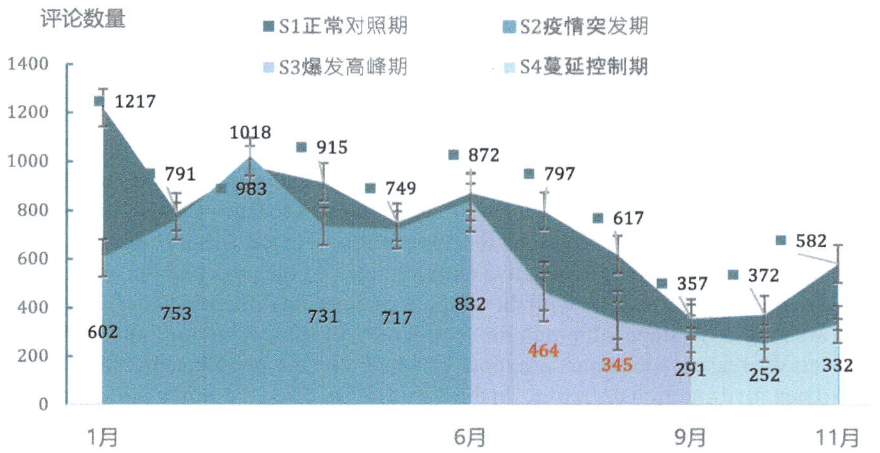

Fig. 5.3 Area diagram of temporal evolution of emotion diffusion value

consumers' attention and caused emotional anxiety. The emotional diffusion value showed a sharp increase trend and was higher than all the emotional diffusion changes in S1 and S2 time intervals. Consumers perceive and make judgments quickly, and the overall purchasing intensity drops sharply. The number of comments in July and August decreased by 41.8% and 44.1% respectively compared with the same period last year. Consumers' emotions on imported fresh products spread rapidly.

4. Spread control period S4 (September–November 2020), the official press conference experts pointed out that for imported fresh products, "do a good job of food safety five requirements, you can rest easy to eat", at the same time, the relevant departments to organize prevention and response measures, the number of consumer reviews gradually rebounded, the purchase of strength has a good trend, although overall compared with the normal control period has declined, but compared with the peak of the outbreak, the emotional diffusion value has the intention to shrink.

5.4.3 *Temporal Evolution Characteristics of Affective Energy Value*

Based on the above sentiment analysis method, the evolution process of consumer emotion is analyzed according to the divided time window. The emotional polarity of online comments in each time window is calculated according to formula 5.3. As can be seen from Fig. 5.4, overall, consumers have a positive attitude toward the fresh products imported from cross-border e-commerce, and the proportion of positive emotion in the four periods is greater than the sum of the proportion of neutral and negative emotion, indicating that consumer emotion has been in a positive and good state. The analysis of consumer emotion fluctuation was divided into each time window. Compared with the normal control stage in S1, consumers' emotion fluctuation on imported fresh products in S2 period after the outbreak of the epidemic was not large, while the positive emotion proportion of consumers increased significantly and the negative emotion proportion decreased in S3 period during the outbreak peak of positive test events of imported fresh packaging. In the S4 stage of the spread control period of imported fresh products, the proportion of positive emotion decreased slightly, but the proportion of negative emotion reached the peak and the rising trend was obvious. In combination with the changes of emotion diffusion value in Fig. 5.3, it shows that in S3 stage, although the number of consumers buying imported fresh products decreases, consumers are more satisfied with the products, and the proportion of negative emotion decreases. In the S4 stage, based on the explanation of WHO and the monitoring and deployment of the General Administration of Customs and other measures on the import test of fresh frozen products, the effective control of imported fresh events has promoted consumers to buy up, but the spread of imported fresh events has a certain impact on the emotional polarity of consumers, and the proportion of consumers' negative emotions has increased, and the requirements for imported fresh products are higher.

Focus on the analysis of consumers' negative emotion fluctuations and further subdivide the categories of imported fresh products. As can be seen from Fig. 5.5, the proportion of negative emotion in consumer reviews is basically maintained at a low level, with the highest proportion accounting for only 11.3% and the lowest 8.9%. The proportion of negative comments on imported fruit products is relatively high, while the negative comments on imported dairy products are relatively low.

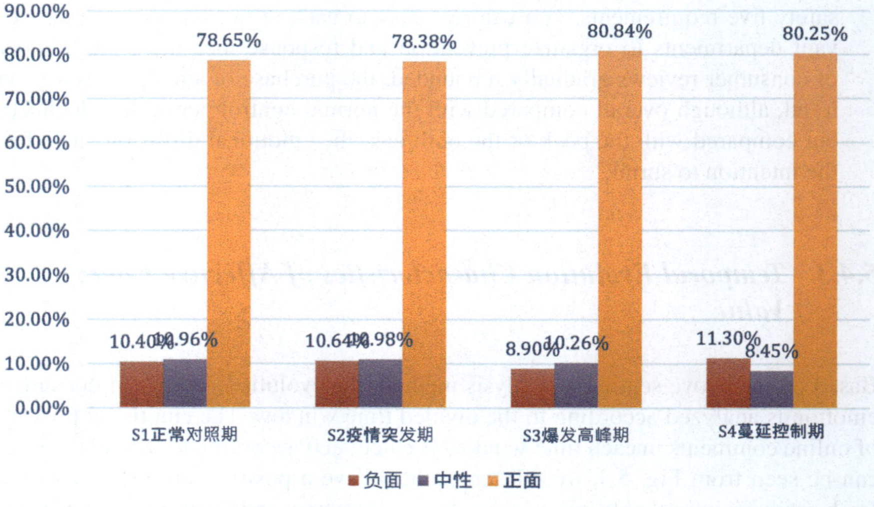

Fig. 5.4 Trend of emotional polarity

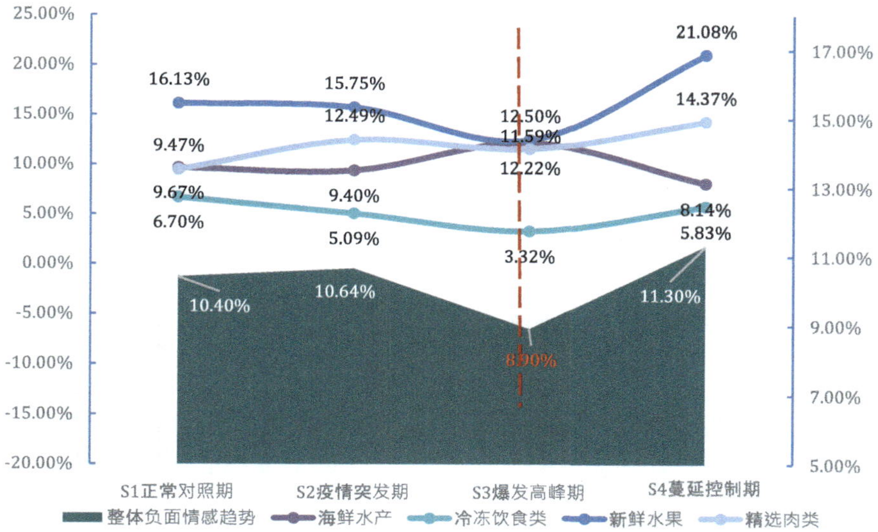

Fig. 5.5 Temporal evolution of negative emotion

Meanwhile, according to the Table 5.8, seafood and aquatic products accounted for 80% of the imported fresh incidents in the S3 stage. Compared with Figs. 5.5 and 5.6, the negative comments on imported fresh seafood and aquatic products in the S3 stage increased significantly, indicating that consumers had a rapid perception of emergencies and had negative emotional fluctuations on the imported fresh seafood and aquatic products involved.

The temporal variation of the polarity intensity of consumer emotion is described from a microscopic perspective. The value of consumer emotion intensity calculated by formula 5.2 is shown in Figs. 5.7 and 5.8. Although overall, consumers have a positive attitude toward imported fresh products purchased on the cross-border e-commerce platform, the positive event of the outer packaging test has a certain impact on the value of consumer emotional intensity. The range value from high intensity to low intensity is significantly larger, indicating that the intensity of consumer emotional fluctuations becomes greater. Among them, the intensity of emotional fluctuation has a greater impact on seafood and aquatic products and selected meat products.

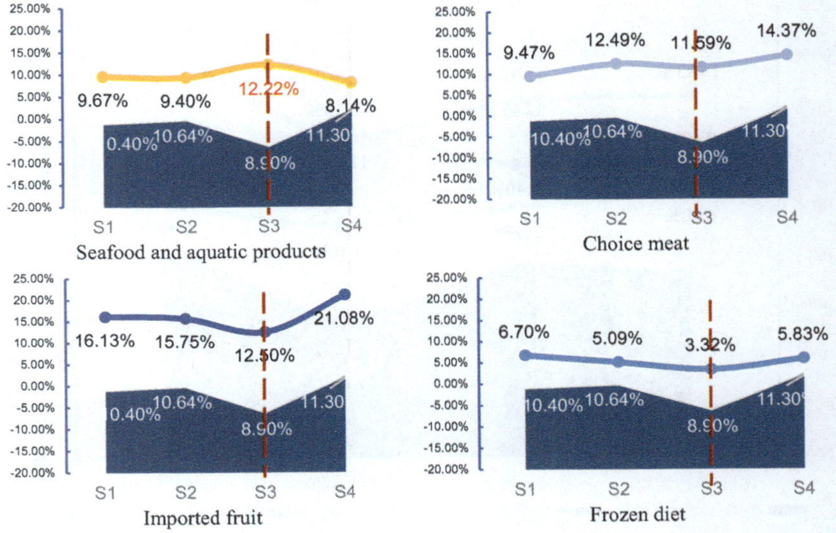

Fig. 5.6 Temporal evolution of negative emotion by product category

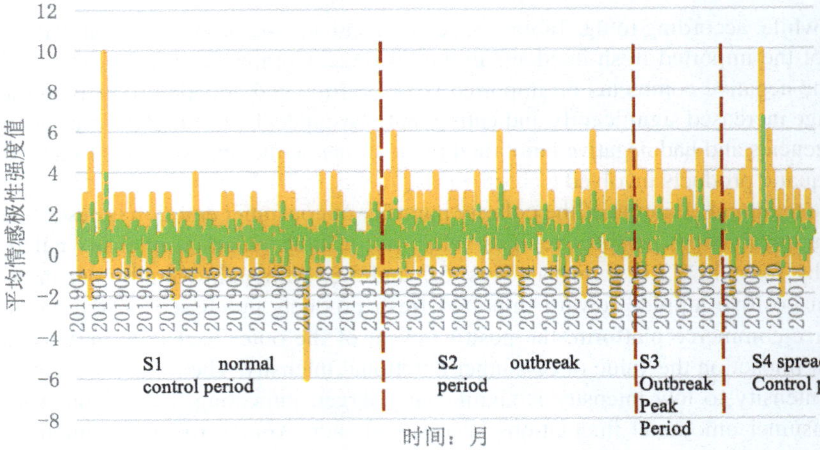

Fig. 5.7 Temporal variation map for evaluating polarity intensity

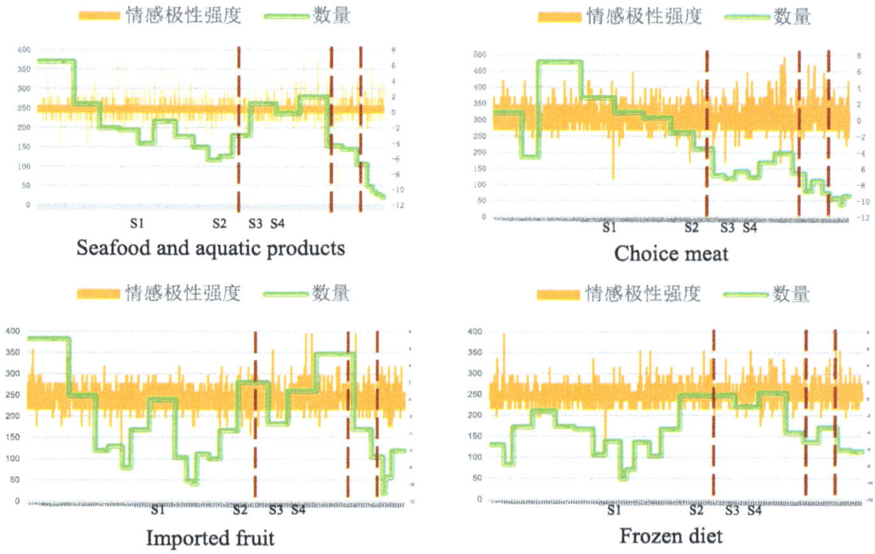

Fig. 5.8 Time series variation of polarity intensity evaluated by product category

Chapter 6
Construction of Cross-Border E-commerce Policy Evaluation Model

This chapter constructs a cross-border e-commerce policy evaluation model based on the policy execution process model proposed by Smith, analyzes the dimensions of cross-border e-commerce policy evaluation, sorts out the data needed for this study, and finally explains the research methods used in this study.

6.1 Cross-Border E-commerce Policy Evaluation Model

The Smith Policy Implementation Model points out that the main factors affecting policy implementation include ideal policy schemes, implementing agencies, target groups, and environmental factors. Therefore, this article combines this model to analyze the policy subjects, policy schemes, policy action fields, and policy evolution process from the perspectives of bibliometrics and data visualization, evaluates the effects of policies from the perspective of econometrics, and explores the environmental factors affecting the development of cross-border e-commerce [[1]], as shown in Fig. 6.1.

1. Analysis of the cooperation network of cross-border e-commerce policy subjects. The subjects of cross-border e-commerce policy are central or local government agencies responsible for the formulation, implementation, practice, supervision, and evaluation of cross-border e-commerce policies, such as central government agencies (the State Council and its subordinate State Council Office, General Administration of Customs, etc.) and local government agencies. Cooperation between policy subjects is conducive to the implementation of policy schemes, and this article uses relational visualization methods to analyze the cooperation situation of policy subjects.

L. Xiong and H. Wang, *User Driven Cross-Border E-Commerce Platform Competition and Policy Analysis*, Advanced Studies in E-Commerce,
https://doi.org/10.1007/978-981-97-3835-9_6

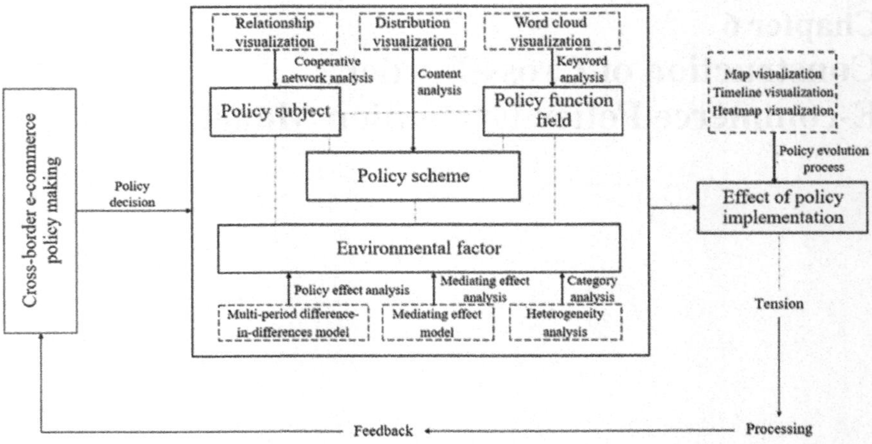

Fig. 6.1 Cross-border e-commerce policy evaluation model

2. Content analysis of cross-border e-commerce policy schemes. Cross-border e-commerce policy tools are divided into environmental, supply, demand, and evaluation types. From the perspective of "shape-push–pull-evaluation", the cross-border e-commerce text content is classified and coded through policy tool classification methods, and the distribution visualization method is further used to conduct multi-dimensional analysis of the measurement results [[2]].
3. Keyword analysis of the action field of cross-border e-commerce policy. According to the different action fields of policies in cross-border e-commerce, cross-border e-commerce policies can be divided into pilot promotion policies, tax policies, payment policies, regulatory policies, informatization policies, logistics policies, and cross-border e-commerce talent policies, etc., reflecting the State Council, Ministry of Commerce, State Taxation Administration, General Administration of Customs and other government agencies' specific guidance for the standardized development of the internal field of cross-border e-commerce. Through the keyword analysis of the action field of cross-border e-commerce policy, the focus and possible development trends of the policy can be focused [[3]].
4. Visualization analysis of the evolution process of cross-border e-commerce. The evolution of cross-border e-commerce policy is based on the year, the time range of the core policies issued at the central level is from 2013 to 2019, and the time range of the cross-border e-commerce comprehensive test zone policy is from 2015 to 2019. The evolution stages and characteristic rules of cross-border e-commerce policy are explored through timeline visualization, map visualization, and heat map visualization methods.

5. Effect evaluation analysis of cross-border e-commerce policy. The main goals of cross-border e-commerce policy include attracting more enterprises to enter the industry, creating a good market environment to facilitate larger-scale transactions, and thereby promoting the development of foreign trade. Therefore, this article uses a multi-period difference-in-differences model to evaluate the policy effects from the perspectives of foreign trade, cross-border e-commerce express delivery, and cross-border e-commerce enterprises [[4]].
6. Analysis of the mediating effect of cross-border e-commerce policy. The implementation of cross-border e-commerce policy is influenced by the interaction of political, economic, technological, and social environments. Firstly, the political environment, which includes national policies and other political factors that play a role in the activities of participating entities in the industry development. Secondly, the economic environment, which includes factors affecting the development of cross-border e-commerce in the stages of economic activity production, circulation, distribution, and consumption. Thirdly, the technological environment, which includes factors related to the optimization of technology, patents, standards, etc., in the cross-border e-commerce industry under technological development and change. Fourthly, the social environment, which includes social factors that integrate human subjective consciousness in social activities, such as social networks and public opinion orientation. Therefore, this paper uses the mediating effect model to analyze the impact of environmental factors on the effectiveness of cross-border e-commerce policy.
7. Analysis of the heterogeneity of cross-border e-commerce policy. When the country sets up cross-border e-commerce comprehensive test zones in batches, the policy input for cross-border e-commerce in each test zone is also different, and the policy effects of cross-border e-commerce in different regions have differences. Therefore, this study divides the comprehensive test zones into different categories and analyzes the policy effects of each category of comprehensive test zones in turn.

6.2 Cross-Border E-commerce Policy Data

The cross-border e-commerce data studied in this paper includes cross-border e-commerce policy data and cross-border e-commerce comprehensive test zone data. The cross-border e-commerce policy data is the text of cross-border e-commerce policies issued by the State Council and its subordinate departments from 2013 to 2019, and the cross-border e-commerce comprehensive test zone policy data is the relevant data of the cross-border e-commerce comprehensive test zones established from 2015 to 2019, as shown in Table 6.1.

Among them, the fields of "policy text form", "policy text nature", "policy tool type", and "policy action field" in the cross-border e-commerce policy data are represented by continuous integer data. The nature of the policy text includes national normative documents, departmental normative documents, departmental

Table 6.1 Cross-border e-commerce policy data

Data category	Data name	Data format	Data type	Remarks
Cross-border e-commerce policy data	Policy number	Numeric type	int	
Cross-border e-commerce policy data	Policy name	String type	text	
Cross-border e-commerce policy data	Policy subject	String type	text	Multiple policy subjects are separated by "、"
Cross-border e-commerce policy data	Implementation time	Date-time type	date	
Cross-border e-commerce policy data	Encoding or not	Byte type	byte	1 represents the encoded data record, and 0 represents the raw data
Cross-border e-commerce policy data	Policy text form	Numeric type	int	Successive numbers represent different forms
Cross-border e-commerce policy data	Nature of policy text	Numeric type	int	Successive numbers represent different forms
Cross-border e-commerce policy data	Types of policy instruments	Numeric type	int	Successive numbers represent different policy instruments
Cross-border e-commerce policy data	Policy text content	String type	longtext	Successive numbers represent different forms
Cross-border e-commerce policy data	Policy function field	Numeric type	int	Successive numbers represent different policy fields
Integrated pilot zone data	Integrated pilot zone number	Numeric type	int	
Integrated pilot zone data	Integrated pilot zone name	String type	text	
Integrated pilot zone data	Geographical coordinates x	Numeric type	float	Longitude of integrated pilot zone
Integrated pilot zone data	Geographical coordinates y	Numeric type	float	Latitude of integrated pilot zone
Integrated pilot zone data	Set up time	Date-time type	date	
Integrated pilot zone data	Time of policy introduction	Date-time type	date	

(continued)

Table 6.1 (continued)

Data category	Data name	Data format	Data type	Remarks
Integrated pilot zone data	Number of policies introduced	Numeric type	int	
Integrated pilot zone data	Foreign import and export trade volume	Numeric type	float	
Integrated pilot zone data	Cross-border express delivery quantity	Numeric type	float	
Integrated pilot zone data	Number of cross-border e-commerce enterprises	Numeric type	int	

work documents, and administrative approval documents [[5]]; the form of the policy text includes guidance and approval, notice, announcement, opinion, and letter, these policy texts have different natures and varying degrees of legal effect; the types of policy tools include environmental, supply, demand, and evaluation types; the fields of policy action include pilot promotion policy, cross-border supervision policy, cross-border tax policy, cross-border payment policy, cross-border logistics policy, and informatization construction. The "whether coded" field indicates whether the data record is the original policy document, if it is the original policy text data, it is 0, and the policy text data that has been coded is 1.

6.3 Cross-Border E-commerce Policy Evaluation Method

6.3.1 Cross-Border E-commerce Policy Literature Measurement

The measurement of cross-border e-commerce policy literature quantifies the structural attributes of cross-border e-commerce-related policy literature over the years, revealing features such as policy themes, goals, and impacts and is the migration application of policy literature measurement in the field of cross-border e-commerce analysis [[6]]. According to the characteristics of the development of the cross-border e-commerce ecosystem, the literature measurement of cross-border e-commerce policy will be carried out from the aspects of policy characteristics, citation network, keywords, and policy tools. In the field of policy action, it will focus on the analysis of various links of cross-border e-commerce, as shown in Table 6.2.

Table 6.2 Bibliometric analysis method of cross-border e-commerce policy

Research method	Bibliometrics of cross-border E-commerce policy
Characteristic quantitative analysis of policy elements	1. Taking the policy subjects as the object to analyze the functions of cross-border e-commerce policy subjects, such as the State Council, customs, Ministry of Commerce, Administration of Foreign Exchange, and other institutions; 2. Taking the policy field as the object to analyze the role of policies in various links of cross-border e-commerce, such as pilot promotion policies and policies in the fields of regulation, taxation, payment, logistics, and informatization[[7]]; 3. Taking the policy form as the object to analyze the composition of cross-border e-commerce policy system, such as notice, guidance opinion, opinion, announcement, reply, and letter; 4. Taking the number of policies as the object to analyze the time trend and evolution characteristics of cross-border e-commerce policies
Citation analysis	1. Taking the cooperation network of policy subjects as the object to analyze the subject cooperation of cross-border e-commerce policy system; 2. Taking the policy reference relationship as the object to analyze the relationship between the cross-border e-commerce policies of the State Council and its subordinate departments
Keyword analysis	1. Taking the policy word frequency as the object to mine the key concerns of cross-border e-commerce policy 2. Taking keywords as the object to mine the key topic change rule of cross-border e-commerce policy
Policy instrument analysis	Taking the combination of cross-border e-commerce policy instruments as the object to analyze the resource input of policies from the types of supply, environment, demand, and evaluation

6.3.1.1 Cross-Border E-commerce Policy Visualization

Due to the different stages of the implementation of cross-border e-commerce policies, the cooperation relationships among policy entities are complex, and the cross-border e-commerce pilot zones are distributed across the country. The measurement of policy documents involves complex data such as policy quantity characteristics, text content, and geographical location. Therefore, how to display policy rules and policy features efficiently and intuitively is an important content of policy document measurement. Therefore, based on the measurement of cross-border e-commerce policy documents, this paper further analyzes the relevant content with the analysis method of measurement visualization and explores the feature rules of the evolution of cross-border e-commerce policies. This paper uses Echarts technology to visualize the measurement of cross-border e-commerce policy documents, as shown in Table 6.3.

Based on the research of policy data collection and preprocessing process, this paper will focus on the visualization mapping process of cross-border e-commerce policy data. The data mapping process of visualization analysis is divided into the following five steps:

Step 1: Prepare the DOM container, prepare a DOM container with height and width on the HTML page, as the rendering container of Echarts, that is, the carrier of visualization mapping.
Step 2: Create an Echarts instance and create an Echarts instance in the DOM, each Echarts instance occupies a DOM node.
Step 3: Option configuration, implement the specific style of visualization mapping, such as data management, visual mapping, timeline, and other user interaction components. This step is also the key part of visualization mapping, where the data analysis purpose of human–computer interaction can be achieved through the interaction components of the series.
Step 4: Data loading and updating. Data loading can be divided into synchronous and asynchronous loading. Directly loaded data is set in the series of step 3 in the form of an array, and asynchronously loaded data is loaded from the preprocessed data.json file.
Step 5: Load the Echarts instance and set the configured option to the corresponding Echarts instance. Form a visualization chart for analysts to study and reference.

In the visualization analysis of the measurement of cross-border e-commerce policy documents, considering the characteristics of policy continuity, policy correlation, geographical distribution characteristics of cross-border e-commerce pilot zones, etc., this study uses timeline charts, word cloud charts, relationship charts, and heat maps to visualize the measurement of policy documents.

The timeline chart of cross-border e-commerce policy maps the data sets of different years of cross-border e-commerce policy on the same chart, which can realize the dynamic visualization analysis of policy-related information with the change of time [[8]], as shown in Fig. 6.2.

The word cloud chart of cross-border e-commerce policy is an analysis of policy text content. By displaying the frequency of policy text words in different sizes, the focus of the policy can be intuitively analyzed, as shown in Fig. 6.3.

By linking various policies or policy entities together through the relationship between cross-border e-commerce policy goals or policy entities, it can not only

Table 6.3 Visualization analysis of cross-border e-commerce policies by using Echarts

Bibliometric content of cross-border e-commerce policies	Visual analysis of cross-border e-commerce policies	Implementation mode
Policy characteristics Policy subject, policy field, policy form, policy quantity	Cross-border e-commerce policy data linkage analysis	Based on the Dataset component, it stores data in various formats such as two-dimensional array and object array of cross-border e-commerce policy data, separately declares policy data sets for reuse by multiple components to realize visual mapping based on specified data
	Cross-border e-commerce policy geographic coordinate analysis	Based on the Geo component, it is used for geographic mapping of policy data during the nationwide implementation of cross-border e-commerce policies to realize the analysis of policy data in the map dimension
	Cross-border e-commerce policy timeline analysis	Based on the Timeline component, policy data at different times can be switched in the same visual graph to realize the analysis of policy differences in different years
Citation network Subject cooperation network, policy citation network	Cross-border e-commerce policy subject network analysis	With the help of Geph software, it is used to analyze the cooperative relationship between policy subjects in the case of multi-subject joint publication
	Cross-border e-commerce policy citation analysis	Based on the Graph component, Node is used to represent cross-border e-commerce policy documents, and Links is used to represent the relationship between the objectives of policy documents. On the basis of network relationship analysis, Category data items are added to distinguish by color, and each Category represents policies in the same field
Keyword	Cross-border e-commerce policy word frequency analysis	Based on the WordCloud component, the word frequency of cross-border e-commerce policy text content is formed into text graphics of different shapes and sizes according to the different numerical values, so as to realize the key focus analysis of policy content
Policy instrument	Cross-border e-commerce policy thermodynamic analysis	Based on the VisualMap component, the specified dimensions of cross-border e-commerce policy data are mapped to corresponding visual elements, such as graphic category, size, transparency, and tone, so as to realize the multi-dimensional analysis of policy data

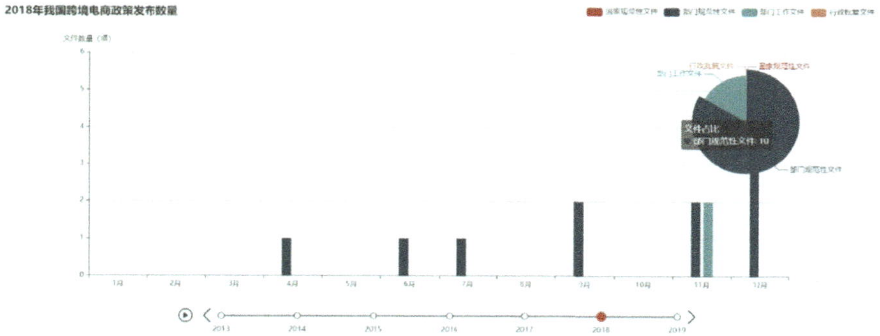

Fig. 6.2 Visualization analysis of cross-border e-commerce policy by using Echarts

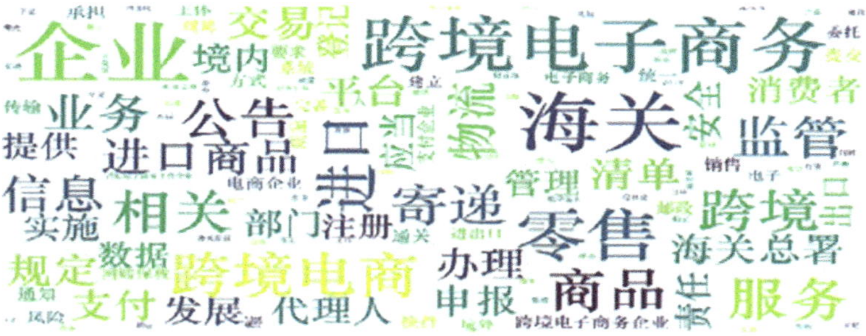

Fig. 6.3 Word cloud map analysis of cross-border e-commerce policy

reflect the relationship between policies, but also intuitively analyze the category of policies, as shown in Fig. 6.4.

The heat map of cross-border e-commerce policy is based on data visual mapping and conducts time series analysis and color gradient mapping on data in chronological order, which can analyze the feature changes of cross-border e-commerce policy in continuous time periods, as shown in Fig. 6.5.

6.3.2 *Evaluation of Cross-Border E-commerce Policy Effects*

According to the national conditions of our country, the cross-border e-commerce pilot zones were not established at one time, but were established in five batches from 2015 to 2020. Therefore, this paper uses a multi-period double difference model to study the effects of cross-border e-commerce policies [[9]], as shown in Eq. 6.1.

The multi-period difference-in-differences model does not directly reflect the group variables in the difference-in-differences model, $Treated_i$, time variables *Time*,

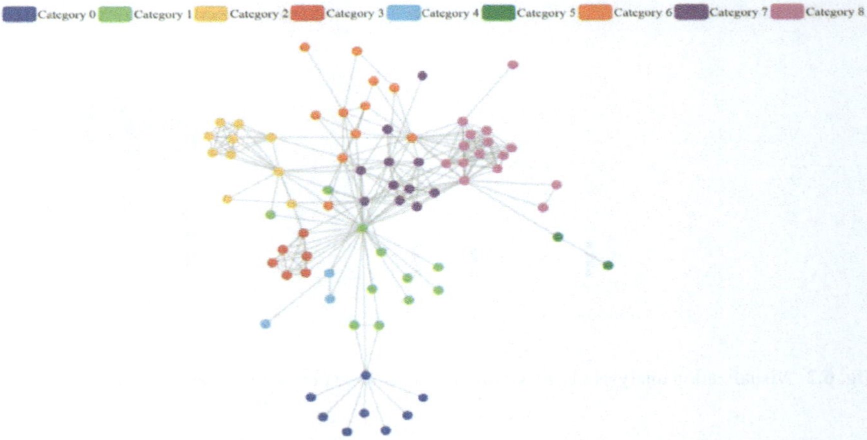

Fig. 6.4 Network relationship analysis of cross-border e-commerce policy

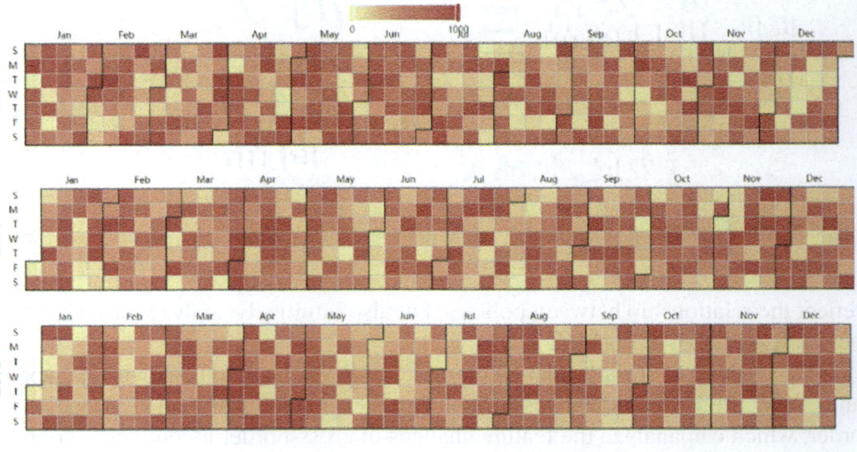

Fig. 6.5 Heatmap analysis of cross-border e-commerce policy word frequency

difference variables $Treated_i * Time$, but instead analyzes further with the transformed dummy variable $Exper_{it}$. Here, i represents the city, t represents the year, and y_{it} represents the development of cross-border e-commerce. In formula 6.2, T_i is the intergroup dummy variable, indicating whether the city is set up as a cross-border e-commerce comprehensive test area. The value for the test area city is 1, representing the experimental group, and the value for other cities is 0, representing the control group. P_t is the policy dummy variable, indicating whether the city is affected by the policy of the cross-border e-commerce comprehensive test area. That is, from the year the policy is implemented, the value is 1, and before that, it is 0. $Exper_{it}$ is the dummy variable for policy effect. In the experimental group, only when the city is set up as a comprehensive test area and subsequent policies are implemented, the dummy variable $Exper_{it}$ is 1, in other cases, this value is 0, and the control group always has a value of 0.

$$y_{it} = \beta_0 + \beta_1 * Exper_{it} + \lambda * \sum_n X_{it} + \mu_i + f_t + \varepsilon_{it} \tag{6.1}$$

$$Exper_{it} = T_i * P_t \tag{6.2}$$

The multi-period double difference method is used to analyze and evaluate the effect of the policy in the cross-border e-commerce comprehensive test area, fully considering the differences in the establishment years of the test area from 2015 to 2019, incorporating different test area establishment times into the research analysis, avoiding the experimental errors caused by single-point analysis, and fully conforming to the reality of different years of establishment of the cross-border e-commerce comprehensive test area [[10]].

This article divides the cross-border e-commerce comprehensive test area into experimental and control groups and evaluates the policy effect of the cross-border e-commerce comprehensive test area through the multi-period double difference method. It is necessary to test the parallel trend of this method to explain the validity of the experiment. In addition, to prevent the randomness of empirical analysis, a placebo test is further adopted, setting a virtual policy time for repeated experiments to test the robustness of the method and the validity of the empirical results.

References

1. Dong F, Wang M (2015) Understanding parking decisions with a Bayesian network[J]. Trans plann Technol 38(6):585–600
2. Xie G, Gao H, Huang B et al (2018) A driving behavior awareness model based on a dynamic Bayesian network and distributed genetic algorithm[J]. Int J Comput Intell Syst 11(1):469–482
3. Julie S (2011) The beauty of data visualization[M]. Machinery Industry Press
4. Wei C (2013) Basic principles and methods of data visualization[M]. Science Press
5. Wang Q, Sun H, Zhang Q (2017) A Bayesian network model on the public bicycle choice behavior of residents: A case study of Xian[J]. Math Probl Eng. https://doi.org/10.1155/2017/3023956
6. Rezaee A, Raie AA, Nadi A et al (2011) Sensor fault tolerance method by using a Bayesian network for robot behavior[J]. Adv Robot 25(16):2039–2064
7. Lazkano E, Sierra B, Astigarraga A et al (2007) On the use of Bayesian networks to develop behaviours for mobile robots[J]. Robot Auton Syst 55(3):253–265
8. Rezaee A, Raie A, Nadi A et al (2011) Using Bayesian network for robot behavior with sensor fault[J]. Elektronika ir elektrotechnika 108(2):91–96
9. Min HJ, Cho SB (2010) Adaptive behaviors of reactive mobile robot with Bayesian inference in nonstationary environments[J]. Appl Intell 33(3):264–277
10. Li LX, Abdul Rahman SS (2018) Students' learning style detection using tree augmented naive Bayes[J]. Royal Soc Open Sci 5(7):172108

Chapter 7
Cross-Border E-commerce Policy Metrics and Visualization Research

Based on the cross-border e-commerce policy evaluation model proposed in Chapter 6, this chapter explores the structural features of cross-border e-commerce policies from the perspectives of policy subjects, policy action fields, policy tools, and policy evolution and analyzes and evaluates the resource allocation of policies based on the idea of policy literature metrics and with the help of visualization methods.

7.1 Sample Selection and Data Processing

(1) Policy Source and Policy Screening

Policy texts mainly come from the official websites of the People's Republic of China Central People's Government, Ministry of Commerce, State Taxation Administration, General Administration of Customs, and other departments, as well as the PKU Law database and related legal and news websites. Due to the different names of cross-border e-commerce during its development, this paper uses "cross-border e-commerce", "cross-border e-commerce", "cross-border trade e-commerce", "cross-border trade e-commerce" as keywords to collect policy texts whose titles contain the above keywords from various websites and databases, and obtained 49 central-level core cross-border e-commerce policy texts issued by the State Council and its subordinate departments.

Considering the effectiveness of policy texts, remove the notice of the former General Administration of Quality Supervision, Inspection and Quarantine on soliciting opinions on the "Detailed Rules for the Supervision and Management of Food Safety for Cross-Border E-commerce Imports under the Bonded Model" [[1]], the letter on publicly soliciting opinions on the "Cross-Border E-commerce Service Specification" [[2]], the reply of the Comprehensive Department of the State Administration of Foreign Exchange on the pilot project of cross-border e-commerce foreign exchange payment business by various payment institutions [[3]], the reply of the

L. Xiong and H. Wang, *User Driven Cross-Border E-Commerce Platform Competition and Policy Analysis*, Advanced Studies in E-Commerce,
https://doi.org/10.1007/978-981-97-3835-9_7

General Administration of Customs on the implementation plan of the pilot project of cross-border trade e-commerce bonded import in Fuzhou and Pingtan [[4]], and the reply of the General Administration of Food and Drug Supervision on the supervision issues of food cross-border e-commerce enterprises [[5]]. and various training notices, a total of 37 core policy texts were selected.

(2) Policy Unit Encoding

After the policy text is determined, first, according to the policy name, policy subject, policy field, implementation time, policy form, policy nature, and policy tool classification method, the metadata features of each cross-border e-commerce policy document are classified and encoded (see Table 7.1).

Then, the policy documents are traced back, and each cross-border e-commerce policy text is divided into independent policy text content units according to the encoding principle, so that each policy text content unit clearly expresses its meaning, and is numbered according to the order of the policy unit in the policy, a total of 310 policy units were obtained, as shown in Table 7.2.

Taking the data in Table 7.2 as an example, the "Whether Encoded" field is 1 means that the data has been encoded, 0 means it is original text data, the "Policy Text Nature" field is 1 means that the nature of the policy text belongs to the national normative document, "Policy Tool Type" is 0 means original text data, 1 means environmental type, 3 means demand type, 4 means evaluation type, "Policy Action Field" field is 0 means original text data, 2 means cross-border regulatory policy, 3 means cross-border tax policy, 4 means cross-border payment policy.

7.2 Cross-Border E-commerce Policy Subject Visualization Analysis

According to the difference of the policy issuing body, the core policy subject types of cross-border e-commerce are divided into single subject and multiple subjects: (1) Single-subject issuance refers to the comprehensive guidance policies issued solely by the State Council and the State Council Office at the macro level to guide the healthy and rapid development of cross-border e-commerce activities and also includes departmental policies issued solely by the ministries and agencies under the State Council focusing on a certain field, respectively guiding and regulating certain aspects of the development of cross-border e-commerce ecology. (2) Multiple subject issuances refer to the related supporting policies jointly formulated and issued by the State Council, various ministries or directly affiliated institutions, providing support and guarantee for the healthy development of cross-border e-commerce. Among them, there are 38 single-subject issuances, and multiple-subject issuances include 2-subject, 3-subject, 4-subject, 6-subject, etc., a total of 11 policy documents (see Fig. 7.1).

In the single-subject issuances, the early ones were mainly issued by the State Administration of Foreign Exchange, mainly targeting the foreign exchange and

Table 7.1 China cross-border e-commerce policy document analysis dimension coding principles1

Dimensions of policy analysis	Coded keywords	Dimensions of policy analysis	Coded keywords
1. Policy name	Publication number	4.Implementation date	2013 – 2019
2. Policy subjects	The State Council and its subordinate departments	5. Policy form	Notices, opinions, announcements, etc
3. Policy role areas		5. Nature of policy	National normative documents, departmental normative documents, departmental working documents, and administrative approval documents
3.1 Pilot promotion policies	Support, promote, further, and popularize	6. Policy instruments	
3.2 Cross-border regulatory policies	Supervision, management, import list, norms	6.1 Supply type	Capital, technology, personnel, training, guidance, streamlining administration, delegating power, organization, and leadership
3.3 Cross-border tax policy	Taxes, levies	6.2 Demand type	Price subsidies, tax incentives, government procurement
3.4 Cross-border payment policy	Payments, payment institutions, foreign exchange payments	6.3 Environmental type	Target planning, standards, regulations, infrastructure, tax incentives, international cooperation, credit system
3.5 Cross-border logistics policy	Consignment, express delivery	6.4 Evaluation type	Reporting, inspection, statistics
3.6 Information construction	Unified version, information system, data	7. Policy content	Word segmentation Stop List (see appendix)

payment business of the cross-border e-commerce ecology, and later ones were mainly issued by the General Administration of Quality Supervision, Inspection, and Quarantine and the General Administration of Customs in the regulatory field (see Fig. 7.2).

Importing the policy subject issuance data into the gehpi software can reveal that among the issuing bodies, a network of cross-border e-commerce policy subject combinations has been formed, with the General Administration of Customs,

Table 7.2 Cross-border e-commerce policy coding and processing data (partial data)2

Policy name	Policy main body	Time	Whet–her Code	Textual nature of the policy	Policy tools type	Policy text content	Policy role field
Guosuofa [2013]No. 89	Department of State General Office	2013	0	1	0	The development of cross-border e-commerce is important for expanding international market share…	0
Guochangfa [2013]No. 89	Department of State General Office	2013	1	1	1	(1)Determine the e-commerce export business entities…	2
State administration and Development [2013]No. 89	Department of State General Office	2013	1	1	4	(2) Establish a new customs supervision model for e-commerce exports and conduct special statistics…	2
Guokangfa [2013]No. 89	Department of State General Office	2013	1	1	1	(3) Establish e-commerce export inspection and supervision model…	2
Guokangfa [2013]No. 89	Department of State General Office	2013	1	1	1	(4) Support the normal collection and settlement of foreign exchange by e-commerce export enterprises…	2

(continued)

Table 7.2 (continued)

Policy name	Policy main body	Time	Whet–her Code	Textual nature of the policy	Policy tools type	Policy text content	Policy role field
Guokangfa [2013]No. 89	The State Council General Office	2013	1	1	1	(5) Encourage banking institutions and payment institutions to provide payment services for cross-border e-commerce..	4
Guokangfa [2013]No. 89	Department of State General Office	2013	1	1	3	(6) Implement tax policies adapted to e-commerce exports...	3

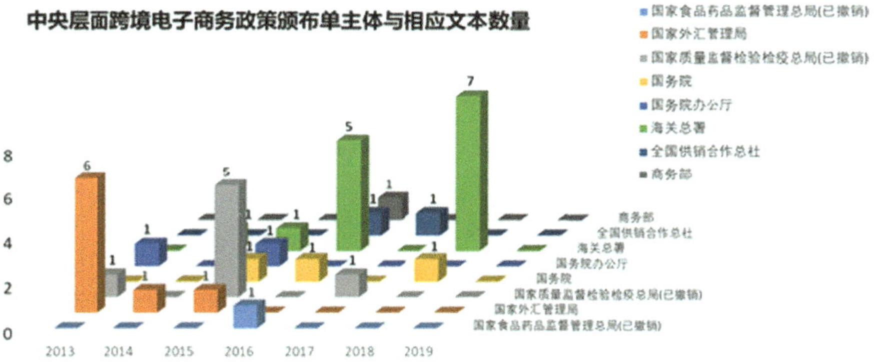

Fig. 7.1 The number of entities issuing cross-border e-commerce policies at the central level and the number of corresponding documents

Ministry of Finance, State Taxation Administration, Ministry of Commerce, General Administration of Quality Inspection, etc., jointly formulating cross-border e-commerce policy subject combination issuance network, and the State Post Bureau, Ministry of Transport, State Administration for Market Regulation, Food and Drug Administration, Ministry of Industry and Information Technology, etc., assisting in policy formulation (see Fig. 7.3).

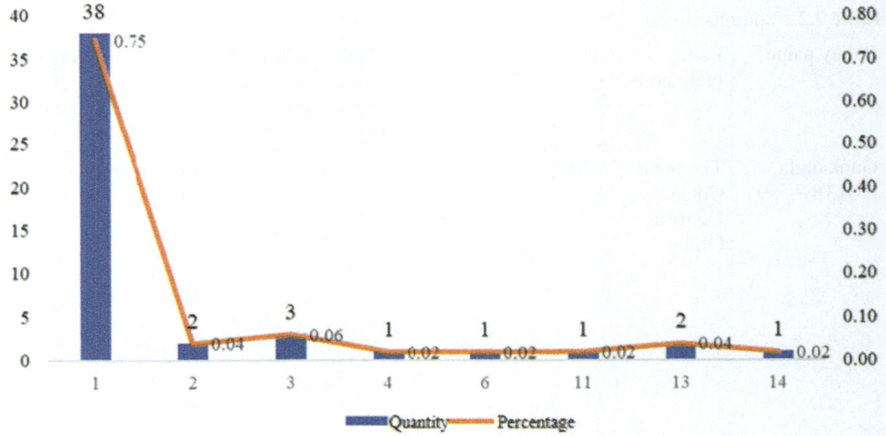

Fig. 7.2 China's central-level cross-border e-commerce policy issued a single body and the corresponding number of texts

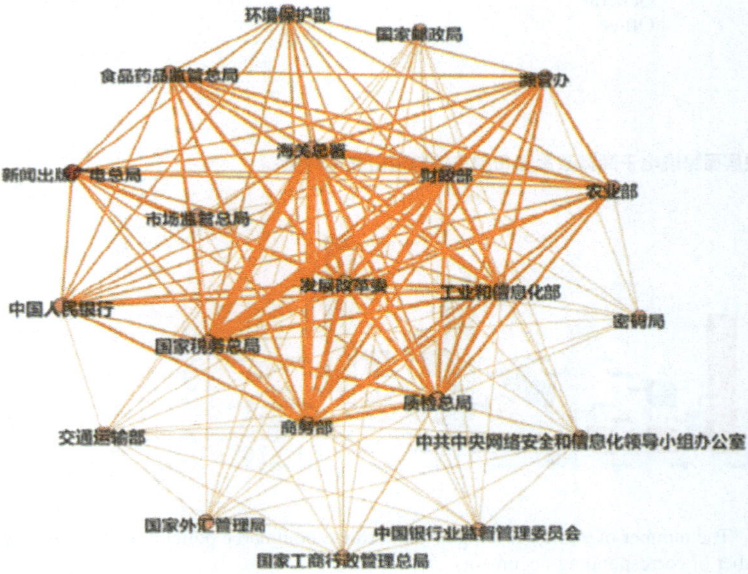

Fig. 7.3 Visual analysis of the role of cross-border e-commerce policies

Further analysis of the network feature indicators of the 21 policy subjects, as shown in Fig. 7.4. From the figure, the connectivity index network diameter is 2, indicating that cooperation is relatively common in this network, the graph density of 0.7 and 0.882 clustering coefficient indicate that the network is relatively dense, and

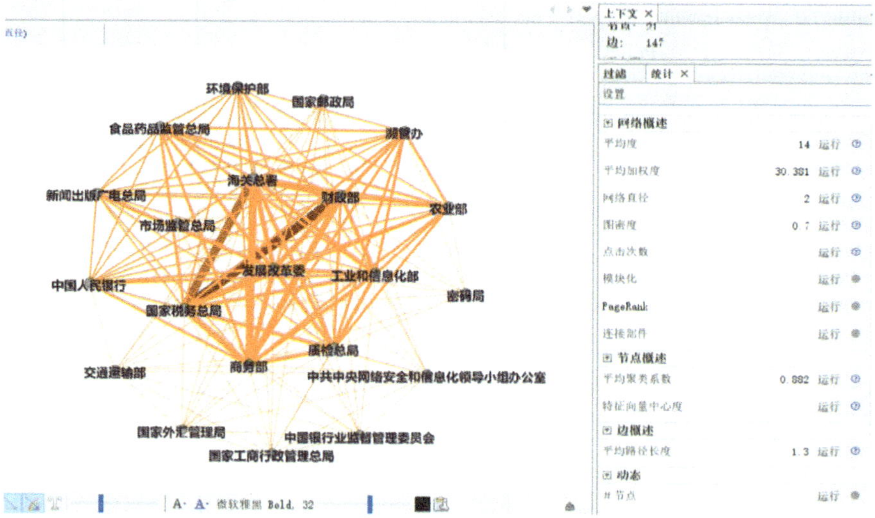

Fig. 7.4 Network characteristic indicators of cross-border e-commerce policy entities

the average number of cooperating institutions for each department is 14, indicating a high degree of cooperation between departments.

7.3 Cross-Border E-commerce Policy Action Field Visualization Analysis

Depending on the areas where policies are implemented, China's cross-border e-commerce policies can be divided into comprehensive promotion policies, cross-border tax policies, cross-border payment policies, cross-border supervision policies, cross-border informatization policies, and cross-border logistics policies. Comprehensive development promotion policies (16.2%) mainly include supporting cross-border e-commerce retail exports, promoting the healthy and rapid development of cross-border e-commerce, and setting up cross-border e-commerce comprehensive pilot zones. Cross-border tax policies (18.9%), cross-border payment policies (5.4%), and cross-border logistics policies (2.7%) provide support for the development of cross-border e-commerce. Cross-border supervision policies (40.5%) strongly regulate the cross-border e-commerce market, and cross-border e-commerce informatization policies (16.2%) can promote the development of the cross-border e-commerce industry and regulatory efficiency (as shown in Table 7.3).

However, government departments have not separately formulated cross-border e-commerce talent policies, but only included them in the content of relevant cross-border e-commerce policies. For example, the 2015 "Guiding Opinions on Promoting

Table 7.3 Areas in which the policy plays a role3

Areas	Policy	Main content	Specific gravity
Promoting development across the board	1, 6, 7, 16, 24, 26	Support cross-border e-commerce retail exports, promote the healthy and rapid development of cross-border e-commerce, and set up comprehensive pilot zones for cross-border e-commerce	16.2%
Cross-border e-commerce regulation	3, 5, 9, 10, 11, 12, 17, 19, 20, 22, 25, 27, 28, 31, 36	Standardize cross-border e-commerce system, supervision of import and export goods, monitoring of credit and risk system, standardize enterprise registration procedures, etc	40.5%
Cross-border e-commerce tax	2, 8, 14, 15, 21, 30, 33	Corporate tax payment, value-added tax, refund (exemption), etc	18.9%
Cross-border e-commerce payments	4, 13	Payment institution pilot application, rights and obligations, etc	5.4%
Cross-border e-commerce logistics	37	Delivery service enterprise main body, mode and system, etc	2.6%
Informatization construction	18, 23, 29, 32, 34, 35	Single window, cross-border unified edition system, data exchange mechanism, etc	16.2%

the Healthy and Rapid Development of Cross-Border E-Commerce" issued by the State Council Office proposed to jointly carry out cross-border e-commerce talent training with universities and vocational education institutions.

In the field of comprehensive promotion, policies mainly promote the development of cross-border e-commerce in the areas of innovation, supervision, logistics, risk, service, and cross-border e-commerce comprehensive pilot zones in the form of "strengthening", "supporting", and "promoting", as shown in Fig. 7.5a.

In terms of cross-border e-commerce taxation, policies mainly regulate the tax aspects of cross-border e-commerce in terms of retail imported goods, exported goods, value-added tax, consumption tax, and dutiable price in the form of "execution", "notification", "principle", "regulation", etc., as shown in Fig. 7.5b.

In terms of cross-border e-commerce payment, policies mainly regulate the declaration and promotion of payment business by cross-border e-commerce payment institutions in terms of payment institutions, banks, foreign exchange, transactions, etc., in the form of "regulation", "management", "requirement", "submission", etc., as shown in Fig. 7.5c.

In terms of cross-border e-commerce supervision, the main method is for customs to supervise cross-border e-commerce retail, enterprises, goods, quality, safety, bonded, inspection and quarantine, logistics, etc., in the form of "should", "regulation", "implementation", etc., as shown in Fig. 7.5d.

In terms of cross-border e-commerce logistics, the main method is to provide cross-border delivery services in the form of "improvement", "development", and

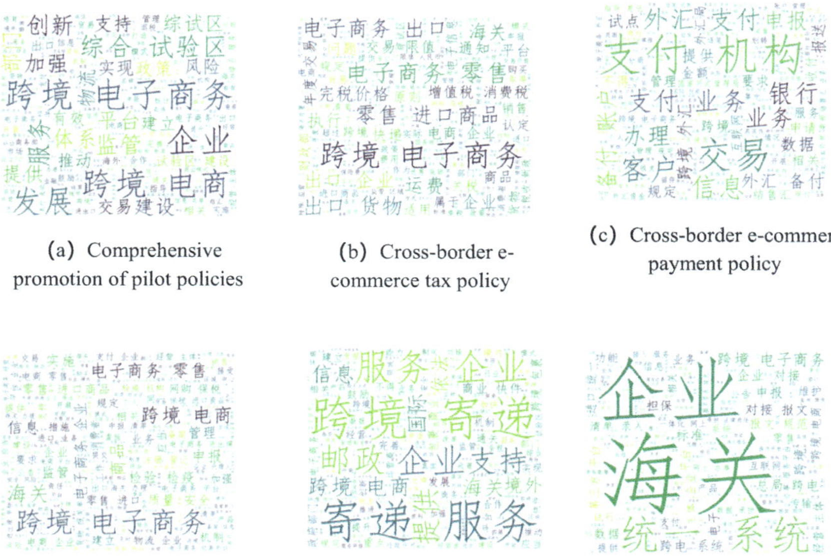

(a) Comprehensive promotion of pilot policies

(b) Cross-border e-commerce tax policy

(c) Cross-border e-commerce payment policy

(d) Cross-border e-commerce regulatory policy

(e) Cross-border e-commerce logistics policy

(f) Cross border e-commerce informatization policy

Fig. 7.5 Cross-border e-commerce policy word cloud analysis by domain (a) Comprehensive promotion of pilot policies, (b) Cross-border e-commerce tax policy, (c) Cross-border e-commerce payment policy, (d) Cross-border e-commerce regulatory policy, (e) Cross-border e-commerce logistics policy, (f) Cross-border e-commerce informatization policy

"encouragement", as shown in Fig. 7.5e; in terms of cross-border e-commerce informatization construction, the main participants are customs and enterprises, and currently, the data information of enterprises is docked with the unified system of customs according to a unified standard, as shown in Fig. 7.5f.

7.3.1 Visualization Analysis of Cross-Border E-commerce Policy Tools

In China's central-level cross-border e-commerce policies, the number of environmental policy tools used is the highest, accounting for 74.51% of all policy analysis units, followed by supply-type and evaluation-type policy tools, which account for 14.52% and 8.06% respectively, and demand-type policy tools account for only 2.9% (see Fig. 7.6). This shows that China's cross-border e-commerce policy structure is dominated by environmental policies, which is in line with the reality that China's cross-border e-commerce policy is in the exploration stage, and shows that the government is currently working hard to improve and regulate the cross-border e-commerce environment. Supply-type and evaluation-type policy tools promote each other, and demand-type policy tools are extremely scarce, which is a key point to be paid attention to in the subsequent improvement of policies.

(1) Environmental Policy Tools Dominate the Regulation

In the development of cross-border e-commerce, policies mainly regulate the environment directly or indirectly through legal systems, business supervision, public services, etc. In terms of environmental policy tools, they mainly revolve around the relevant definitions and regulatory regulations of cross-border e-commerce (64.5%). This indicates that the cross-border e-commerce industry cannot completely replicate the experience of international trade and e-commerce development. It needs to deeply analyze this special form of cross-border e-commerce and strengthen the exploration and regulation of emerging cross-border e-commerce formats. As cross-border e-commerce gradually develops, the industry's demand for credit systems, risk prevention, business supervision, public services, etc., is gradually increasing, and the policy system supporting cross-border e-commerce business is gradually being valued.

(2) Supply and Evaluation-Type Dual Promotion

Supply-type (14.5%) and evaluation-type (8.6%) policy tools promote the development of cross-border e-commerce through guidance and feedback. From the perspective of supply-type policy tools, decision support accounts for 51.1%, including decision-making deployment, organizational leadership, and simplification of administration. Service guidance accounts for 37.8% as a supplement, while support provided in terms of funds, talent, and technology is relatively weak,

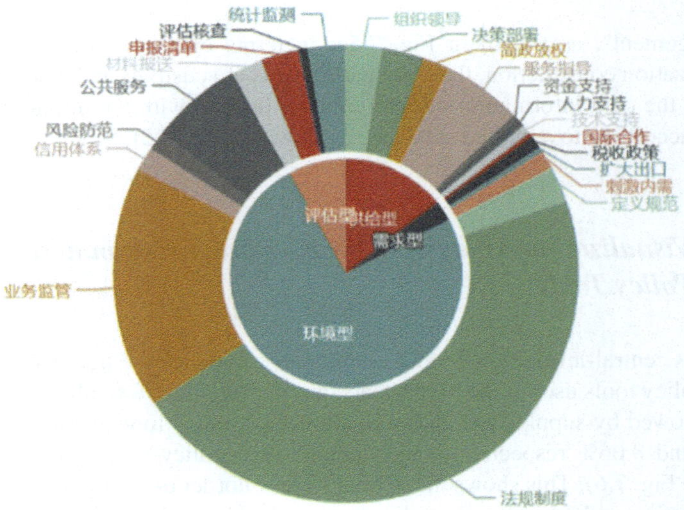

Fig. 7.6 Combined application of policy tools1

accounting for only 10% in total. Evaluation-type policy tools mainly include statistical evaluations by departments such as customs and the Ministry of Commerce, and business statistics and data declarations by payment institutions, embedded in supply-type and environmental-type policy tools in the form of policy combinations. For example, the State Council requires the establishment of a new type of customs supervision model for e-commerce exports and special statistics, and the State Administration of Foreign Exchange requires branches to be responsible for self-examination of abnormal transactions found in daily monitoring work.

7.4 Demand-Type Policy Tools Are Seriously Lacking

The use of demand-type tools is significantly lacking, accounting for only 2.9% of all cross-border e-commerce policy tools. Cross-border e-commerce demand-type policy tools include international cooperation, tax norms, expanding exports, and stimulating domestic demand. In order to expand the international market and increase the activity of China's cross-border e-commerce, the General Office of the State Council, the Ministry of Commerce, etc., proposed to strengthen cooperation with countries and regions along the "Belt and Road" in the field of e-commerce, and to open up safe and efficient cross-border e-commerce channels; the State Post Bureau, the Ministry of Commerce, and the General Administration of Customs jointly issued a document aimed at promoting cooperation with the destination or origin country of cross-border parcels, especially the docking with the customs of key export countries for cross-border e-commerce in countries and regions along the "Belt and Road", North America, Europe, etc., to improve the level of overseas information clearance and international demand.

Policy tools are applied differently in different areas of cross-border e-commerce (see Fig. 7.7). The color difference in the figure represents different categories. From left to right on the horizontal axis are: pilot promotion policy, cross-border supervision policy, cross-border tax policy, cross-border payment policy, cross-border logistics policy, and information policy tool structure. The size of the rectangle represents the frequency of application of policy tools in this policy area. As can be seen from the figure, environmental policy tools are most used in the field of cross-border e-commerce supervision. In the areas of pilot promotion development, cross-border e-commerce logistics, and information construction, the application of evaluation and demand-type policy tools is very limited.

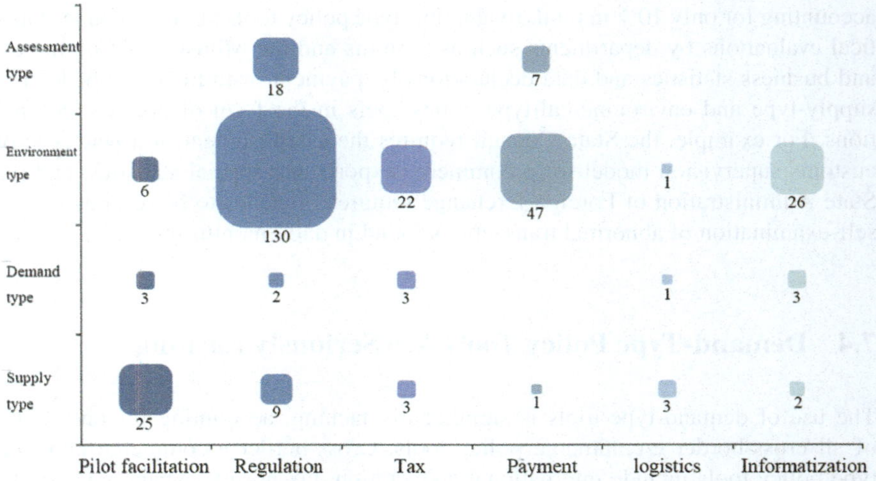

Fig. 7.7 Application of policy tools in various areas of cross-border e-commerce

7.4.1 *Visualization of the Evolution Process of Cross-Border E-commerce Policy*

7.4.1.1 Stages of Cross-Border E-commerce Policy Evolution

The central-level cross-border e-commerce policy refers to a series of policies proposed by the State Council and various ministries to regulate the order of the cross-border e-commerce industry and promote the healthy and rapid development of the cross-border e-commerce ecosystem. This section analyzes the development status of cross-border e-commerce over the years, the differences in policy effects on the links of the cross-border e-commerce ecosystem, the focus areas of policies at different times, and the application of policy tools, dividing cross-border e-commerce policies into four stages: preliminary exploration, support and promotion, standard promotion, and comprehensive development (see Fig. 7.8). Moreover, China's central-level cross-border e-commerce policies from 2013 to 2019 peaked at different levels in 2013, 2016, and 2018. The policies implemented at different stages cover cross-border e-commerce pilots, regulatory systems, quality supervision, customs taxation, cross-border payments, cross-border logistics, and information construction, etc.

From the analysis of the characteristics of each stage of cross-border e-commerce policy, not only can the laws and focus of policy changes be mined, but also the effects of policy implementation can be preliminarily judged based on the focus of the policy, therefore, this article uses Echarts visualization method to study the output of cross-border e-commerce policy.

(1) Preliminary Exploration Stage (Before 2012)

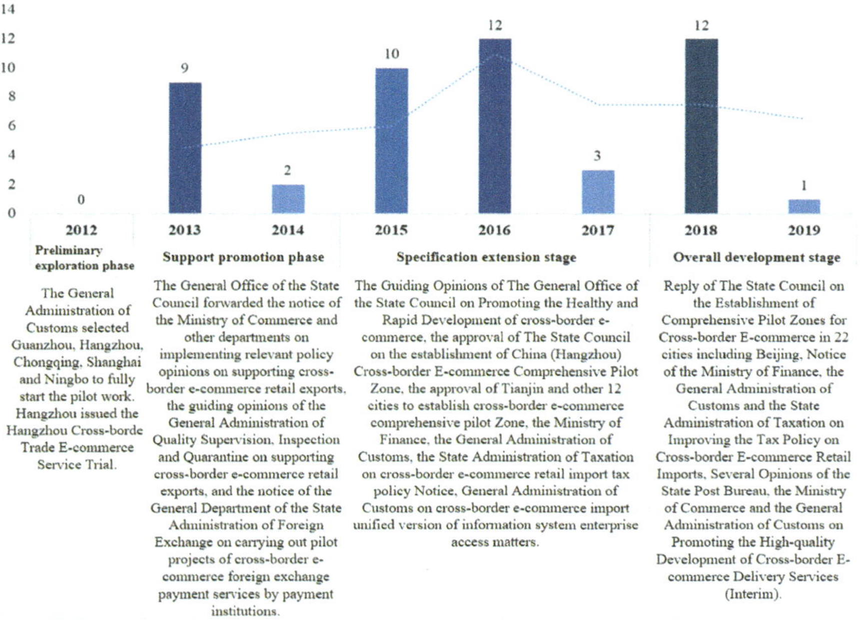

Fig. 7.8 Central-level core cross-border e-commerce policy development stage

Before 2012, the state did not introduce direct policies to promote the development of cross-border e-commerce, and the cross-border e-commerce ecosystem was in its initial formation. In terms of imports, the overseas personal shopping service mainly participated and promoted by overseas students, rose, and platforms focusing on shopping services gradually appeared, forming an initial shopping market. In terms of exports, cross-border e-commerce platforms represented by Alibaba International, Dunhuang Network, and AliExpress successively emerged. Domestic suppliers posted product information on these platforms and sold products directly to foreign intermediaries through international logistics. The foreign intermediaries then sold the products to the final customers.

At this stage, suppliers, consumers, and the core entities of cross-border shopping and cross-border platforms are gathered into the system. Cross-border e-commerce began to face problems such as difficulty in ensuring product quality and safety, low customs clearance efficiency, inability to settle foreign exchange and refund taxes, and traditional regulatory policies could not be directly applied to cross-border e-commerce, which posed an urgent need for the formulation and implementation of cross-border e-commerce policies. In 2012, the General Administration of Customs selected Shanghai, Chongqing, Hangzhou, Ningbo, and Zhengzhou to set up cross-border trade e-commerce service pilots, focusing on the research of cross-border e-commerce-related basic information standards, the formulation of management systems, and the improvement of customs clearance management and service levels.

(2) Support and Promotion Stage (2013 – 2014)

During the support and promotion stage of cross-border e-commerce policy (2013 – 2014), the State Council and its ministries officially issued policies to support cross-border e-commerce retail exports. Government departments began to intervene in the cross-border e-commerce ecosystem and focused on payment and regulatory links. The policy mainly involved cross-border e-commerce transactions, cross-border e-commerce payment pilots, and business declaration, etc. Payment institutions and foreign exchange institutions officially became part of the cross-border e-commerce ecosystem (see Figs. 7.9 and 7.10), with high-frequency words and word frequency in policy texts as shown in Table 7.4.

Combining word frequency analysis with the development of cross-border e-commerce in the promotion stage, in the field of cross-border e-commerce payment, by setting up pilot projects for cross-border e-commerce foreign exchange payment business in Shanghai, Beijing, Chongqing, Zhejiang, and Shenzhen, it has brought convenience for domestic entities to trade goods and services on international e-commerce platforms, effectively ensuring the safety of cross-border e-commerce transactions and reducing the risk of foreign exchange payments through Internet channels. In the field of cross-border e-commerce supervision, the General Administration of Customs has added "cross-border trade e-commerce" supervision method and "bonded cross-border trade e-commerce" supervision method, refining and clarifying the supervision work of cross-border e-commerce goods transit. In the field of cross-border e-commerce taxation, financial departments and tax departments have formulated different tax systems for specific cross-border goods. In the field of informatization construction, local governments and customs have begun to build cross-border e-commerce public service platforms and cross-border e-commerce

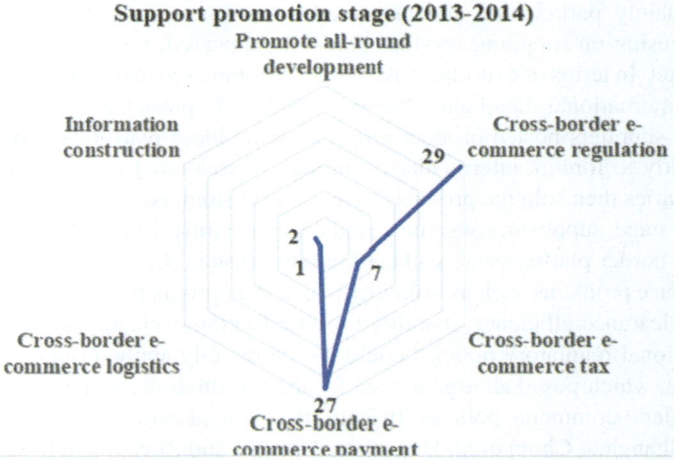

Fig. 7.9 Support policy measurement in the promotion phase

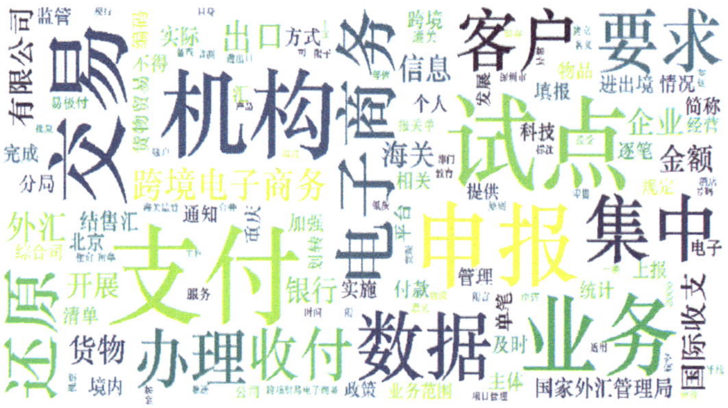

Fig. 7.10 Policy word cloud in support promotion phase

customs service platforms, which are helpful for obtaining cross-border e-commerce enterprise information and improving overall customs clearance efficiency.

7.5 Standardization and Promotion Stage (2015 – 2017)

In the early stage of cross-border e-commerce ecology, cross-border e-commerce policies mainly focused on standardizing cross-border supervision, but there were still problems of unfair tax burden caused by postal tax under the old rules in the field of cross-border e-commerce taxation. During the standardization and promotion stage of the policy (2015 – 2017), our country aimed to optimize the business environment and strengthen cross-border e-commerce supervision, mainly standardizing cross-border e-commerce taxation, cross-border e-commerce informatization construction, and pilot development (see Figs. 7.11 and 7.12).

From the perspective of promoting the healthy and high-quality development of our country's cross-border e-commerce ecology, the high-frequency words and word frequency of policy texts are shown in Table 7.5.

Combining the high-frequency words of cross-border e-commerce policy with the development of cross-border e-commerce in the standardization and development stage, in 2016, although the series of policies formulated by government departments for traditional cross-border e-commerce tax issues caused a large fluctuation in the transaction volume of cross-border e-commerce, the subsequent targeted transitional policies effectively alleviated the pressure caused by the reform of cross-border e-commerce tax policy. In addition, the cross-border e-commerce ecology includes enterprise registration, information release, product selection, payment settlement, inspection and quarantine, tax refund and other links, facing problems such as multiple departments involved, mismatched data between departments, and

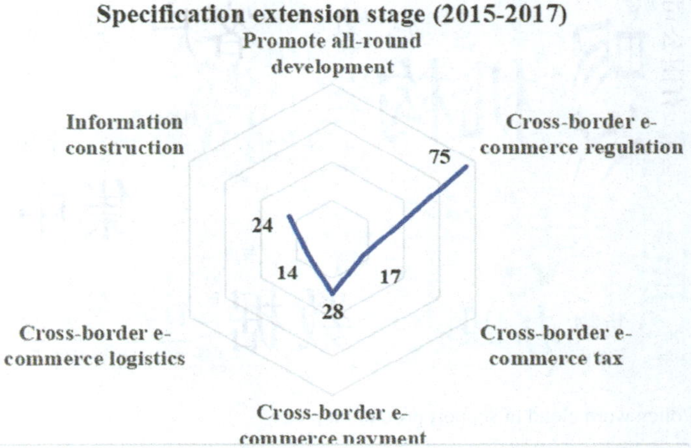

Fig. 7.11 Policy measurement in the standard promotion stage

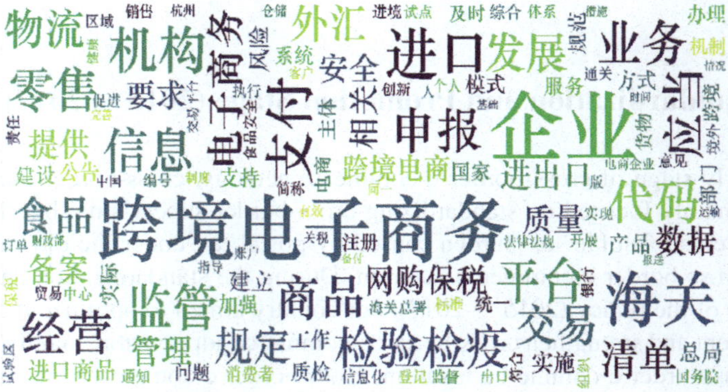

Fig. 7.12 Policy word cloud in the regulation promotion phase

a sharp increase in small packages for customs clearance, the General Administration of Customs uses the cross-border e-commerce customs clearance service platform for distribution and tax refund, and government departments build cross-border e-commerce public service platforms for data collection and enterprise supervision.

In addition, the improvement of the unified version system of cross-border e-commerce retail import and the informatization management system of cross-border e-commerce retail import and export inspection and quarantine and the approval of 12 cities such as Tianjin to establish cross-border e-commerce comprehensive experimental zones have injected great vitality into the development of our country's cross-border e-commerce ecology.

Table 7.4 2013 – 2014 cross-border e-commerce policy.

High-frequency Words	Word frequency	High-frequency words	Word frequency	High-frequency words	Word frequency
Payment	235	Cross-border e-commerce	77	Settlement and sale of foreign exchange	42
Pilot	217	Export	76	Within borders	38
Agencies	190	Forex	71	Notices	37
Trading	175	Cargo	66	Statistics	37
Declare	168	Enterprise	63	Individual	35
Business	155	The Message	55	Body	35
Data	113	Limited Company	52	Items	34
Concentration	107	Bank	51	Cross-border	56
E-commerce	95	Balance of payments	48	Checklist	23
The Client	91	Customs	47	Management	23
Receiving and Paying	79	National Forex	45	Supervision	23

7.6 Comprehensive Promotion Stage (2018 and Later)

Since 2018, with the introduction of the "People's Republic of China E-commerce Law", our country's cross-border e-commerce policy has entered a comprehensive development stage, especially in the fields of cross-border e-commerce supervision, informatization construction, cross-border e-commerce logistics, etc., as shown in Figs. 7.13 and 7.14.

Combining the high-frequency words of cross-border e-commerce policy with the comprehensive promotion stage of cross-border e-commerce development, in the field of cross-border e-commerce taxation and supervision, departments such as the General Administration of Customs and the Ministry of Finance. Successive standardization work has been carried out on matters such as the customs registration and management of cross-border e-commerce companies, the improvement of tax collection on retail imports of cross-border e-commerce, and the supervision of import and export goods. In the field of cross-border e-commerce logistics, in February 2019, the State Post Bureau, the Ministry of Commerce, and the General Administration of Customs jointly issued "Several Opinions on Promoting the High-Quality Development of Cross-Border E-commerce Delivery Services" to ensure the safe delivery of cross-border items and reduce logistics costs. In the field of pilot promotion and informatization construction, the number of comprehensive pilot areas for cross-border e-commerce increased from 13 cities established before 2018 (established in 2015 and 2016) to 105 cities nationwide. The mature practices of the "two platforms" of online comprehensive services and offline industrial parks, as well as the

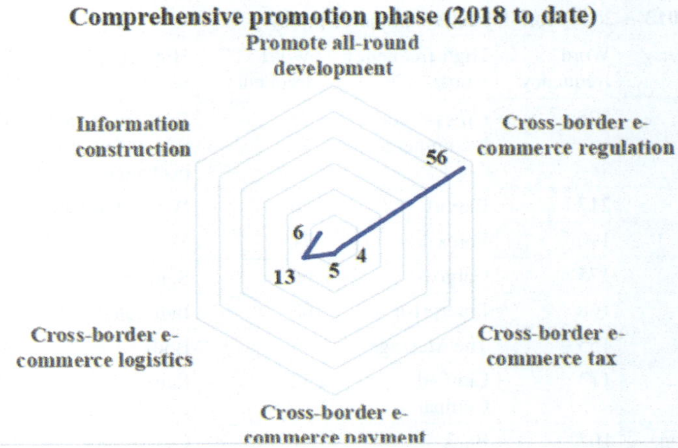

Fig. 7.13 Policy word cloud in the overall promotion phase

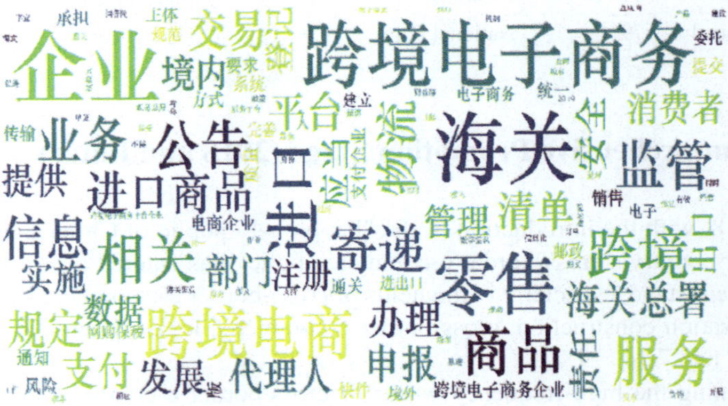

Fig. 7.14 Policy measurement in the overall promotion phase

"six systems" of information sharing, financial services, intelligent logistics, risk prevention and control, etc., explored by the first few batches of comprehensive pilot areas, are being replicated and promoted nationwide, making China's cross-border e-commerce ecosystem increasingly rich and complex. The high-frequency words and word frequencies of policy texts are shown in Table 7.6.

Table 7.5 High-frequency words and word frequencies of cross-border e-commerce policy from 2015 to 2017

High-frequency Words	Word frequency	High-frequency words	Word frequency	High-frequency words	Word frequency
Enterprise	337	Regulations	75	Quality inspection	42
Cross-border e-commerce	294	Checklist	75	Specifications	41
Customs	180	E-commerce	73	Body	40
Import	156	Online shopping bonded	71	Registration	40
Pay	145	Safety	71	Mechanics	40
Agencies	135	Quality	67	Unified	38
Supervision	124	Filing	65	E-commerce	37
Merchandise	114	Management	63	Cargo	35
The Information	113	Data	62	Cross-Border	35
Operating	111	Import and export	61	Consumer	34
Code	110	Cross-border e-commerce	61	General	34
Declaration	108	Imported goods	61	General administration of customs	34
Business	104	Products	59	Opinions	33
Retail	104	Risks	57	Notices	33
Platform	100	Service	49	System	32
Inspection and quarantine	95	System	46	Registration	32
Trading	87	Announcement	45	Standard	32
Food	81	Fortify	45	Trade	32
Logistics	80	Country	43	Execute	31
Forex	76	Support	43	Informatization	31

7.6.1 Cross-Border E-commerce Policy Evolution Characteristics

(1) Form of Cross-Border E-commerce Policy Text

The forms of cross-border e-commerce policy texts analyzed in this article include notifications, guiding opinions, replies, letters, announcements, and opinions. From 2013 to 2019, cross-border e-commerce policies were mainly in the form of notifications and announcements (see Fig. 7.15). These two types of texts account for 59.17% of the total (30.6% and 28.57% respectively), and they mainly guide specific

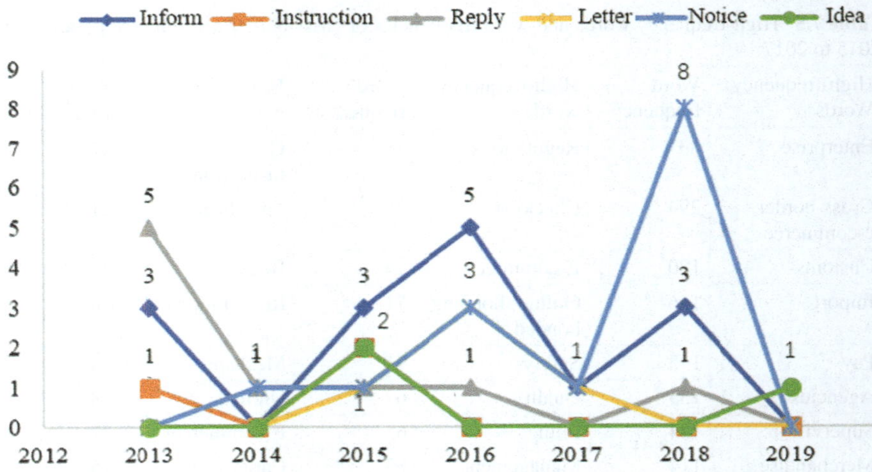

Fig. 7.15 Statistics on the forms of cross-border e-commerce policy documents at the central level

areas of cross-border e-commerce, have a wide range of knowledge, and are directly related to cross-border e-commerce companies.

"Announcement" type policy texts mainly focus on the supervision of import and export goods in the payment and information systems of cross-border e-commerce platform companies, while "notification" type policy texts mainly focus on cross-border e-commerce tax policies.

There are nine "reply" documents. The "reply" documents of cross-border e-commerce are mainly used for the central departments to reply to the requests of localities or enterprises. Among them, three replies are the State Council's replies on the establishment of cross-border e-commerce comprehensive pilot zones, and six are the comprehensive department of the State Administration of Foreign Exchange's replies on payment institutions to carry out cross-border e-commerce foreign exchange payment business pilots. There are a total of five "letters". The "letters" of cross-border e-commerce have communication and flexibility and have a discussion and guidance role in the construction of cross-border e-commerce comprehensive pilot zones and the standardization of cross-border e-commerce services.

There are three "guiding opinions" and "opinions". Among them, "guiding opinions" guide the development strategy of cross-border e-commerce from a macro level, setting the tone for the development of cross-border e-commerce in terms of overall direction and principles, while "opinions" implement specific measures for cross-border e-commerce from a micro level, emphasizing the feasibility of operations and methods. The rich forms of cross-border e-commerce policy texts show that the government, in the process of regulating and developing cross-border e-commerce, has both affirmed the strategic direction and provided ample space for exploration and experimentation.

(2) Nature of Cross-Border E-commerce Policy Text

Policy documents are generally divided into national normative documents, departmental normative documents, departmental work documents, and administrative approval documents according to the policy subject and the role of the policy. In 2013 and 2014, during the support and promotion phase, the development of cross-border e-commerce was mainly promoted by administrative approval documents to activate market entities; from 2015, the cross-border e-commerce policy entered the standard promotion phase, and the proportion of national normative documents and departmental normative documents gradually increased. In addition, to deeply integrate into the new business format and strengthen cognition and management, the number of cross-border e-commerce departmental work documents has also increased year by year; after 2018, as various departments gradually integrate into each link of the ecosystem, departmental normative documents have become the main cross-border e-commerce policy text, aiming to regulate the healthy development of each link of the ecosystem. This result also more powerfully confirms the argument of the four stages of cross-border e-commerce policy development mentioned above (see Table 7.7).

(3) High-Frequency Words in Cross-Border E-commerce Policy

Heatmap of cross-border e-commerce policy word frequency (see Fig. 7.16) through the combination of calendar and heatmap chart types, using continuous data distribution, the depth of color represents the frequency. The deeper the color, the more it tends toward pure red, indicating that this content is the policy direction that was more focused on in that year. In this way, the word frequency data of cross-border e-commerce policy texts from 2013 to 2019 are processed after text mining. In the heatmap, the horizontal axis represents the frequency change of the policy word in different years, and the vertical axis represents the emphasis of the policy content in the same year.

From the figure, in 2013 and 2014, "payment" was the focus of attention. As the cross-border e-commerce ecosystem gradually improved, transaction payments also matured, so the focus on "payment" gradually weakened; after 2015, the cross-border e-commerce industry gradually exploded, so "customs" and "supervision"-related cross-border e-commerce policy content became the focus, and government departments mainly strengthened the supervision of this industry; from 2013 to 2019, the attention to "risk" of cross-border e-commerce also increased year by year, the importance of "quality" and "dynamics" showed a cyclical pattern of intermittent prominence, and "enterprises" have always been an important subject of policy content.

(4) Citation Relationship of Cross-Border E-commerce Policy

According to the relationship between cross-border e-commerce policies, a policy reference derivative relationship diagram is constructed (see Fig. 7.17). The red circle in the middle represents the cross-border e-commerce policy formulated by the State Council. The surrounding blue, brown, brick red, and purple colors represent the policies of the departments under the State Council in taxation, customs supervision, foreign exchange, payment, and comprehensive test area approval. From the figure, it can be seen that during the support and promotion stage (2013 – 2014), the main documents were issued by the Foreign Exchange Bureau (Exchange Comprehensive

Table 7.6 High-frequency words and word frequency of cross-border e-commerce policy in 2018 – 2019

High-frequency Words	Word frequency	High-frequency words	Word frequency	High-frequency words	Word frequency
Enterprise	151	Platform	39	Cross-border e-commerce enterprises	27
Customs	138	Transact	39	Post	26
Cross-border e-commerce	114	General Administration of Customs	39	Requirements	25
Retail	99	Declare	39	Undertake	24
Imports	77	Pay	38	Sales	24
Cross-border e-commerce	70	Within borders	36	System	24
Service	65	Agent	35	E-commerce business	23
Related	65	Safe	34	Unify	22
Merchandise	65	Departments	34	Risk	21
Cross-Border	63	Development	33	Ways	20
Supervision	58	Consumer	33	Payment business	20
Shipping	56	Management	33	Body	20
Announcements	55	Supplied	32	Submit	19
Business	48	Implementation	31	Express	19
The Message	46	Should	30	Notices	19
Logistics	46	Responsibility	30	Quality	18
Imported goods	45	Registration	29	Clear stages	18
Trading	43	Export	28	Transmission	18
Regulations	41	Data	28	E-commerce	18
Checklist	40	Registration	27	Electronics	18

Reply) based on the cross-border e-commerce policy formulated by the State Council; during the standard promotion stage (2015–2017), the main documents were issued by the tax department (Tax Management Letter), and the finance department based on the cross-border e-commerce policy formulated by the State Council; during the comprehensive promotion stage (2018 and later), the General Administration of Customs, the Ministry of Commerce, and the Finance Department (Commerce and Finance) issued documents based on the cross-border e-commerce policy formulated by the State Council.

The reference relationship diagram reflects that after the central government introduced policies to promote the development of cross-border e-commerce, the departments under the State Council referred to this policy to further introduce policies

Table 7.7 Nature and characteristics of documents issued at each stage of cross-border e-commerce policies5

Stage Nature	Support facilitation phase	Regulation promotion stage	Overall promotion stage
National normative documents	9.1%	20%	0
Department specification documents	27.3%	40%	84.6%
Departmental working papers	9.1%	36%	15.4%
Administrative approval documents	54.5%	4%	0

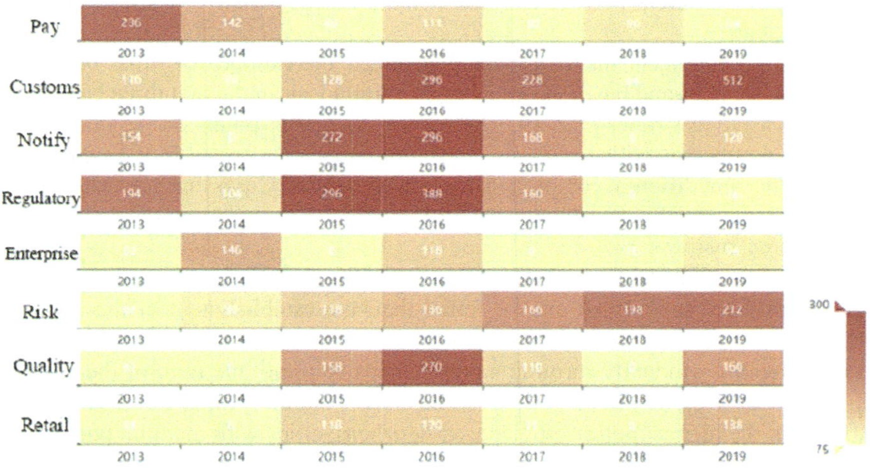

Figure 7.16 cross-border e-commerce policy word frequency heat map

covering cross-border e-commerce foreign exchange, payment, taxation, and supervision. However, the current policy reference situation still does not cover all aspects of the cross-border e-commerce ecosystem, such as logistics, informatization, talent cultivation. It is necessary to further form a cross-border e-commerce policy system corresponding to the cross-border e-commerce ecosystem.

(5) Cross-Border E-commerce Policy Efficiency

In the cross-border e-commerce ecosystem, suppliers, consumers, cross-border e-commerce platforms, and other communities are directly related to cross-border e-commerce transactions. The implementation of policies allows the main participants in cross-border e-commerce to maximize their business through self-adjustment.

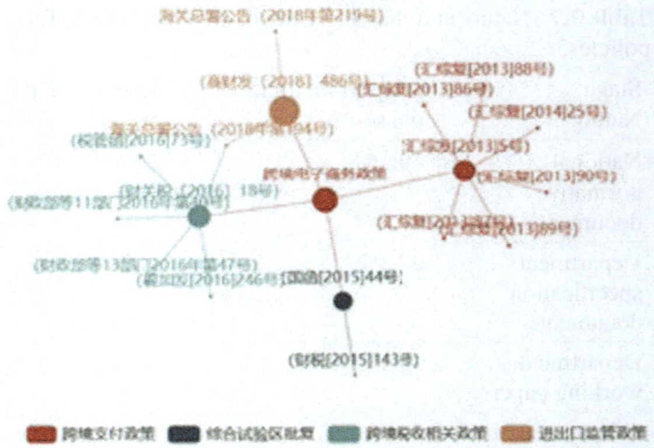

Fig. 7.17 Policy reference derivation relationship diagram

Therefore, the ratio of cross-border e-commerce policy input to business volume in a unit time at different periods can reflect the efficiency change of the policy to a certain extent.

Figure 7.18 reflects the relationship between the number of cross-border e-commerce policies and business volume in a certain year in the first three batches of comprehensive test zones in 2019. The size of the scatter points on the map represents the number of policy releases, and different scatter points in the coordinate system represent different comprehensive test zone cities. Cities that are farther away from the y-axis in the coordinate system indicate a larger volume of cross-border e-commerce business.

Figure 7.19 reflects the evolution of policy efficiency in the comprehensive test zone from 2014 to 2019. It can be found that: the establishment of the comprehensive test zone gradually shifted from the eastern part to the central and northeastern regions, gradually forming a comprehensive trend; the ratio of the number of cross-border e-commerce policies to business volume formed three categories: cities with the highest policy efficiency (Shenzhen), cities with medium policy efficiency (Hangzhou, Shanghai, Guangzhou, Yiwu, Dongguan), and cities where policy efficiency needs to be improved.

From the differences and changes in the policy efficiency of the comprehensive test zone, it can be found that the policy documents of the first two types of comprehensive test zone cities are basically in a continuous release state, which can reflect to a certain extent the differences in policy efficiency of different comprehensive test zones in promoting the business volume of cross-border e-commerce in the region. In conjunction with the cross-border e-commerce ecosystem proposed earlier, this suggests that newly established comprehensive test zones need to fully exploit local advantages according to local conditions, develop suitable industries, and carry out scientific evaluation and dynamic adjustment of policies according to the current development situation. In addition, from a national perspective, the inherent attributes of a city will affect the development of cross-border e-commerce, each comprehensive test zone should fully play the advantages of geographical location, industrial structure,

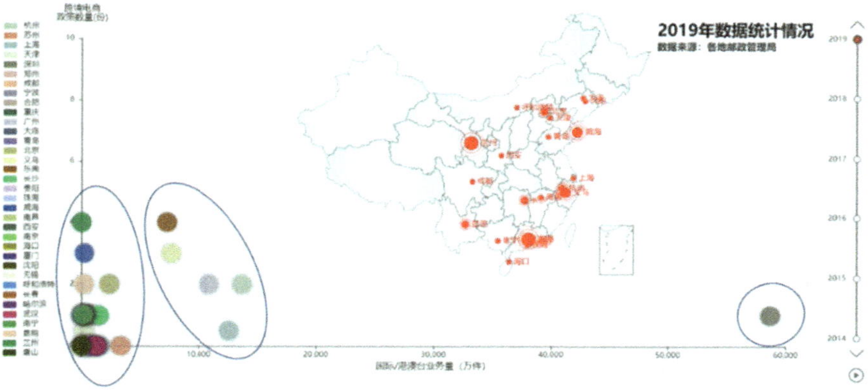

Fig. 7.18 Policy efficiency in the comprehensive pilot area (2019)

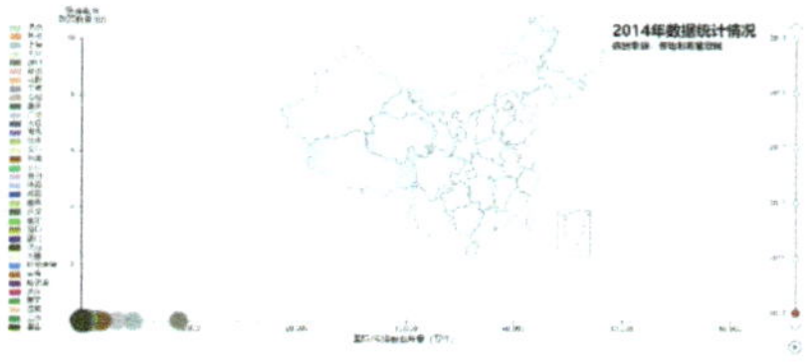

Policy Efficiency of the Comprehensive pilot area (2014)

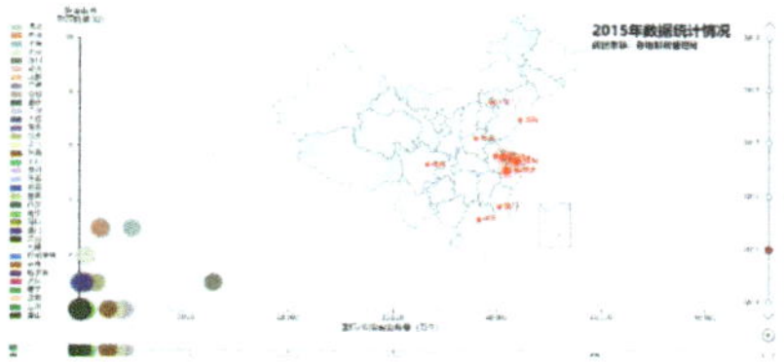

Policy efficiency of comprehensive pilot areas (2015)

Policy Efficiency of the Comprehensive pilot Area (2016)

Policy Efficiency of the Comprehensive pilot Area (2017)

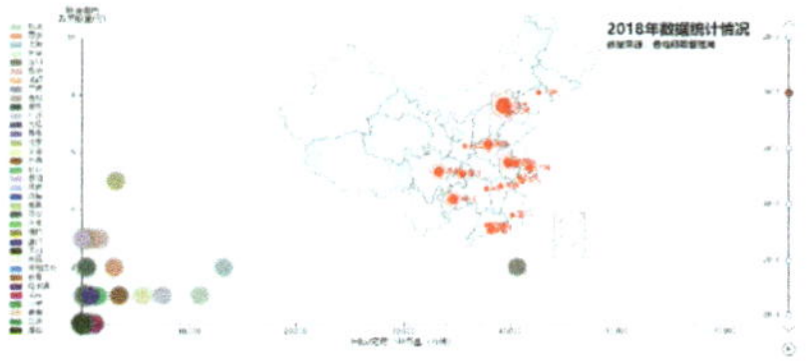

Policy Efficiency of the Comprehensive pilot Area (2018)

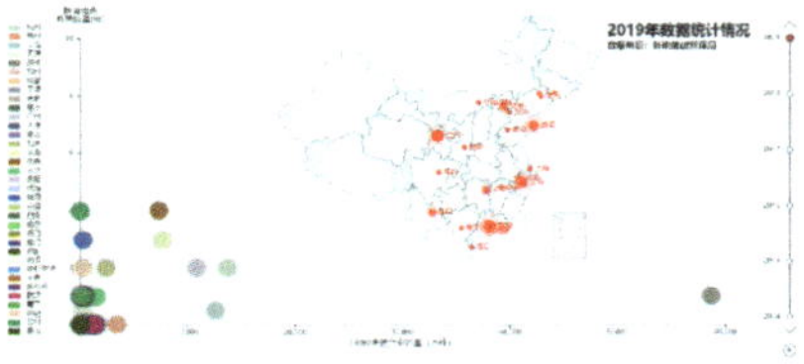

Policy Efficiency of the Comprehensive pilot Area (2019)

Fig. 7.19 Variation of policy efficiency differences in the comprehensive pilot area

population size, science and technology, etc., in the cross-border e-commerce ecological environment, strengthen the exchange and cooperation between comprehensive test zones, in order to achieve the healthy development of the national cross-border e-commerce ecology.

References

1. Peking University Law Treasure (2015) Notice of the general administration of quality supervision, inspection and quarantine on soliciting opinions on the "detailed rules for the supervision and management of food safety for cross-border e-commerce imports under the bonded online shopping model" [EB/OL]. Retrieved from http://www.pkulaw.cn/fulltext_form.aspx?Gid=1090526280&Db=protocol. Accessed on 26 Oct 2015
2. Department of E-commerce and Informatization, Ministry of Commerce (2016) Letter on publicly soliciting opinions on the "standards for cross-border commodity e-commerce business services" (draft for soliciting opinions) [EB/OL]. Retrieved from http://www.mofcom.gov.cn/article/h/redht/201603/20160301279134.shtml. Accessed on 21 Mar 2016
3. Hualv Network (2013) Reply of the comprehensive department of the state administration of foreign exchange on the pilot project of cross-border e-commerce foreign exchange payment business by Beijing Tongrongtong Information Technology Co., Ltd. and 4 other payment institutions [EB/OL]. Retrieved from https://www.66law.cn/tiaoli/51784.aspx. Accessed on 16 Sep 2013
4. Fuzhou News Network (2016) Reply of the general administration of customs on the implementation plan for cross-border e-commerce bonded imports in Fuzhou and Pingtan [EB/OL]. Retrieved from http://news.fznews.com.cn/fuzhou/20160125/56a5cd4c9ffef.shtml. Accessed on 25 Jan 2016
5. China Food Network (2016) Reply of the general office on the supervision issues of cross-border e-commerce food enterprises [EB/OL]. Retrieved from http://www.cnfood.com/news/show-222929.html. Accessed on 29 Aug 2016

Chapter 8
Study on the Policy Effect Evaluation of Cross-Border E-commerce

From the bibliometric and visualization analysis in Chapter 7, it can be found that the policy efficiency of the cross-border e-commerce comprehensive test area varies. Therefore, this chapter focuses on discussing and evaluating the implementation effect of the comprehensive test area policy and analyzes the impact of environmental factors in the cross-border e-commerce ecosystem on policy execution.

8.1 Sample Selection and Data Source

(1) Sample Selection of Cross-Border E-commerce Comprehensive Test Area

This article takes the cross-border e-commerce comprehensive test area as the entry point for the comprehensive promotion policy field of cross-border e-commerce and selects the comprehensive test area pilot policy implemented by the State Council as the research object. The main reasons are as follows: in recent years, the cross-border e-commerce comprehensive test areas approved by the State Council have gradually spread across the country, and their policy implementation scope is wider. The comprehensive test area policy can promote the comprehensive development of the city's cross-border e-commerce industry, and the policy direction is more representative; the comprehensive test areas are established in batches over time, implementing a model of "first trial, first implementation, and gradual promotion". This characteristic has the nature of a "quasi-natural experiment", which can provide a good sample set for empirical research.

(2) Data, Variables, and Descriptive Analysis

In the research on measuring the development level of cross-border e-commerce, Wu Fen uses import and export turnover as the explained variable to measure the level of foreign economic development [[1]], Zhang Xibao selects the number of city express deliveries to reflect the level of cross-border e-commerce transactions [[2]], Zhang

L. Xiong and H. Wang, *User Driven Cross-Border E-Commerce Platform Competition and Policy Analysis*, Advanced Studies in E-Commerce,
https://doi.org/10.1007/978-981-97-3835-9_8

Xia Heng believes that the number and scale of enterprises can reflect the development of the cross-border e-commerce industry [[3]]. Therefore, referring to existing research and the availability of related data, this article mainly uses the total amount of imports and exports (*frtrade*), the number of international and Hong Kong, Macao, and Taiwan express parcels (*express*), and the number of registered cross-border e-commerce companies (*company*) as the explained variables to measure the development of China's cross-border e-commerce pilot zones. The original data of this article comes from the China City Statistical Yearbook, local post and telecommunications bureaus, local transportation bureaus, and the Tianyancha official website. The total import and export volume reflects the city's foreign trade development in that year, the number of international and Hong Kong, Macao, and Taiwan express parcels reflects the city's cross-border e-commerce business development in that year, and the number of registered cross-border e-commerce companies reflects the city's cross-border e-commerce industry development in that year, including different entities in the cross-border e-commerce industry: suppliers, marketers, payment companies, and all registered companies in the cross-border e-commerce industry.

Existing research has confirmed that the establishment of cross-border e-commerce pilot zones has promoted local trade facilitation [[2]], however, different cross-border e-commerce pilot zones have different cultivation and regulation of local cross-border e-commerce new business formats, so this study further introduces the number of cross-border e-commerce policies to measure the "pilot policy of the comprehensive pilot zone" core explanatory variable, that is, the two explanatory variables of the establishment of the comprehensive pilot zone and the internal policy of the pilot zone are used to measure the development of cross-border e-commerce.

That is: at the national level, whether city i in year t is set up as a cross-border e-commerce pilot zone dummy variable $Exper_{it}$, if there is, take 1; otherwise, take 0; at the local level, the cumulative number of cross-border e-commerce policies $Policy_{it}$ issued by city i by the end of the year t. The data comes from the National Bureau of Statistics, the China City Statistical Yearbook, and the China Transportation Yearbook.

In order to control other factors that affect the development of cross-border e-commerce in the comprehensive test area, combined with existing related literature and real mechanism analysis, this paper takes city scale (*people*)[[2]], economic development (*grp*)[[2]], government scale (*gov*)[[4]], and transportation development (*transport*)[[5]] as control variables in the model. The data comes from the National Bureau of Statistics, the China City Statistical Yearbook, and the China Transportation Yearbook which reflects the government's ability to provide public services and its role in promoting the development of cross-border e-commerce; the level of transportation development (*sport*)[[2]], innovation capability (*inno*)[[1]], level of information development (*info*)[[2]], and industrial structure (*indu*)[[2]] are selected as control variables. The city size (*people*) reflects the degree of aggregation of city producers, suppliers, and consumers, and suppliers and consumers are necessary conditions for the development of cross-border e-commerce ecology; the level of economic development (*grp*) is the foundation for the development of cross-border e-commerce, reflecting the ability to aggregate various economic resources; the size of the government (*gov*). The role of urban public infrastructure in providing "hard power" and "soft power" support for cross-border e-commerce not only can provide cross-border e-commerce public services such as public service platforms, but also regulate and standardize the cross-border e-commerce ecosystem through regulatory departments; the optimization and upgrading of industrial structure (*indu*) is an important factor in promoting the improvement of urban "soft power", especially the development of service industries represented by customs declaration, marketing, finance, etc., provides the driving force for the development of the cross-border e-commerce ecosystem; the degree of transportation development (*transport*) will greatly affect the development of cross-border e-commerce logistics; the development of informatization (*info*) represented by the expansion of the Internet, is an essential factor for cross-border e-commerce sales and transactions. All variables and meanings are shown in Table 8.1.

8.2 Evaluation of the Policy Effect of the Cross-Border E-commerce Comprehensive Test Area

8.2.1 Multi-Period Double Difference Method Baseline Model

For the five batches of cross-border e-commerce comprehensive test areas that have been established, considering the demonstration role of the first few batches of comprehensive test areas, this article selects the cities of the first four batches of cross-border e-commerce comprehensive test areas in our country as samples, the first three batches of comprehensive test areas as the experimental group, and the fourth batch of comprehensive test area cities as the control group, to empirically analyze the policy effect of the establishment of the cross-border e-commerce comprehensive test area on local cross-border trade and economic growth. Specifically, this article sets the 35 cross-border e-commerce comprehensive test area cities established in the first three batches in 2015, 2016, and 2018 as the experimental group, and the 24 cities established in the fourth batch in 2019 as the control group, constructing virtual variables for the experimental group and the control group, setting the experimental group as 1 (i.e., the comprehensive test areas established before 2019 are set as the experimental group), and the control group as 0 (i.e., the comprehensive test areas established in 2019 and later are set as the control group). If according to the double difference method, the baseline regression model constructed is as shown in formula (8.1):

$$y_{it} = \beta_0 + \beta_1 * Time + \beta_2 * Treated_i + \beta_3 * Time * Treated_i + \beta_4 * X_{it} + \varepsilon \quad (8.1)$$

In the formula, the y_{it} is the dependent variable, measuring the development level of the cross-border e-commerce pilot zone, with specific indicators including foreign

Table 8.1 Descriptive statistics of major variables1

Variables Type	Variables	Meaning	sample number	Mean	Criteria poor	Mini-mum value	Max value
Be explained Variables	lnfrtrade	Foreign trade, take the correct value[[1]]	354	6.93	1.82	0.57	11.67
	lnexpress	Number of cross-border deliveries, take the correct value[[2]]	352	4.61	2.78	6.27	10.98
	company	Total number of filings by cross-border e-commerce enterprises[[3]]	279	2.49	1.47	0	6.44
Policy Variables	Exper	Whether it is set up as a comprehensive pilot area (at the national level)	354	0.34	0.47	0	1
	Policy	Cumulative number of policies issued from the establishment of comprehensive pilot zones to a certain year (at the regional level)	354	0.40	0.88	0	5
Controls Variables	lnpeople	City size, take logarithm[[2]]	354	6.34	0.97	0.93	8.05
	lngrp	Economic development, take the logarithm[[2]]	354	8.42	1.20	4.54	16.94
	lngov	Size of government, take logarithm[[1]]	354	6.52	1.01	2.93	9.03
	indu	Industrial structure[57]	354	54.46	11.37	24.95	90.8
	lninfo	Level of informatization development, logarithm[57]	354	5.18	1.08	1.14	8.39

(continued)

Table 8.1 (continued)

Variables Type	Variables	Meaning	sample number	Mean	Criteria poor	Mini-mum value	Max value
	lntransport	Degree of traffic development, logarithm[[2]]	354	9.66	0.90	5.86	11.58
	lninno	Innovation ability, take logarithm[[2]]	354	9.66	1.79	1.79	12.47

trade, international and Hong Kong, Macao and Taiwan express delivery quantity and company quantity, X_{it} is the set of other control variables, β is the coefficient of the explanatory variable, ε is the random error term. However, the formula only applies to the situation where the pilot zones are established in the same batch. From 2015 to 2021, 105 cities were designated as pilot zones in five batches at different years. If the time for each city to be approved as a pilot zone is set uniformly, it will not conform to the actual situation and will affect the accuracy of the experimental results. Therefore, this study further optimizes the model into a multi-period double difference benchmark model, as shown in formula (8.2).

$$y_{it} = \beta_0 + \beta_1 * Exper_{it} + \lambda * \sum_{n} X_{it} + \mu_i + f_t + \varepsilon_{it} \tag{8.2}$$

In formula 8.3, the multi-period double difference model does not directly reflect the group variable of the original double difference model *Treated*, time variable *Time* and difference variable $Time * Treated_i$, and converted into a dummy variable $Exper_{it}$ for further analysis, where, i represents the city, t represents the year, y_{it} represents the level of cross-border e-commerce development.

$$Exper_{it} = T_i * P_t \tag{8.3}$$

In formula (8.3), T_i is a between-group dummy variable, indicating whether the city is set up as a cross-border e-commerce pilot zone. If so, it is valued at 1, otherwise it is 0, P_t is a policy dummy variable, valued at 1 in the year of the pilot zone establishment and thereafter, otherwise it is 0. Then, $Exper_{it}$ is a dummy variable for whether each city is a pilot zone, i.e., if the experimental group city i The period before being established as a comprehensive test area, dummy variable $Exper_{it}$ is 0, the year of the establishment of the comprehensive test area and the years after $Exper_{it}$ is 1, the control group is all 0. $\sum_n X_{it}$ are economic, social, transportation, informatization and other control variables (see Table 8.2), the model controls regional fixed effects μ_i and time fixed effects f_t, β_0 is the constant term, γ is the regression coefficient of the control variables.

In this empirical study, the focus is on β_1 regression result, if $\beta_1 > 0$, it indicates that the establishment of the comprehensive test area can promote the development

Table 8.2 Variable selection and description2

Category of Variables	Variables	Indicators	Measurement
Explained variables	frtrade	foreign trade	Total City Import and export Volume, China City Statistical Yearbook
	express	Logistics level	City international Hong Kong, Macao and Taiwan express volume, the official website of each city post and telecommunications bureau
	company	Cross-border e-commerce enterprises	The total number of cross-border e-commerce enterprises registered in the city, Tianyan check the official website
Explanatory variables	Exper	Grouping variable	Whether it is approved to be set up as a comprehensive pilot area
	Policy	Policy variables	Total number of cross-border e-commerce policies implemented in the region
Control variables	people	City size	Urban Population, China Urban Statistical Yearbook
	grp	Economic size	Gross National Product of the region, China Urban Statistical Yearbook
	gov	Size of government	Public Finance Expenditure, China Urban Statistical Yearbook
	indu	Upgrading of industrial structure	Proportion of Tertiary Industry, China Urban Statistical Yearbook
	info	Information development level	Number of Internet broadband access users, China City Statistical Yearbook
	transport	Level of transport development	Highway freight volume, official website of each city transportation bureau
	innovate	The ability to innovate	Number of patent applications of the city in the current year, China City Statistical Yearbook
	Year	A given year	Year – The year when the cross-border e-commerce Comprehensive Experimental Zone was established

of cross-border e-commerce in this area compared to the control group, otherwise, it does not promote the development of cross-border e-commerce. Based on formula (8.2), to test the impact of the number of policies implemented after the establishment of the comprehensive test area on the city's cross-border e-commerce, this paper further uses *policy* as a policy dummy variable for analysis, representing the comprehensive test area i the cumulative number of cross-border e-commerce policy documents issued in the t year, as shown in formula (8.4):

$$y_{it} = \beta_0 + \beta_1 * Policy_{it} + \lambda * \sum_n X_{it} + \mu_i + f_t + \varepsilon_{it} \tag{8.4}$$

$$Policy_{it} = T_i * P_t \tag{8.5}$$

In formulas (8.4) and (8.5), *i* represents the city, *t* represents the year, Q_i is a group dummy variable, representing the cumulative number of cross-border e-commerce policies issued by the city, P_t. It is a policy dummy variable, set to 1 for the year and thereafter when established as a cross-border e-commerce pilot zone, otherwise 0.

8.2.2 Empirical Analysis Results

As a policy measure strongly supported by our government for the development of foreign trade, the cross-border e-commerce pilot zone provides an important impetus for the development of foreign trade. This article is based on the quasi-natural experiment samples of 59 pilot zones established from 2014 to 2019 and uses a multi-period double difference model to analyze the impact of pilot zone policies on the development of our country's foreign trade. Under the two situations of not joining and joining control variables, the results of the impact of the establishment of pilot zones at the national level and the total amount of policies implemented after the establishment of the pilot zones on the development of cross-border e-commerce are described through formulas (8.2) and (8.4), Tables 8.3 and 8.4.

From the above observation results, it can be found that whether it is "whether to establish a pilot zone" or "the number of pilot zone policies", the results are more significant after joining the control variables, indicating that it is necessary to join the control variables.

Table 8.3 Overall impact of the establishment of comprehensive pilot areas on cross-border e-commerce3

Explained variable	Lnfrtrade		Inexpress		company	
variable	(1)	(2)	(1)	(2)	(1)	(2)
Exper	0.307** *	0.107	0.8***	0.387***	111.103***	84.454***
Inpeople		1.246		2.533**		2195.368***
Ingrp		0.059		0.05		1.171
Ingov		0.309**		0.694***		215.164***
indu		0.423		0.259		162.963
Ininfo		0.056		0.47***		13.603
Intransport		0.175		0.22		38.813

*** $p < 0.01$, ** $p < 0.05$, * $p < 0.1$

Table 8.4 Overall impact of the number of policies in the comprehensive pilot area on cross-border e-commerce4

Explained variable	Lnfrtrade		lnexpress		company	
variable	(1)	(2)	(1)	(2)	(1)	(2)
Policy	0.09***	0.047***	0.166***	0.049*	50.499***	38.469***
lnpeople		0.866		0.776**		1621.951***
lngrp		0.069		0.037		1.254
lngov		0.331**		0.575**		245.292***
indu		0.337		0.516		49.759
lninfo		0.062		0.452***		35.299*
lntransport		0.197		0.278		50.293

*** $p < 0.01$, ** $p < 0.05$, * $p < 0.1$

For the two explained variables of cross-border express (*Inexpress*) and the number of cross-border companies (*company*), regardless of whether control variables are included, the fitting coefficients are significantly positively correlated, indicating that the establishment of the pilot zone can significantly promote the development of the cross-border e-commerce logistics industry, attract more companies to enter the cross-border e-commerce industry, and increase the volume of cross-border e-commerce transactions.

For the level of import and export trade (*Inftrade*), Table 8.3 reflects that its impact has not significantly increased before and after the establishment of the pilot zone. The reason may be that more specific supporting policies are needed to consolidate its effect after the establishment of the pilot zone. This issue is also explained from Table 8.4: the level of import and export trade in the pilot zone (*Inftrade*) is positively correlated with the policy, further indicating that after the specific policy implementation in the comprehensive test area, the total import and export value of the city where the comprehensive test area is located has a significant upward trend. Therefore, for cities, if they want to achieve the goal of promoting cross-border e-commerce development, being designated as a comprehensive test area is only the first step. What's more important is to propose supporting policies with local characteristics and targeted based on the actual business environment.

8.2.3 Model Robustness Test

(1) Parallel Trend Test

Whether the parallel trend assumption holds or not is a condition for the effectiveness of the difference-in-differences method. If the parallel trend assumption holds, the impact of the establishment of the comprehensive test area on cross-border e-commerce will only occur after each city is designated as a comprehensive test area.

Before this, there is no significant difference in the trend of changes in the cross-border e-commerce variables of the city. Therefore, based on formula 0, this article sets up the following model:

$$y_{it} = \beta_{\bar{0}} + \sum\nolimits_{p=-4}^{p=4} \beta_p * Year_{it} + \gamma * \sum_{n} X_{it} + \mu_i + f_t + \varepsilon_{it} \tag{8.6}$$

In formula (8.6), $Year_{it}$ is a dummy variable. If city i was designated as a comprehensive test area between 2014 and 2019, if the t year is before or after city i was designated as a comprehensive test area in the p year, then $Year_{it}$. The value is 1 if the year exceeds p, otherwise the value is 0. Here p is set to 4, which measures the development of cross-border e-commerce in the city 4 years before and after the establishment of the cross-border e-commerce comprehensive test area. If β_{-4} to β_{-1} do not have a uniform change pattern, it indicates that the parallel trend assumption holds.

Specifically, in STATA software, follow the steps below:

Step 1: Generate the difference between the policy implementation year and the current year of the sample *distance*.

Step 2: Generate the dummy variables d_j and dj for the jth year before and after the policy implementation of the experimental group, where j is up to 4, representing 4 years before and after the policy implementation.

d_j: If the sample is the "experimental group" and it is the "jth period before policy implementation", the value is 1, otherwise the value is 0.

dj: If the sample is the "experimental group" and it is the "jth period after policy implementation", the value is 1, otherwise the value is 0.

After the first two steps, the data table will add nine columns: distance, d_4, d_3, d_2, d_1, d1, d2, d3, d4, as shown in Fig. 8.1.

	city	year	policy_year	distance	d_1	d_2	d_3	d_4	d_5	d1	d2	d3	d4
1	杭州	2014	2015	-1	1	0	0	0	0	0	0	0	0
2	苏州	2014	2016	-2	0	1	0	0	0	0	0	0	0
3	上海	2014	2016	-2	0	1	0	0	0	0	0	0	0
4	天津	2014	2016	-2	0	1	0	0	0	0	0	0	0
5	深圳	2014	2016	-2	0	1	0	0	0	0	0	0	0
6	郑州	2014	2016	-2	0	1	0	0	0	0	0	0	0
7	成都	2014	2016	-2	0	1	0	0	0	0	0	0	0
8	宁波	2014	2016	-2	0	1	0	0	0	0	0	0	0
9	合肥	2014	2016	-2	0	1	0	0	0	0	0	0	0
10	重庆	2014	2016	-2	0	1	0	0	0	0	0	0	0
11	广州	2014	2016	-2	0	1	0	0	0	0	0	0	0
12	大连	2014	2016	-2	0	1	0	0	0	0	0	0	0
13	青岛	2014	2016	-2	0	1	0	0	0	0	0	0	0
14	北京	2014	2018	-4	0	0	0	1	0	0	0	0	0
15	义乌	2014	2018	-4	0	0	0	1	0	0	0	0	0
16	东莞	2014	2018	-4	0	0	0	1	0	0	0	0	0
17	长沙	2014	2018	-4	0	0	0	1	0	0	0	0	0
18	贵阳	2014	2018	-4	0	0	0	1	0	0	0	0	0
19	珠海	2014	2018	-4	0	0	0	1	0	0	0	0	0
20	威海	2014	2018	-4	0	0	0	1	0	0	0	0	0
21	南昌	2014	2018	-4	0	0	0	1	0	0	0	0	0
22	西安	2014	2018	-4	0	0	0	1	0	0	0	0	0
23	南京	2014	2018	-4	0	0	0	1	0	0	0	0	0
24	海口	2014	2018	-4	0	0	0	1	0	0	0	0	0

Fig. 8.1 Year processing of parallel trend testing process

Step 3: Conduct a parallel trend test using regression method and draw a parallel trend graph.

Take d_4, d_3, d_2, d_1, d1, d2, d3, d4 as explanatory variables, control time effects and fixed effects, control variable regression, and draw the regression coefficient in the 95% confidence interval based on the results of the regression.

According to the above steps, the total amount of imports and exports, cross-border express delivery, and the number of cross-border e-commerce companies are tested for parallel trends, respectively representing the changes in the coefficients of these three explained variables before and after the establishment of the comprehensive test area. From Figs. 8.2, 8.3, 8.4, it can be found that the changes in the coefficients of β_{-4} to β_{-1} do not show a certain pattern, and the coefficients are not significantly different from 0, all within the 95% confidence interval. Therefore, it can be judged that the parallel trend assumption holds, that is, before the cross-border e-commerce policy takes effect, the difference in changes between the experimental group and the control group is not large, which can demonstrate the effectiveness of the multi-period difference-in-differences method.

(2) Placebo Test

In actual research, the parallel trend test and placebo test methods can often be used together to test the robustness of empirical results. For example, when Lv Yue and others studied the promotion effect of the "Belt and Road" initiative on foreign investment using the difference-in-differences method, they used the parallel trend test method to examine the change trends of the experimental group and the control group and used the hypothetical virtual policy time and randomly selected experimental group to conduct a placebo test [[5]]; Fang Fang and others constructed a virtual policy time variable for parallel trend testing and placebo testing, confirming

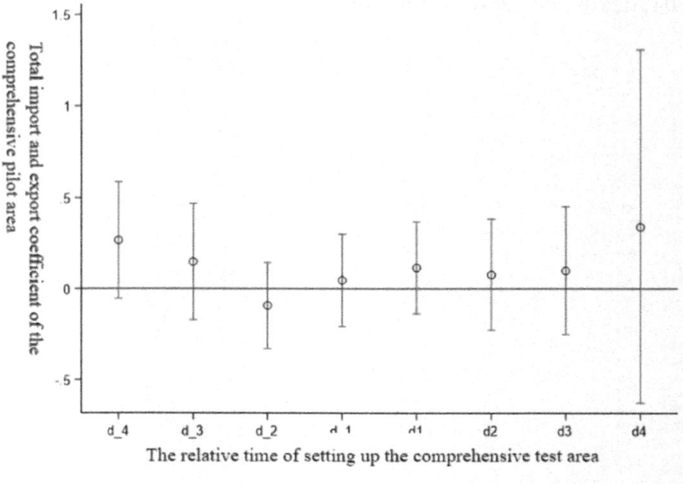

Fig. 8.2 Parallel trend of total import and export volume in the comprehensive test area SEQ 图9- * ARABIC 1

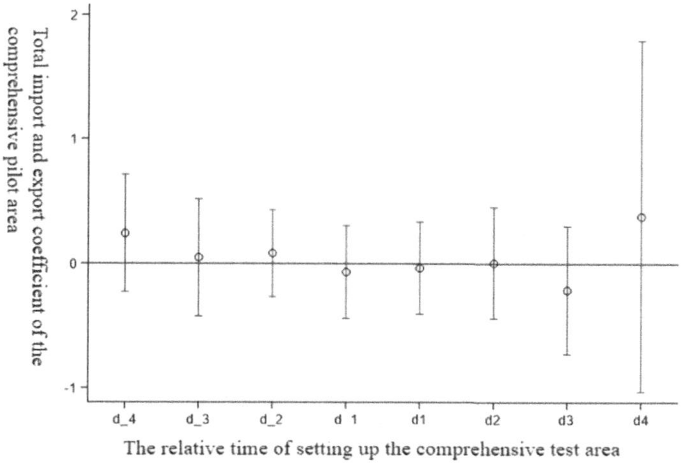

Fig. 8.3 Parallel trend of cross-border express volume in the comprehensive pilot area SEQ 图9- * ARABIC 2

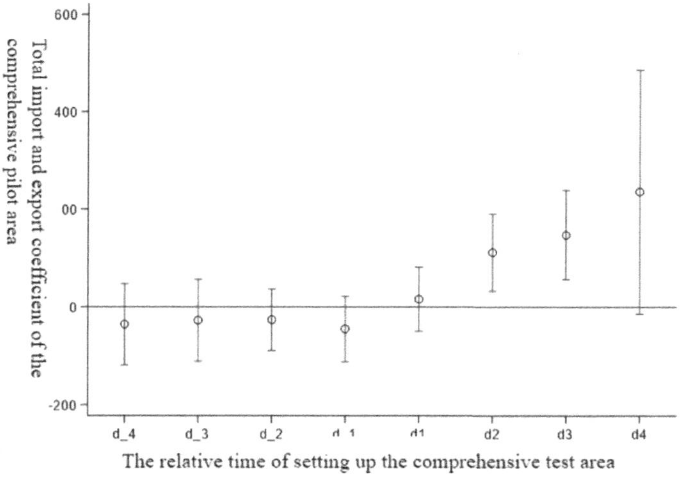

Fig. 8.4 Parallel trend of cross-border express delivery volume in the comprehensive pilot area SEQ 图9- * ARABIC 3

the effectiveness of the double difference model of environmental regulation and urban manufacturing economic efficiency [[6]].

Another key to the effectiveness of the multi-period difference-in-differences experiment is to exclude the interference of other unobservable variables on the estimation results. Although some control variables have been added in the baseline regression, and city fixed effects and time control effects have been added, controlling the impact of city characteristics that do not change with time on the quality of city development, there may still be some unobservable variables that affect the estimation results of this article.

This paper randomly selects a year between 2014 and 2019 as the policy time for each city to conduct an indirect placebo test. If other unobservable variables do not interfere with the estimated results, the estimated coefficient of the explanatory variable will be insignificant; however, if the estimated results at the virtual policy point do not match the expectations, i.e., the estimated coefficient is significant, it means that in addition to the impact of the comprehensive test area policy, there are also some potential factors affecting the development of cross-border e-commerce in each city.

Therefore, to eliminate the possibility of potential unobserved factors affecting the research results, this paper uses the total amount of imports and exports (lnfrtrade), cross-border express delivery (lnepress), and cross-border e-commerce companies (company) as the explained variables, and randomly repeats formula 0–500 times, correspondingly generating 500 β_1 estimated values, and draws the distribution of 500 estimated coefficients and their corresponding p values. If these 500 estimated coefficients are randomly distributed around 0, and the estimated coefficients do not meet the significance condition, i.e., p value> 0.1, it indicates that there is no systematic difference in the experiment, eliminating the possibility of unobserved factors affecting the results.

Specific operations in STATA software:

Step 1: Generate a backup matrix.

Step 2: Sampling, group the data according to the comprehensive test area cities, and randomly select a year from the *year* variable in each city as the virtual policy time.

Step 3: Convert the matrix into a vector and form an estimated coefficient distribution diagram.

Figures 8.5, 8.6, 8.7 record the distribution of the estimated coefficients of the three explained variables, the total amount of imports and exports, cross-border express delivery, and e-commerce companies in the comprehensive test area, after 500 times. The estimated coefficient distributions of the three experiments are all concentrated around zero and approximately follow a normal distribution, and most of the estimated values' p. The value is greater than 0.1, which means the estimated coefficient of the fictitious policy time variable is not significant. Therefore, it proves that the randomly generated virtual time years have no policy effect, and it can be inferred that the promotion effect of the comprehensive test area policy on the development of cross-border foreign trade and cross-border logistics of the experimental group is real. Therefore, it proves that the comprehensive test area policy effectively promotes the development of the cross-border e-commerce industry.

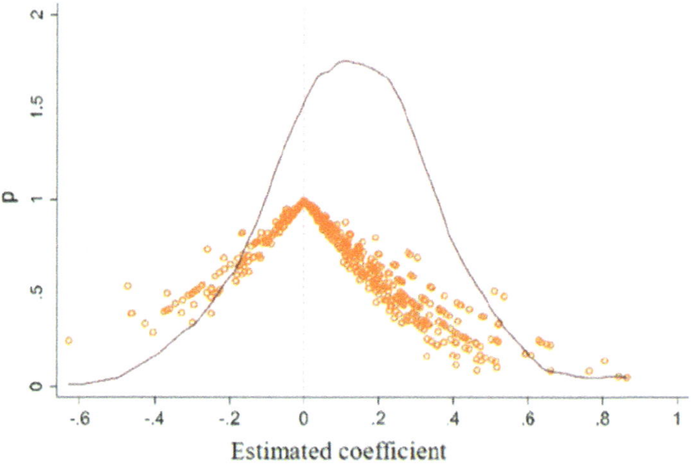

Fig. 8.5 Estimated coefficient of total import and export volume in the comprehensive pilot zone

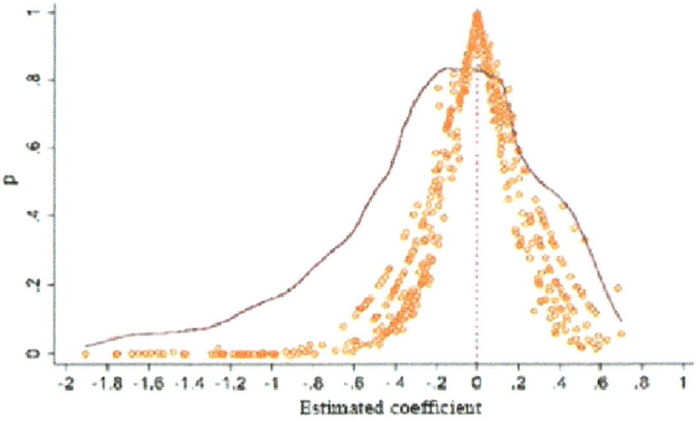

Fig. 8.6 Estimated coefficients for cross-border express delivery in the comprehensive pilot zone

8.2.4 Analysis of the Mediating Effect of Cross-Border E-commerce Policy

Empirical research results show that the establishment of cross-border e-commerce comprehensive test zones has a certain promoting effect on the development of cross-border trade, which leads to a question: from which dimensions does the establishment of the comprehensive test zone promote cross-border trade? The evolution model of cross-border e-commerce ecosystem points out that the development of cross-border e-commerce depends on the political, economic, technological, and

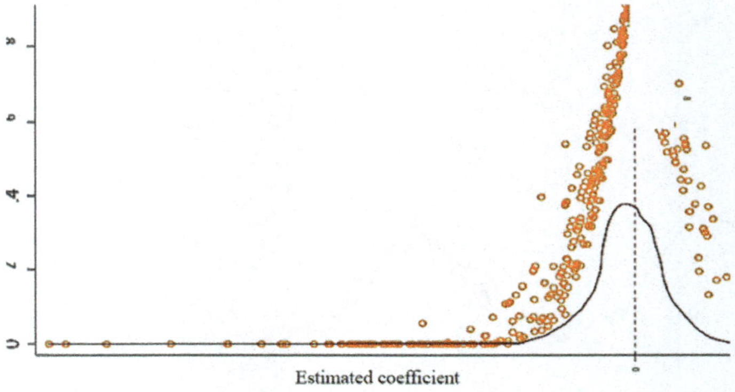

Fig. 8.7 Estimated coefficient of cross-border e-commerce enterprises in the comprehensive pilot area

social ecological environment. First, the policy environment promotes and regulates cross-border e-commerce. Second, economic development promotes cross-border e-commerce. Third, technological changes support cross-border e-commerce. Fourth, social progress promotes cross-border e-commerce.

8.2.4.1 The Mediating Effect of Environmental Factors on Cross-Border E-commerce Policy

Combining the Smith model, this study further analyzes the promoting effect of economic, technological, and social environment on the implementation effect of cross-border e-commerce comprehensive test zone policy and uses the classic stepwise regression method to verify the mediating effect. In the first step, the establishment policy variable of the comprehensive test zone (*Exper*) and cross-border express (*Inexpress*) are regressed, as shown in formula (8.7). If the regression coefficient is significant, it can be explained that the establishment of the comprehensive test zone can significantly promote the development of cross-border e-commerce in the city of the comprehensive test zone; in the second step, the establishment policy item of the comprehensive test zone is regressed with the four types of environmental factors in the cross-border e-commerce ecosystem, as shown in formula (8.8). If the corresponding regression coefficient is significant, it means that the establishment of the comprehensive test zone can significantly improve various types of environments in the cross-border e-commerce ecosystem; in the third step, the establishment policy variable of the comprehensive test zone and the environmental factor mediating variable are put into the model and regressed with cross-border express, as shown in formula (8.9). If the cross term is still significant, it means that the establishment of the comprehensive test zone can further promote the development of cross-border e-commerce through environmental factors. The three-step model is as follows:

$$Y_i = c * Exper_i + e_1 \tag{8.7}$$

$$M_i = a * Exper_i + e_2 \tag{8.8}$$

$$Y_i' = c' * Exper_i + b * M_i + e_3 \tag{8.9}$$

Table 8.5 explains the selection of mediating variables. Specifically, with cross-border express (*Inexpress*) is the dependent variable, with four types of cross-border e-commerce ecological environment as the mediating variables. Among them, the cross-border e-commerce Baidu index is the expression of the behavior intention of many netizens, reflecting the popularity of cross-border e-commerce among the public and can serve as an important basis for corporate decision-making behavior in participating in the cross-border e-commerce market to a certain extent. The city size (*people*), economic development (*grp*), government size (*gov*), transportation development (*transport*), level of information development (*info*), and industrial structure (*indu*) and other indicators are selected as control variables, and regression analysis is performed controlling for these variables.

8.2.5 Intermediary Effect Analysis Results

Taking the intermediary effect analysis of the technical environment as an example, in STATA software, first, the variable "cross-border express" and the variable "comprehensive test area establishment" are regressed, that is, formula (8.10), to obtain the estimated coefficient c; then the variable "technical environment" and the variable "comprehensive test area establishment" are further regressed, that is, formula (8.11); finally, the variable "cross-border express" and "comprehensive test area establishment", "technical environment" are regressed again, that is, formula (8.12), at this time the estimated coefficients c' and b are obtained,

$$Inexpress_i = c * Exper_i + e_1 \tag{8.10}$$

First step:xtreg lnexpress x lnpeople lngrp lngov lninfo lntransport indu, fe

$$innovate_i = a * Exper_i + e_2 \tag{8.11}$$

Second step:xtreg innovate x lnpeople lngrp lngov lninfo lntransport indu, fe

$$Inexpress_i = c' * Exper_i + b * innovate_i + e_3 \tag{8.12}$$

Third step:xtreg lnexpress x innovate lnpeople lngrp lngov lninfo lntransport indu, fe.

Table 8.5 Mediating effect variable selection description5

Category of Variables	Variables	Indicators	Measurement
Explained variables	lnexpress	Cross-border express delivery	International and Hong Kong, Macao and Taiwan express mail quantity, official website of Post and Telecommunications Bureau
Mediating variable	policy	Political environment	Total number of policies implemented in the region
	innovation	Technological environment	Number of patent applications in the region that year, China Urban Statistical Yearbook
	consumption	Economic environment	Annual Average Urban Income, China Urban Statistical Yearbook
	bdindex	Social context	Cross-border e-commerce Baidu Index, Baidu Index official website
Control variables	people	City size	Urban Population, China Urban Statistical Yearbook
	grp	Economic size	Gross regional Product, China Urban Statistical Yearbook
	gov	Government size	Public Finance Expenditure, China Urban Statistical Yearbook
	indu	Upgrading of industrial structure	Proportion of Tertiary Industry, China Urban Statistical Yearbook
	info	Informatization development level	Number of Internet broadband access users, China City Statistical Yearbook
	transport	Traffic development degree	Highway Freight volume, official website of the Bureau of Transportation

As explained in Chapter 3 for the analysis of intermediary effects, c is the total effect of the establishment of the comprehensive test area on the scale of cross-border e-commerce transactions, c' is the direct effect, a is the effect of the establishment of the comprehensive test area on the technical environment, b is the effect of the technical environment on cross-border e-commerce, $a*b$ is the intermediary effect of the comprehensive test area promoting cross-border e-commerce through technology, therefore, the intermediary effect of the technical environment can be expressed as: $a * b = c - c'$. The process of analyzing the mediating effects of policy, economic, and social environment is consistent with the above.

The regression results after controlling for variables are shown in Table 8.6. Firstly, it can be found that: the "three-step" regression results show that the comprehensive test area significantly promotes the development of cross-border e-commerce scale by optimizing the technical environment, economic environment, and social environment, and the environmental mediation effect is verified; secondly, the mediation effects of technology, policy, economy, and social environment are calculated separately. The mediating effect of the policy environment is

$c - c' = 0.387 - 0.0831 = 0.3039$, the mediating effect of the technical environment is $c - c' = 0.387 - 0.324 = 0.063$, and the mediating effect of the economic environment is $c - c' = 0.387 - 0.202 - 0.185$, the mediating effect in the social environment is $c - c' = 0.387 - 0.351 = 0.036$.

Among the environmental factors, the mediating effect of policy implementation is the strongest, followed by the promoting effect of the economic environment. Although the technological environment promotes cross-border e-commerce transactions the mediating effect of policy on the technological environment still largely needs to be strengthened. In addition, the decrease in the coefficient of the cross terms of technology, economy, and social environment factors is relatively small, indicating that the cross-border e-commerce pilot zone is still in the development and construction stage. The mechanism to promote industrial development by improving the implementation effect of cross-border e-commerce policies through the optimization of technology, economy, and social environment is still weak. The potential of policy implementation effects after the establishment of the pilot zone needs to be further released.

Based on the above analysis, the mediating effect of the cross-border e-commerce ecological environment factors discussed in this study on the policy implementation effect is established. The establishment of the cross-border e-commerce comprehensive experimental zone can promote the improvement of the political, social, technological, and social environment of the cross-border e-commerce ecosystem in the pilot zone and further promote the expansion of the cross-border e-commerce industry scale through the role of environmental factors. However, in the cross-border e-commerce ecology, it is necessary to strengthen the promoting effect of the establishment of the pilot zone on the technological and social environment and further promote the development of cross-border e-commerce.

8.3 Analysis of the Heterogeneity of Cross-Border E-Commerce Policies

The experiment shows that the policy of the cross-border e-commerce pilot zone can significantly promote the growth of cross-border e-commerce enterprises, the improvement of logistics level, and the expansion of foreign trade. The mediating effect analysis has shown that in the cross-border e-commerce ecology, the role of the technological environment, economic environment, and social environment in policy transmission is significant. In the development process of the cross-border e-commerce pilot zone, whether the inherent attributes of the city will affect the implementation effect of the policy becomes a content that can be further explored. Therefore, this article further considers the effects of different geographical locations, population sizes, and the "Belt and Road" strategy on the effect of pilot zone policy.

Table 8.6 The intermediary effect results of eco-environmental factors in the comprehensive pilot area of cross-border e-commerce

Variable	lnexpress							
Exper	0.387***	0.0831***	0.387***	0.324***	0.387***	0.202***	0.387***	0.351***
Policy		1.523***						
Innovation				9641.9***				
consumption						4461.04***		
Bdindex								13.805**
control variable	control	control	control	control	control	control	control	control
N	353	346	353	353	353	353	354	354
R^2	0.9464	0.6344	0.9464	0.9468	0.9464	0.9465	0.9464	0.9462

*** $p < 0.01$, ** $p < 0.05$, * $p < 0.1$

8.3.1 The Impact of Geographical Location on the Implementation of Cross-Border E-Commerce Policy

According to the division of economic zones by the National Bureau of Statistics, China's provincial administrative regions are divided into four regions: east, west, central, and northeast [[7]]: the eastern region includes Beijing, Tianjin, Hebei, Shanghai, Jiangsu, Zhejiang, Fujian, Shandong, Guangdong, and Hainan, a total of ten provinces (cities); the central region includes Shanxi, Anhui, Jiangxi, Henan, Hubei, and Hunan, a total of six provinces (autonomous regions); the western region includes Sichuan, Inner Mongolia, Guizhou, Yunnan, Tibet, Shaanxi, Gansu, Qinghai, Ningxia, Xinjiang, Chongqing, and Guangxi, a total of 12 provinces (autonomous regions); the northeastern region includes Liaoning, Jilin, and Heilongjiang, a total of three provinces. Therefore, this article separately conducts a benchmark regression on the comprehensive test areas of the four regions, and the empirical results are shown in Table 8.7.

Observations show: (1) The comprehensive test area policy has significantly promoted foreign trade in cities in the northeast and western regions, and greatly promoted the growth of cross-border e-commerce companies in the northeastern, central, and western regions; (2) The total foreign trade, cross-border express delivery, and cross-border e-commerce companies in the eastern region did not show a significant growth trend after the establishment of the cross-border e-commerce comprehensive test area.

The possible reasons are: (1) In recent years, with the implementation of strategic policies such as "Western Development", "Belt and Road", and "Revitalization of the Northeast", the investment and industrial opportunities in the western and northeastern regions have increased, and the trend of economic globalization has made the geographical advantages of the west and northeast more prominent. (2) There are more channels and methods for the development of enterprises in the economically developed eastern region, and most of the powerful e-commerce companies are in the eastern region, such as Shanghai's Cross-Border Pass, Shenzhen's Aoqi E-commerce, Hangzhou Alibaba's AliExpress, and Beijing's Dunhuang Network occupy most of the market share, making it difficult for new cross-border e-commerce companies in this region to develop, and fierce market competition drives companies to explore emerging markets in the inland areas of our country.

8.3.2 The Impact of City Size on the Implementation of Cross-Border E-commerce Policy

Cities of different sizes have different infrastructure, innovation capabilities, and economic capabilities, and the execution effects of comprehensive test area policies will also vary. The city size is divided by population, 5 million, 5 million–10 million,

Table 8.7 Regional heterogeneity test results of cross-border e-commerce comprehensive experimental area

Region	Variable	lnfrtrade		lnexpress		company	
East	exper	0.075		0317 *		23.421	
	policy		0.033		0.014		5.089
	control variable	control	control	control	control	control	control
	N	353	353	353	353	353	353
	R^2	0.171	0.184	0.352	0.404	0.380	0.562
Northeast part	exper	0.133*		0.213		54.86***	
	policy		0.047**		0.017		34.9***
	control variable	control	control	control	control	control	control
	N	353	353	353	353	353	353
	R^2	0.173	0.183	0.345	0.404	0.358	0.540
Middle part	exper	0.083		0.125		59.109**	
	policy		0.041**		0.02		36.538***
	control variable	control	control	control	control	control	control
	N	353	353	353	353	353	353
	R^2	0.173	0.190	0.355	0.403	0.347	0.541
West	exper	0.137*		0. 14		54.34***	
	policy		0.056***		0.021		39.363***
	control variable	control	control	control	control	control	control
	N	353	353	353	353	353	353
	R^2	0.177	0.195	0.346	0.402	0.349	0.556

*** *p<0.01*, ** *p<0.05*, * *p<0.1*

and more than 10 million, respectively, for cities of different population sizes to conduct benchmark regression, and the empirical results are shown in Table 8.8. The study found that: for cities with a population of less than 5 million and more than 10 million, the effect of the comprehensive test area policy is more significant, with strong foreign trade driving ability and greater attraction to enterprises; for cities with a population of 5 million–10 million, whether it is the establishment of the comprehensive test area or the implementation of the policy, the role in import and export foreign trade is not obvious.

The reason for this phenomenon may be: for cities with a population of less than 5 million, the cross-border e-commerce comprehensive test area policy can strengthen the gathering of resources such as funds and talents, provide market development opportunities for small and medium-sized cities, and then generate a strong impetus

Table 8.8 Test results of city size heterogeneity in cross-border e-commerce comprehensive pilot area

Region	Variable	Infrtrade		Inexpress		company	
< 5 million	exper	0.09		0.062		26.007	
	policy		0.043**		0.12		36.742***
	control variable	control	control	control	control	control	control
	N	353	353	353	353	353	353
	R^2	0.229	0.234	0.403	0.403	0.447	0.535
5 to10 million	exper	0.038		0.093		43.80	
	policy		0.022		0.14		34.253***
	control variable	control	control	control	control	control	control
	N	353	353	353	353	353	353
	R^2	0.226	0.262	0.403	0.403	0.451	0.528
> 10 million	exper	0.036		0.056		3.112	
	policy		0.086***		0.36		26.973***
	control variable	control	control	control	control	control	control
	N	353	353	353	353	353	353
	R^2	0.220	0.241	0.403	0.403	0.463	0.531

*** *p<0.01, ** p<0.05, * p<0.1*

to promote the development of cross-border e-commerce; for cities with a population of more than 10 million, large-scale human resources and strong consumption levels, advanced technology and a complete industrial chain can further promote the development of foreign trade.

8.3.3 *The Impact of the "Belt and Road" Strategy on the Implementation of Cross-Border E-commerce Policy*

The purpose of the development of cross-border e-commerce is to promote the optimization, upgrading, transformation, and development of our country's foreign trade. It is an important foothold for our country's "Belt and Road" national strategy. According to the "China's 'Belt and Road' Plan" announced by the State Council Information Office [[8]], this section further screens the cities in the cross-border e-commerce comprehensive test area of the "Belt and Road" cities and tests the heterogeneous role of the "Belt and Road" on the development of cross-border e-commerce. The baseline regression of the cities along the Belt and Road and other regional cities is carried out separately, and the empirical results are shown in Table 8.9.

Table 8.9 Test results of strategic heterogeneity in cross-border e-commerce comprehensive experimental area

Rigon	Variable	lnfrtrade		lnexpress		company	
Belt and Road Cities	exper	0.106		0.424**		20.828	
	policy		0.007		0.014		4.623
	control variable	control	control	control	control	control	control
	N	353	353	353	353	353	353
	R^2	0.221	0.236	0.346	0.329	0.452	0.595
Other City	exper	0.014		0.37***		35.89	
	policy		0.059**		0.079**		57.335***
	control variable	control	control	control	control	control	control
	N	353	353	353	353	353	353
	R^2	0.221	0.236	0.346	0.329	0.452	0.595

*** *p<0.01, ** p<0.05, * p<0.1*

As the research shows, the establishment of the cross-border e-commerce comprehensive test area does not significantly differ in policy effects for cities along the "Belt and Road", but the policy implementation within the test area significantly affects non-"Belt and Road" key cities based on the establishment of the test area, with positive significant impacts on foreign trade (lnfrtrade), cross-border express delivery (lnexpress), and cross-border companies (company). The reason may be that the influence of the "Belt and Road" strategy is more widespread and profound, and the policy effect of the test area in the cities along the route is covered, making the estimated value not significant, while other cities are directly intervened by cross-border e-commerce policies due to the lack of direct impact of the "Belt and Road" strategy, resulting in significant policy effects. Therefore, during the implementation of the test area policy, it is necessary to fully consider the impact of other strategic policies and promote policy coordination to maximize the goals under multiple policy situations.

8.4 Conclusion and Enlightenment

8.4.1 Research Summary

This book selects Tmall International website as the representative object for cross-border platform research, selects the category with the largest proportion of user consumption preferences and the most representative research individuals under this category as the research source, and uses online evaluation information as the data source. Based on nearly 80,000 pieces of data, it explores user cross-border consumption behavior preference analysis and comparative analysis of consumption behavior preferences between cross-border and non-cross-border platforms, and draws the following conclusions:

(1) The four-dimensional customer perceived value driving model consists of value-driven, technology-driven, brand-driven, and service-driven. Through keyword frequency statistics, it is found that the words with the highest frequency are "concealing effect", "duration", "taste", "genuine guarantee", etc., with the highest scores of 4202, 4307, 4610, and 3708, respectively, followed by "duration", "logistics", "packaging", etc. This indicates that users on cross-border retail import platform websites pay most attention to value-driven factors, brand-driven factors, and technology-driven factors. Merchants and even platforms need to not only strengthen the improvement of the value attributes of products, that is, the core value of competitiveness, but also strictly control the source channels of products, and improve the timeliness cost and service cost of international logistics.

(2) From the consumer's perspective, it is found that the importance of customer perceived value driving factors is inconsistent, among which the importance of value-driven, brand-driven, and technology-driven is the highest and needs to be focused on; the value-driven factor ranked first is related to consumer demands. Purchasing different products has different functional values, which is also the most basic perceived demand of consumers. Whether this value is satisfied or not will affect the conditional probability of other driving factors, and the attention to brand-driven reflects the consumer's behavior verification when shopping on this platform.

(3) Through the data modeling comparison between cross-border and non-cross-border platforms, it is found that the customer perceived value of non-cross-border platforms tends to be value-driven, far greater than technology-driven and brand-driven factors, among which the estimated technology-driven factor is related to the relatively complete domestic logistics system; while the customer perceived value of cross-border platforms can be classified from large to small as: value-driven factors, brand-driven factors, and technology-driven factors, but the importance values of the three are relatively small. In other words, domestic platform users pay more attention to value-driven factors (product characteristics, etc.), under the same circumstances, overseas platform users pay more attention to brand-driven factors, which may be related to the lack of patent agency rights or the mixed shops on the domestic platform, and further verification and research are needed.

This book analyzes the competitive advantage of imported cross-border e-commerce platforms from the perspectives of platform companies and users, and is committed to exploring the key factors affecting the competitive advantage of platforms from different perspectives. The research conclusions are as follows:

Based on the perspective of platform companies, this paper takes small and medium-sized B2C import cross-border e-commerce platforms in our country as the research object and uses enterprise survey data as the empirical basis. It studies the impact of different factors under the two dimensions of cross-border e-commerce transaction subjects and import modes, and the matching between factors on the competitive advantage of the platform. The research results show that the product category and the degree of product popularity have a significant impact on the competitive advantage of the platform, and the website traffic of comprehensive e-commerce and long-tail e-commerce is larger and more competitive; in addition, the matching of the mixed import mode and long-tail e-commerce can better meet consumer needs, promote consumer use of the platform, and help enhance the competitive advantage of the platform.

In the research from the user's perspective, this paper builds an evolutionary model of cross-border e-commerce consumers' emotional preference, takes online reviews of Jingdong Fresh platform as the research object, builds an emotional dictionary, divides time Windows, and analyzes consumers' emotional diffusion value and emotional energy value under different time Windows. The results show as follows: In terms of emotional diffusion value, consumers have strong perception ability. During the outbreak period, consumers' behavior of purchasing imported fresh products on cross-border e-commerce platforms decreases significantly, and their overall purchasing power decreases, that is, the emotional diffusion value increases. In the period of spread control, consumer purchasing power recovered slightly, and the emotional diffusion was convergent. In terms of emotional energy value, consumer emotion has always been in a positive and good state, but compared with other categories of fresh products, consumers have a rapid perception of the incident, and there are negative emotional fluctuations on the seafood and aquatic imported fresh products involved, and the intensity of fluctuations is large, which seriously affects the purchase of seafood and aquatic imported fresh products.

To study the impact of policies on the development of cross-border e-commerce as deeply as possible, this book takes cross-border e-commerce policy as the research object and constructs a cross-border e-commerce policy evaluation model in combination with the policy implementation process model. Firstly, the main body of cross-border e-commerce policy, the field of action, policy tools, and policy development context were evaluated and analyzed through policy literature metrology and data visualization methods. Secondly, an empirical analysis of the policy effect of the cross-border e-commerce comprehensive test zone was carried out through econometric methods. The main conclusions are as follows:

A new paradigm for cross-border e-commerce policy research is proposed. Starting from the policy implementation process model, a systematic cross-border e-commerce policy evaluation research model is constructed. Firstly, the policy main body, policy action field, policy tools, and environmental factors of cross-border e-commerce are included in the cross-border e-commerce policy evaluation model. Secondly, policy literature metrology, data visualization, and econometric methods are selected to deeply study the policy effect of cross-border e-commerce from the perspectives of policy resource allocation and policy implementation effect.

(2) Cross-border e-commerce policy measurement and visualization. The study found: (1) In terms of policy subject cooperation, the departmental cooperation network is generally dense. Through the visualization of the relationship of joint issuance of cross-border e-commerce policies, it can be found that the current multi-subject joint issuance is mainly based on the cooperation of the General Administration of Customs, the Ministry of Finance, the State Administration of Taxation,

the Ministry of Commerce, and the General Administration of Quality Inspection. By measuring the network characteristics of the subjects, it can be found that cooperation is common in the multi-subject network of departments, and the degree of cooperation between departments is high; (2) in terms of policy action fields, the impact of policies on the cross-border e-commerce ecosystem is gradually deepening, extending from payment and taxation to regulation, logistics, and informatization, but it has not yet fully integrated into the cross-border e-commerce ecosystem, such as the policy content in terms of cross-border e-commerce talent and intellectual property protection is relatively lacking; (3) in terms of policy tool combinations, cross-border e-commerce policies show the characteristics of environmental policy tools dominating, evaluation policy tools relatively weak, and demand policy tools seriously lacking. It should strengthen the guidance of cross-border e-commerce demand and policy evaluation in the policy; (4) in terms of policy evolution, China's cross-border e-commerce policies are divided into four stages: preliminary exploration, support and promotion, standard promotion, and comprehensive development. In terms of policy focus, the attention to cross-border e-commerce risks is gradually increasing, which is helpful for cross-border e-commerce companies to improve their self-protection awareness in the increasingly complex international situation; in terms of policy efficiency, the relationship between the policies and business volume of the first three batches of comprehensive pilot zones forms three levels, and the policy efficiency differences are obvious. Therefore, each cross-border e-commerce comprehensive pilot zone needs to pay more attention to the implementation effect of the policy and promote the high-quality development of the industry.

(3) Evaluation of the implementation effect of cross-border e-commerce comprehensive pilot zone policies. The study found: (1) In terms of the policy effect of the comprehensive pilot zone, the establishment of the comprehensive pilot zone has a promoting effect on the development of cross-border e-commerce, but it needs to further introduce and implement supporting policies to enhance the effect; (2) in terms of the cross-border e-commerce environment, environmental factors have a significant impact on the effect of cross-border e-commerce policies, and the mediating effect of the political environment is prominent. During the development process, the impact of the political environment, technical environment, economic environment, and social environment should be coordinated, especially the mediating role of technological development and social environment on the development of cross-border e-commerce should be paid attention to, and the policy guidance of technology and innovation should be strengthened; (3) in terms of city attributes, it is found that the geographical location of the city, the size of the city, and the differences in the "Belt and Road" strategy will affect the effect of cross-border e-commerce policies. The comprehensive pilot zone policy is conducive to the economic growth of small and medium-sized cities and non-"Belt and Road" cities. Therefore, in the process of policy formulation and implementation, the comprehensive pilot zone should fully combine the advantages and disadvantages of the city and the possible impact of related strategies to maximize the implementation effect of the policy.

8.5 Management Enlightenment

This book, based on customer perceived value theory and Bayesian network, starts from the background of cross-border e-commerce retail import, and comprehensively analyzes the consumer's demand perception factors and preferences for cross-border products under the two stages of product purchase and use experience, showing certain research enlightenment, mainly including:

(1) Based on the research of cross-border consumer behavior driving factors and preferences through online word-of-mouth, this book innovatively studies cross-border consumer behavior preferences from a consumer micro-perspective based on objective event data. Previous scholars' research on online shopping behavior has mostly focused on two directions, one part focuses on the influencing factors of online shopping behavior, and the other part focuses on the mechanism characteristics of online shopping behavior; among them, there are few literature on consumer behavior research based on the cross-border field, and some cross-border consumer behavior research mainly proposes hypotheses based on past literature and discusses the verification of conceptual models, lacking empirical verification of objective data; a small amount of research is based on survey questionnaires, expert interviews or official data to discuss the conceptual model of cross-border online shopping behavior, and individual research is based on empirical discussion of online reviews of a product, this research does not involve the entire process of cross-border consumer behavior, and the data is one-sided and lacks extensibility and predictability. This book builds a model based on a solid theoretical foundation, and captures a large amount of online review data of 30 products from the consumer's perspective to empirically derive a systematic, comprehensive, and mixed model structure. The research shows that there are similarities in the consumption structure of different products, which provides support for the extensibility of the conclusion, and clarifies the dimensions of customer perceived value of representative product categories, promoting the learning and prediction of other category product preferences.

(2) A customer perceived value driving model that includes the entire consumption stage of product purchase and uses experience under the background of cross-border online shopping behavior has been constructed, clarifying the intrinsic relationship between different driving dimensions, and exploring the latest application category of Bayesian network model. Past literature research has mostly focused on consumer behavior at different consumption stages under cross-border channels, or research on the influencing factors of single-dimensional consumer behavior, and the research results often only get a related action relationship model, and there is no data probability action model. This book applies the Bayesian network model for repeated training and learning of data. The model generates the corresponding model structure based on objective micro-data and includes the probability relationship between each driving dimension (or secondary driving indicator), extending and broadening the application field of Bayesian networks, providing a new solution for future consumer behavior research. The research results of this book show that the network structure model obtained through continuous training and learning of the Bayesian network

has a high accuracy and validity, and is a relatively efficient and feasible research method.

(3) Further expanded and discussed the preference factors and importance of consumer behavior for purchasing overseas products under cross-border platforms and non-cross-border platforms, and deeply analyzed the necessity and importance of cross-border platforms based on this. Previous research did not simultaneously study and discuss consumer behavior preferences from two channels and compare them. This book establishes a four-dimensional driving model based on the consumer's perspective, sets the same experimental environment, and obtains the network structure diagram of the two channels and the probability distribution of each driving indicator through training and learning. The research results show that there are similarities in the customer value dimension preferences perceived by consumers when purchasing overseas products through different channels, but there are differences in the secondary driving indicators under specific dimensions. Value driving is the most important factor perceived by consumers, and brand driving has a huge difference in importance in different channels. Consumers on cross-border platforms pay more attention to product origin and brand awareness, which fully reveals the necessity and importance of cross-border platforms, providing indirect decision support for the country's attention to the policy adjustment of cross-border platforms.

Based on the data analysis results of Chapter 6 of this book and according to the current situation of Chinese consumers' cross-border purchases, it is concluded that imported cross-border e-commerce platforms can enhance their competitive advantages in the following aspects:

(1) In line with consumers' cross-border purchasing preferences, increase the variety of goods offered on the platform. A wide range of goods not only meets consumers' one-stop shopping needs and improves their shopping efficiency, but also helps to enhance the user stickiness of cross-border e-commerce platforms. Compared to vertical e-commerce, comprehensive e-commerce is more favored by users, has more competitive advantages, and is conducive to improving platform performance. In the early stages of establishment, import cross-border e-commerce platforms may be limited by funds, manpower, technology, etc., preventing them from directly positioning as comprehensive platforms. However, as the company expands, the platform should focus on combining consumers' cross-border purchasing preferences, increasing the categories of goods operated, and gradually transitioning from vertical e-commerce to comprehensive e-commerce, thereby enhancing its competitive advantage and improving platform performance.

(2) Based on mass demand, gradually meet personalized needs. The convenience and normalization of cross-border purchases have led consumers' demand for overseas goods to gradually develop in a diversified and personalized direction. They are no longer limited to buying popular hot-selling products, but are more willing to shift their attention to niche products that can highlight their personality and express their unique characteristics. When import cross-border e-commerce platforms choose the types of goods to operate based on the popularity of the goods, they should be good at discovering changes in consumer behavior. While based on mass demand, they should also strive to collect good things from around the world,

discover high-quality niche products, continuously meet users' personalized needs, transition from hot-selling e-commerce to long-tail e-commerce, and continuously enhance the user stickiness of the platform, improve its competitive advantage and sustainable development capabilities.

(3) Achieve a reasonable match between the trading entity and the import model to improve platform performance. Different types of trading entities and import models have their unique advantages and disadvantages, and the choice of trading entity type and import model by cross-border e-commerce platforms should be a complementary result. Survey data results show that when the platform is positioned as a long-tail e-commerce, its matching hybrid import model can better demonstrate the platform's competitive advantage. Therefore, when import cross-border e-commerce platforms determine their market positioning in combination with their own development status, they should not only consider the characteristics of the trading entity and import model, but also comprehensively analyze the matching effect of the two, and choose a reasonable, appropriate, and sustainable development matching combination to maximize the platform's competitive advantage and performance.

(4) Continuously optimize and improve the functions of the cross-border e-commerce platform. When consumers make cross-border purchases, the first thing they encounter is the import cross-border e-commerce platform, and the platform's functions, convenience, system stability, page design, etc. directly affect consumers' use of the platform, thereby affecting the platform's competitive advantage. From the analysis of platform competitive advantage from the user's perspective, the interactive features of import cross-border e-commerce platforms are features that users generally pay high attention to, and this feature affects the platform's competitive advantage to a certain extent. Therefore, import cross-border e-commerce platforms should first provide excellent functions, and continuously optimize on this basis to meet the ever-changing needs of users, thereby improving the core competitive advantage of the platform.

References

1. Fen W (2017) Research on trade facilitation and the development of China's cross-border e-commerce [D]. Zhejiang University
2. Xibao Z, Yitao S, Baochang X (2020) Trade facilitation and the development of china's cross-border e-commerce – an empirical analysis based on the double difference method [J]. East Chin Econ Manag 34(02):94–103
3. Xiaheng Z (2020) Evaluation of the efficiency of input of production factors in cross-border e-commerce [J]. J Beijing Univ Post Telecommun (social science edition) 22(01):30–35
4. Zhitian Z, Jianzheng Y (2014) Identification, verification and comprehensive evaluation of cross-border e-commerce capabilities of small and medium-sized manufacturing enterprises [J]. Syst Eng 10:53–62
5. Yue L, Yi L, Songbo W, Yong W (2019) The promoting effect of the "belt and road" initiative on foreign investment – a double difference test based on China's greenfield investment 2005–2016 [J]. Econ Res 54(09):187–202

6. Fang F, Lan Y, Yahong Z (2020) Environmental regulation, enterprise evolution and urban manufacturing productivity [J]. J Manag Sci 23(04):22–37
7. National Bureau of Statistics (2020) Frequently asked questions: statistical systems and classification standards [EB/OL]. Retrieved from http://www.stats.gov.cn/tjzs/cjwtjd/201308/t20130829_74318.html
8. National Development and Reform Commission, Ministry of Foreign Affairs, Ministry of Commerce (2015) Vision and actions on jointly building silk road economic belt and 21st-century maritime silk road [Z]. Beijing

Appendix 1
2013–2022 Cross-Border E-commerce Core Policies

Serial Number	Policy	Body of the document	Time
1	The General Office of the State Council forwarded the notice of the Ministry of Commerce and other departments on the implementation of relevant policy opinions to support cross-border e-commerce retail exports	General Office of the State Council	2013
2	Notice of the Ministry of Finance and the State Administration of Taxation on Cross-border E-commerce Retail Export Tax Policy	The Ministry of Finance, the State Administration of Taxation	2013
3	A guideline from the General Administration of Quality Supervision, Inspection, and Quarantine on supporting cross-border e-commerce retail exports	General Administration of Quality Supervision, Inspection and Quarantine (revocation)	2013

(continued)

L. Xiong and H. Wang, *User Driven Cross-Border E-Commerce Platform Competition and Policy Analysis*, Advanced Studies in E-Commerce,
https://doi.org/10.1007/978-981-97-3835-9

(continued)

Serial Number	Policy	Body of the document	Time
4	Notice of the General Department of the State Administration of Foreign Exchange on Pilot implementation of cross-border E-commerce Foreign exchange payment business by payment institutions	The State Administration of Foreign Exchange	2013
5	Announcement on regulatory matters relating to cross-border E-commerce Import and export goods and articles	General Administration of Customs	2014
6	Reply of the State Council on agreeing to set up China (Hangzhou) Cross-border E-commerce Comprehensive Pilot Zone	The State Council	2015
7	A guideline of the General Office of the State Council on promoting the healthy and rapid development of cross-border e-commerce	General Office of the State Council	2015
8	Notice of the Ministry of Finance and the State Administration of Taxation on the Tax Policy of Export Goods of China (Hangzhou) Cross-border E-commerce Comprehensive Pilot Zone	The Ministry of Finance and the State Administration of Taxation	2015

(continued)

(continued)

Serial Number	Policy	Body of the document	Time
9	Cross-border e-commerce business entities and commodity filing management work standards	General Administration of Quality Supervision, Inspection and Quarantine (revoked)	2015
10	Opinions of the General Administration of Quality Supervision, Inspection and Quarantine on supporting the development of the China (Hangzhou) Comprehensive Pilot Zone for cross-border e-commerce	General Administration of Quality Supervision, Inspection and Quarantine (revoked)	2015
11	Aqsiq's guiding Opinions on Strengthening the inspection and supervision of cross-border E-commerce import and export consumer goods	General Administration of Quality Supervision, Inspection and Quarantine (revocation)	2015
12	Aqsiq's opinions on Further exerting the functions of inspection and quarantine to promote the development of cross-border e-commerce	General Administration of Quality Supervision, Inspection and Quarantine (abolished)	2015
13	Notice of the State Administration of Foreign Exchange on the pilot Project of cross-border Foreign Exchange Payment by payment institutions	State Administration of Foreign Exchange	2015

(continued)

(continued)

Serial Number	Policy	Body of the document	Time
14	Notice of the Department of Customs Collection and Administration and the Department of Canadian Trade of the General Administration of Customs on Clarifying the Customs Value of cross-border E-commerce imports	General Administration of Customs	2016
15	Notice of General Office of the General Administration of Customs on Matters related to the implementation of the New Tax Policy on Cross-border E-commerce	General Administration of Customs	2016
16	A reply from the State Council on agreeing to set up comprehensive pilot zones for cross-border e-commerce in 12 cities including Tianjin	The State Council	2016
17	Notice of the General Administration of Customs on Strengthening the Supervision of cross-border E-commerce online purchases of bonded imports	General Administration of Customs	2016

(continued)

(continued)

Serial Number	Policy	Body of the document	Time
18	Letter of the Department of Customs Collection and Administration of the General Administration of Customs on clarifying the operation of some tax-related functions of the Unified Cross-border E-commerce Retail Import System	General Administration of Customs	2016
19	Announcement on the publication of the list of cross-border e-commerce retail imports	The Ministry of Finance, the Development and Reform Commission, the Ministry of Industry and Information Technology, the Ministry of Agriculture, the Ministry of Commerce, the General Administration of Customs, the State Administration of Taxation, the General Administration of Quality Inspection, the Food and Drug Administration, the Endangered Control Office, the Cryptographic Bureau	2016
20	Announcement on the publication of the list of cross-border e-commerce retail imports (the second batch)	Ministry of Finance, Development and Reform Commission, Ministry of Industry and Information Technology, Ministry of Environmental Protection, Ministry of Agriculture, Ministry of Commerce, People's Bank of China, General Administration of Customs, State Administration of Taxation, General Administration of Quality Inspection, State Administration of Press, Publication, Radio, Film and Television, Food and Drug Administration, Bin Regulation Office	2016
21	Notice of the Ministry of Finance, the General Administration of Customs and the State Administration of Taxation on the Tax Policy of Cross-border E-commerce Retail Imports	The Ministry of Finance, the General Administration of Customs and the State Administration of Taxation	2016

(continued)

(continued)

Serial Number	Policy	Body of the document	Time
22	Notice on Regulatory Matters relating to Cross-border E-commerce Retail Import and Export Commodities 2016	General Administration of Customs	2016
23	Announcement on data access specifications for cross-border e-commerce Retail Import and Export Inspection and Quarantine Information Management System	General Administration of Quality Supervision, Inspection and Quarantine (revoked)	2017
24	Letter on copying and promoting the mature experiential practices formed in the comprehensive pilot zone of cross-border e-commerce exploration	Ministry of Commerce, Office of the Central Leading Group for Cyberspace Administration of the CPC, National Development and Reform Commission, Ministry of Industry and Information Technology, Ministry of Finance, Ministry of Transport, People's Bank of China, General Administration of Customs, State Administration of Taxation, State Administration for Industry and Commerce, General Administration of Quality Supervision, Inspection and Quarantine, China Banking Regulatory Commission, State Post Bureau, State Administration of Foreign Exchange Administration of Commerce	2017
25	Announcement on adjusting the list of cross-border e-commerce retail imported goods	Ministry of Finance, Development and Reform Commission, Ministry of Industry and Information Technology, Ministry of Ecology and Environment, Ministry of Agriculture and Rural Affairs, Ministry of Commerce, People's Bank, General Administration of Customs, General Administration of Taxation, General Administration of Market Supervision, Food and Drug Administration, Cryptology Administration, Endangered Regulation Office	2018
26	A reply from the State Council on agreeing to set up comprehensive pilot zones for cross-border e-commerce in 22 cities including Beijing	The State Council	2018

(continued)

(continued)

Serial Number	Policy	Body of the document	Time
27	Announcement on Matters related to the Administration of Customs Registration of Cross-border E-commerce Enterprises	General Administration of Customs	2018
28	Notice on Regulatory Matters relating to Cross-border E-commerce Retail Import and Export Commodities 2018	General Administration of Customs	2018
29	Announcement on matters related to real-time access to raw data related to cross-border e-commerce platform enterprise payments	General Administration of Customs	2018
30	A circular on improving the tax policy on cross-border e-commerce retail imports	Ministry of Finance, General Administration of Customs, State Administration of Taxation	2018
31	A circular on improving the supervision of cross-border e-commerce retail imports	Ministry of Commerce, Development and Reform Commission, Ministry of Finance, General Administration of Customs, General Administration of Taxation, General Administration of Market Regulation	2018
32	Announcement on matters related to real-time access to raw data related to enterprise payments on cross-border e-commerce platforms	General Administration of Customs	2018
33	Notice on Tax Policy of Retail Export Goods in Cross-border E-commerce Comprehensive Pilot Zone	Ministry of Finance, State Administration of Taxation, Ministry of Commerce, General Administration of Customs	2018

(continued)

(continued)

Serial Number	Policy	Body of the document	Time
34	Announcement on the revision of Enterprise Access Message Specifications for the Unified Version of Cross-border e-Commerce Information System	General Administration of Customs	2018
35	Announcement on Enterprise access to the Unified version of Cross-border E-commerce Information System	General Administration of Customs	2018
36	An announcement on regulating the registration management of cross-border e-commerce payment enterprises	General Administration of Customs	2018
37	Several Opinions on Promoting High-quality Development of Cross-border e-Commerce Delivery Services (Interim)	The State Post Bureau, the Ministry of Commerce and the General Administration of Customs	2019

Appendix 2
Multi-agent Formulation of Cross-Border E-commerce Policies

Number of Entities	Multi-agent case	Number of posts	Main content involved
2	Ministry of Finance, State Administration of Taxation	2 2013 2015	Cross-border e-commerce retail export tax policy, Hangzhou Comprehensive pilot zone export tax policy
3	Ministry of Finance, General Administration of Customs, State Administration of Taxation	2 2016 2018	Cross-border e-commerce retail import tax policy
3	State Post Bureau, Ministry of Commerce, General Administration of Customs	1 2019	High-quality development of cross-border e-commerce delivery services
4	Ministry of Finance, State Administration of Taxation, Ministry of Commerce, General Administration of Customs	1 2018	Tax policy on retail export goods in the comprehensive Pilot zone of cross-border e-commerce
6	Ministry of Commerce, Development and Reform Commission, Ministry of Finance, General Administration of Customs, General Administration of Taxation, General Administration of Market Supervision	1 2018	Cross-border e-commerce retail import regulation

(continued)

L. Xiong and H. Wang, *User Driven Cross-Border E-Commerce Platform Competition and Policy Analysis*, Advanced Studies in E-Commerce,
https://doi.org/10.1007/978-981-97-3835-9

(continued)

Number of Entities	Multi-agent case	Number of posts	Main content involved
11	Ministry of Finance, Development and Reform Commission, Ministry of Industry and Information Technology, Ministry of Agriculture, Ministry of Commerce, General Administration of Customs, State Administration of Taxation, General Administration of Quality Inspection, Food and Drug Administration, Endangered Control Office, Cryptographic Bureau	1 2016	List of cross-border e-commerce retail imports
13	Ministry of Finance, Development and Reform Commission, Ministry of Industry and Information Technology, Ministry of Ecology and Environment, Ministry of Agriculture and Rural Affairs, Ministry of Commerce, People's Bank, General Administration of Customs, State Administration of Taxation, General Administration of Market Regulation, Food and Drug Administration, Cryptology Bureau, Endangered Management Office	2 2016 2018	List of cross-border e-commerce retail imports
14	Ministry of Commerce, Office of the Central Leading Group for Cyberspace Administration of the CPC, National Development and Reform Commission, Ministry of Industry and Information Technology, Ministry of Finance, Ministry of Transport, People's Bank of China, General Administration of Customs, State Administration of Taxation, State Administration for Industry and Commerce, General Administration of Quality Supervision, Inspection and Quarantine, China Banking Regulatory Commission, State Post Bureau, State Administration of Foreign Exchange Administration of Commerce	1 2017	Replicate and promote the mature experience and practice formed in the comprehensive pilot zone of cross-border e-commerce

Appendix 3
Classification of Cross-Border E-commerce Policy Tools

Types of Basic Instruments	Tool name	Keywords	Quantity	Subtotal	Accounting percentage
Supply type	Organizational leadership	Carry out learning, organization and leadership, policy implementation	8	45	14.52%
	Decision deployment	Set up comprehensive pilot areas, decision-making strategic deployment, replication and promotion	9		
	Streamline administration and delegate power	We will encourage innovation and delegate power to lower levels	6		
	Service guidance	Guidance and service, policy consultation, policy improvement	17		
	Financial support	Financial support	1		
	Human Support	Human resource allocation	2		
	Technical support	Technical support, technical consultation	2		
Demand-type	International cooperation	Foreign enterprises enter the market	1	9	2.90%
	Tax policy	Tax incentives, tax rebates	3		

(continued)

L. Xiong and H. Wang, *User Driven Cross-Border E-Commerce Platform Competition and Policy Analysis*, Advanced Studies in E-Commerce,
https://doi.org/10.1007/978-981-97-3835-9

(continued)

Types of Basic Instruments	Tool name	Keywords	Quantity	Subtotal	Accounting percentage
	Expand exports	The Belt and Road, international trade	1		
	Stimulating domestic demand	List of bonded, port construction, and imported commodities	4		
Environmental type	Defining specifications	Determine the main body of e-commerce export business	8	231	74.51%
	Rules and regulations	Policy subject, policy applicable goods, requirements for cross-border e-commerce participants	141		
	Business Supervision	Supervision of various departments	53		
	Credit system	Credit management	5		
	Risk prevention	Risk prevention and control, risk monitoring	4		
	Public service	Single window	20		
Assessment type	Submission of materials	Declaration system, problem report, information submission	7	25	8.06%

Appendix 4
Coding of Cross-Border E-commerce Policy Tools

Types of Basic Tools	Tools name	Definition	Policy unit	Quantity
Supply type	Organizational leadership	Carry out learning, organization and leadership, policy implementation	6–4, 7–12, 16–4, 3–1, 11–7, 26–4, 31–5, 33–2	8
	Decision deployment	Set up comprehensive pilot areas, decision-making strategic deployment, replication, and promotion	6–1, 6–2, 16–1, 16–2, 26–1, 26–2, 15–1, 24–1, 20–1	9
	Streamline administration and delegate power	We will encourage innovation and delegate power to lower levels	12–1, 16–3, 26–3, 10–1, 10–2, 37–4,	6
	Service guidance	Guidance and service, policy consultation, policy improvement	6–3, 6–5, 16–5, 3–6, 4–1, 10–13, 10–14, 11–1, 15–2, 26–5, 37–5, 37–6, 37–7, 37–8, 38–9, 11–9, 13–1	17
	Financial support		7–7	1
	Human Support		10–15, 11–10	2
	Technical Support		10–12, 10–16,	2

(continued)

L. Xiong and H. Wang, *User Driven Cross-Border E-Commerce Platform Competition and Policy Analysis*, Advanced Studies in E-Commerce,
https://doi.org/10.1007/978-981-97-3835-9

(continued)

Types of Basic Tools	Tools name	Definition	Policy unit	Quantity
Demand-type	International cooperation	Foreign enterprises enter the market	37–2	1
	Tax policy	Tax incentives, tax rebates	1–6, 7–5, 33–1	3
	Expand exports	The Belt and Road, international trade	7–11	1
	Stimulating domestic demand	List of bonded goods, port construction and imported goods	10–9, 10–10, 25–1, 30–5	4
Environmental type	Definition specification	Determine the main body of e-commerce export business	1–1, 5–20, 22–20, 28–31, 15–3, 17–1, 4–2, 13–2	8

(continued)

(continued)

Types of Basic Tools	Tools name	Definition	Policy unit	Quantity
	Regulation	Policy subject, policy applicable goods, requirements for cross-border e-commerce participants	2–1, 2–2, 2–3, 2–4, 2–5, 2–6, 4–3, 4–4, 4–5, 4–7, 4–8, 4–9, 4–10, 4–12, 4–13, 4–14, 4–15, 4–16, 4–17, 4–19, 4–20, 4–21, 4–22, 4–23, 4- 24, 5–1, 5–2, 5–3, 5–4, 5–5, 5–6, 5–7, 5–8, 5–11, 5–12, 5–13, 5–14, 5–15, 5–16, 5–18, 5–21, 8–2, 8–3, 9–1, 9–2, 9–6, 9–7, 9–8, 9–9, 9- -10, 9–11, 13–3, 13–4, 13–5, 13–6, 13–7, 13–8, 13–9, 13–10, 13–11, 5, 5, 13, 6, 13, 7, 9, 13, 10, 13, 11, 13–12, 13–13, 13–14, 13–15, 13–16, 13–17, 13–19, 13–30, 14–1, 14–2, 14–3, 17–2, 17–3, 17–4, 17–5, 17–6, 17–7, 17–8, 21–1, 21–2, 21–3, 21–4, 21 -5, 21–6, 21–7, 22–1, 22–2, 22–3, 22–4, 22–6, 22–9, 22–10, 22–11, 22–14, 22–17, 22–18, 22–19, 22–21, 23–3, 23–4, 27–1, 27–2, 30–1, 30–2, 30–3, 30–4, 33–4, 33–5, 35–3, 36–1, 36–2, 36–3, 28–1, 28–2, 28–6, 28–7, 28–9, 28–12, 28–13, 28–14, 28–18, 28–22, 28–23, 28–32, 34–2, 12–2, 31 -1, 31–2, 31–3, 31–6, 29–2, 32–1, 32–2, 32–3, 32–4,	141

(continued)

(continued)

Types of Basic Tools	Tools name	Definition	Policy unit	Quantity
	Business Supervision	Supervision of various departments	1–4, 1–5, 3–2, 3–3, 3–4, 4–26, 5–17, 7–1, 7–4, 7–6, 8–1, 10–5, 10–6, 10–11, 11–2, 12–1, 12–2, 12–4, 12–5, 13–24, 13–26 13–27, 13–28, 13–29, 17–9, 17–10, 22–13, 22–15, 22–16, 33–3, 28–3, 28–4, 28–5, 28–16, 28–17, 28–19, 28–20, 28–24, 28–25, 28–26, 28–28, 28–29, 37–1, 37–10, 37–11, 37–12, 18–2, 31–4, 11–4, 11–5, 11–6, 11–8,	53
	Credit system	Enterprise credit	1–7, 7–9, 37–3, 10–3, 10–7,	5
	Risk prevention	Commodity risk	28–27, 11–3, 12–3	4
	Public service	Single window	3–5, 7–2, 7–8, 7–10, 10–4, 10–8, 18–1, 34–1, 34–3, 34–4, 35–1, 35–2, 12–6, 23–1, 23–2, 23–5, 23–6, 32–1, 32–2, 29–1	20
Assessment type	Submission of materials	Declaration system, problem report, information submission	1–3, 4–6, 17–11, 22–12, 28–15, 13–21, 13–23	7
	Declaration Checklist	List of Goods, List of Articles, Declaration of Import and Export Goods	5–9, 5–10, 22–5, 22–7, 22–8, 28–8, 28–10, 28–11	8
	Evaluation Verification	Evaluation of results	16–6, 26–6	2
	Statistical monitoring	Special statistics, statistical system and statistical declaration	1–2, 4–25, 5–19, 7–3, 11–11, 13–18, 13–20, 13–22,	8

Appendix 5
Part of the Code

```
/* Parallel trend test */
```

Step 1: Generate the difference between the policy implementation year and the current year of the sample, distance.

gen distance = year – policy_year

Step 2: Generate the dummy variables d_j and dj for the jth year before and after the policy implementation of the experimental group, where j is up to 4, representing 4 years before and after the policy implementation.

d_j: If the sample is the "experimental group" and it is the "jth period before policy implementation", the value is 1, otherwise it is 0.

Process:

```
forvalues i=1/4 {
gen d_`i' = 0
replace d_`i' = 1 if treat== 1 & distance== -`i'
}
dj: If the sample is the "experimental group" and it is the "jth
period after policy implementation", the value is 1, otherwise it
is 0.
```

Code:

```
forvalues i=1/4 {
gen d`i' = 0
replace d`i' = 1 if treat== 1 & distance== `i'
}
After the first two steps, the data table will add nine columns:
distance, d_4, d_3, d_2, d_1, d1, d2, d3, d4.
```

Step 3: Use regression method to test parallel trends and draw parallel trend graphs.

```
Take d_4, d_3, d_2, d_1, d1, d2, d3, d4 as explanatory variables,
control time effect and fixed effect, control variable regression:
```


L. Xiong and H. Wang, *User Driven Cross-Border E-Commerce Platform Competition and Policy Analysis*, Advanced Studies in E-Commerce,
https://doi.org/10.1007/978-981-97-3835-9

```
xtreg lnexpress d_4 d_3 d_2 d_1 d1 d2 d3 d4 i.year lnpeople lngrp
lngov indu lninfo lntransport lninno,fe
```

According to the results of the regression, draw the regression coefficient in the 95% confidence interval:

```
coefplot,keep(d_4 d_3 d_2 d_1 d1 d2 d3 d4) levels(95)
vertical lcolor(black) mcolor(black) msymbol(circle_hollow)
ytitle(Cross-border express volume coefficient of the compre-
hensive test area, size(small)) ylabel(, labsize(small)
angle(horizontal) nogrid) yline(0, lwidth(vthin)lpattern(solid)
lcolor(black)) xtitle(Relative time of establishment of the
comprehensive test area, size(small)) xlabel(,labsize(small))
graphregion(fcolor(white) lcolor(white) ifcolor(white)
ilcolor(white)) ciopts(recast(rcap)) xline(10.5, lwidth(vthin)
lpattern(solid)lcolor(black))
/* Placebo test */
```

Step 1: Generate a spare matrix.

```
set matsize 5000
mat b = J(500,1,0)
mat se = J(500,1,0)
mat p = J(500,1,0)
```

Step 2: Sample, group the data according to the comprehensive test area city, and randomly select a year from the year variable in each city as the virtual policy time.

```
forvalues i = 1/500{
use C:\Users\94099\Desktop\Comprehensive Test Area\test1112.dta,
clear
xtset city_id year
bsample 1, strata(city_id) //Group by **id**, randomly select a year
from each group
keep year
save matchyear.dta, replace
mkmat year, matrix(sampleyear)
use C:\Users\94099\Desktop\Comprehensive Test Area\test1112.dta,
clear
xtset city_id year
gen DID = 0
foreach j of numlist 1/25 {
replace DID = 1 if (id == `j' & year >= sampleyear[`j',1])
}
qui xtreg bdindex DID lnpeople lngrp lngov indu lninfo lntransport
lninno i.year, re
mat b[`i',1] = _b[DID]
mat se[`i',1] = _se[DID]
scalar df_r = e(N) - e(df_m) -1
mat p[`i',1] = 2*ttail(df_r,abs(_b[DID]/_se[DID]))
}
```

Step 3: Convert the matrix into a vector and form an estimated coefficient distribution diagram.

```
svmat b, names(coef)
svmat se, names(se)
svmat p, names(pvalue)
drop if pvalue1 == .
label var pvalue1 p-value
label var coef1 estimated coefficient
twoway (scatter pvalue1 coef1, xline(0 -0.03, lwidth(0.2)
lp(shortdash)) xlabel(0(0.01)0, grid) xtitle(estimated coef-
ficient) ytitle(p-value) msymbol(smcircle_hollow) mcolor(orange)
legend(off)) (kdensity coef1, title(Cross-border E-commerce Baidu
Index Placebo Test))
/* Mediating effect lnexpress */
/* Mediating effect Innovation (Technological Environment) */
xtreg lnexpress x lnpeople lngrp lngov lninfo lntransport indu ,fe
xtreg innovate x lnpeople lngrp lngov lninfo lntransport indu ,fe
xtreg lnexpress x innovate lnpeople lngrp lngov lninfo lntransport
indu,fe
/* Visualization */
```

Step 1: Prepare the DOM container, prepare a DOM container with height and width on the HTML page, as the rendering container for echarts, that is, the carrier of visualization mapping.

```
<div id="ID" style="width: 600px; height:400px;"></div>
```

Step 2: Create an echarts instance, create an echarts instance in the DOM, each echarts instance occupies a DOM node exclusively.

```
var dom=document.getElementByID("ID");
var instance=echarts.init(dom);
```

Step 3: Option configuration, implement the specific style of visualization mapping, such as data management, visual mapping, timeline, and other user interaction components. This step is also the key part of visualization mapping, where data analysis purposes can be achieved through a series of interaction components.

```
var option={
xAxis:{…},
yAxis:{…},
series{type: "bar",data:[…]}
};
```

Step 4: Data loading and updating.

Data loading can be divided into and asynchronous loading

Directly load data, set array-form data in the series in step three:

```
instance.setOption(option);
Asynchronously load data, load from the preprocessed data.json
file:
$.get('data.json').done(function (data) {
instance.setOption({
xAxis: {
data:…
```

```
},
series: [{
name:…,
data:…
}]
});
});
```

Step 5: Load the echarts instance, set the configured option to the corresponding echarts instance.

```
myChart.setOption(option);
```

1. Conclusion

"User-Driven Cross-Border E-commerce Platform Competition and Policy Analysis" conducts research using Tmall International as a representative cross-border platform, selecting the category with the largest proportion of user consumption preferences and the most representative research individuals in this category as the research source. Online review information is used as the data source, based on nearly 80,000 pieces of data to explore user cross-border consumption behavior preference analysis and comparative analysis of consumption behavior preferences between cross-border and non-cross-border platforms. It analyzes the competitive advantages of imported cross-border e-commerce platforms from the perspectives of platform companies and users, and is committed to digging out the key factors affecting platform competitive advantages from different perspectives. It takes cross-border e-commerce policy as the research object, combines the policy implementation process model to construct a cross-border e-commerce policy evaluation model, and draws the following conclusions.

(1) The four-dimensional customer perceived value driving model is composed of value-driven, technology-driven, brand-driven, and service-driven. Through keyword frequency statistics, it is found that the words with the highest frequency are "concealing effect", "duration", "taste", "guarantee", etc., with the highest scores of 4202, 4307, 4610, 3708, followed by "duration", "logistics", "packaging", etc. This shows that users of cross-border retail import platform websites pay most attention to value-driven factors, brand-driven factors, and technology-driven factors. Merchants and even platforms need to strengthen the improvement of the value attributes of products, that is, the core value of competitiveness, and strictly control the source channels of products, and improve the timeliness cost and service cost of international logistics.

(2) From the consumer's perspective, it is found that the importance of customer perceived value driving factors is inconsistent, among which the importance of value-driven, brand-driven, and technology-driven is the highest and needs to be focused on. The value-driven factor ranked first, which is related to consumer demands. Purchasing different products has different functional values, which is also the most

basic perceived demand of consumers, whether this value is satisfied or not will affect the conditional probability of other driving factors. The attention to brand-driven reflects the consumer's behavior of seeking proof on this platform.

(3) Through the data modeling comparison of cross-border and non-cross-border platforms, it is found that the customer perceived value of non-cross-border platforms tends to be value-driven, far greater than technology-driven and brand-driven. The estimated technology-driven factor is related to the relatively complete domestic logistics system; while the customer perceived value of cross-border platforms can be classified from large to small as: value-driven, brand-driven, and technology-driven, but the importance of the three is slightly different. In other words, domestic platform users pay more attention to value-driven factors (product characteristics, etc.), under the same circumstances, overseas platform users pay more attention to brand-driven factors, which may be related to the lack of patent agency rights or the mixed shops on the domestic platform, which needs further verification and research.

(4) Based on the perspective of platform companies, this paper takes China's small and medium-sized B2C import cross-border e-commerce platforms as the research object and uses corporate survey data as the empirical basis to study the impact of different factors and the matching between factors under the two dimensions of cross-border e-commerce transaction subjects and import models on platform competitive advantages. The research results show that the product category and the degree of product popularity have a significant impact on the competitive advantage of the platform, and the website traffic of comprehensive e-commerce and long-tail e-commerce is larger and more competitive; in addition, the matching of the mixed import model and long-tail e-commerce can better meet consumer needs, promote consumers' use of the platform, and help improve the competitive advantage of the platform.

(5) Based on the user's perspective, this paper builds an evolutionary model of cross-border e-commerce consumers' emotional preference, takes online reviews of Jingdong Fresh platform as the research object, builds an emotional dictionary, divides time Windows, and analyzes consumers' emotional diffusion value and emotional energy value under different time Windows. The results show as follows: In terms of emotional diffusion value, consumers have strong perception ability. During the outbreak period, consumers' behavior of purchasing imported fresh products on cross-border e-commerce platforms decreased significantly, and emotional diffusion value increased overall. In the period of spread control, consumer purchasing power recovered slightly, and the emotional diffusion was convergent. In terms of emotional energy value, consumer emotion has always been in a positive and good state, but compared with other categories of fresh products, consumers have a rapid perception of the incident, and there are negative emotional fluctuations on the seafood and aquatic imported fresh products involved, and the fluctuation intensity is large.

(6) Propose a new paradigm for cross-border e-commerce policy research. Starting from the policy implementation process model, a systematic cross-border e-commerce policy evaluation research model is constructed. First, the policy subjects, policy action fields, policy tools, and environmental factors of cross-border e-commerce are included in the cross-border e-commerce policy evaluation model.

Then, policy literature metrics, data visualization, and econometric methods are selected to deeply study the effects of cross-border e-commerce policies from the perspectives of policy resource allocation and policy implementation effects.

(7) Cross-border e-commerce policy measurement and visualization. The research found: (1) In terms of policy subject cooperation, the department cooperation network is generally dense. Through the visualization of the relationship of joint issuance of cross-border e-commerce policies, it can be found that the current multi-subject joint issuance is mainly based on the cooperation of the General Administration of Customs, the Ministry of Finance, the State Taxation Administration, the Ministry of Commerce, and the General Administration of Quality Inspection. Through the measurement of the network characteristics of the subjects, it can be found that cooperation is common in the multi-subject network of departments, and the degree of cooperation between departments is high; (2) in terms of policy action fields, the impact of policies on the cross-border e-commerce ecosystem is gradually deepening, extending from payment and taxation to regulation, logistics, and informatization, but it has not yet fully integrated into the cross-border e-commerce ecosystem, such as cross-border e-commerce talents, intellectual property protection. The policy content is relatively lacking; (3) in terms of policy tool combinations, cross-border e-commerce policies show the characteristics of environment-type policy tools dominating, evaluation-type policy tools being relatively weak, and demand-type policy tools being seriously lacking. It should strengthen the guidance of cross-border e-commerce demand and policy evaluation in policies; (4) in terms of policy evolution, China's cross-border e-commerce policies are divided into four stages: preliminary exploration, support and promotion, standard promotion, and comprehensive development. In terms of policy focus, the attention to cross-border e-commerce risks is gradually increasing, which is conducive to cross-border e-commerce companies in the increasingly complex international situation. Improve self-protection awareness; in terms of policy efficiency, the relationship between the policies and business volume of the first three batches of comprehensive test zones forms three levels, and the policy efficiency differences are obvious. Therefore, each cross-border e-commerce comprehensive test zone needs to pay more attention to the implementation effect of policies and promote the high-quality development of the industry.

(8) Evaluation of the implementation effect of cross-border e-commerce comprehensive test zone policy. The study found: (1) In terms of the policy effect of the comprehensive test zone, the establishment of the test zone promotes the development of cross-border e-commerce, but it is necessary to further introduce and implement supporting policies to enhance the effect; (2) in terms of the cross-border e-commerce environment, environmental factors significantly affect the policy effect of cross-border e-commerce, with the mediating effect of the political environment being prominent. During the development process, the impact of the political, technological, economic, and social environments should be coordinated, especially the mediating role of technological development and the social environment on the development of cross-border e-commerce should be paid attention to, and the policy guidance of technology and innovation should be strengthened; (3) in terms of city

attributes, it was found that the geographical location of the city, the size of the city, and the differences in the "Belt and Road" strategy will affect the policy effect of cross-border e-commerce. The comprehensive test zone policy is beneficial to the economic growth of small and medium-sized cities and non-"Belt and Road" cities along the route. Therefore, in the process of policy formulation and implementation, the comprehensive test zone should fully combine the advantages and disadvantages of the city and the possible impact of related strategies to maximize the implementation effect of the policy.

SPRINGER NATURE

GPSR Compliance

The European Union's (EU) General Product Safety Regulation (GPSR) is a set of rules that requires consumer products to be safe and our obligations to ensure this.

If you have any concerns about our products, you can contact us on ProductSafety@springernature.com

In case Publisher is established outside the EU, the EU authorized representative is:

Springer Nature Customer Service Center GmbH
Europaplatz 3
69115 Heidelberg, Germany

The manufacturer's authorised representative in the EU is Springer Nature Customer Service Centre GmbH, Europaplatz 3, 69115 Heidelberg, Germany. If you have any concerns regarding our products, please contact ProductSafety@springernature.com

Printed and bound by CPI Group (UK) Ltd, Croydon, CR0 4YY

30/09/2026

02225300-0007